THE MAJOR VICTORIAN POETS:
RECONSIDERATIONS

THE MAJOR
VICTORIAN POETS:
RECONSIDERATIONS

Edited by
ISOBEL ARMSTRONG

LONDON
ROUTLEDGE & KEGAN PAUL

First published in 1969
by Routledge and Kegan Paul Ltd
Broadway House, 68–74 Carter Lane
London, E.C.4
Reprinted 1969
Printed in Great Britain by
The Garden City Press Limited
Letchworth, Hertfordshire
© Routledge and Kegan Paul Ltd 1969
No part of this book may be reproduced
in any form without permission from
the publisher, except for the quotation
of brief passages in criticism
SBN 7100 6380 6

ACKNOWLEDGEMENTS

All the essays collected here were written especially for this book except my discussion of Browning's style which was originally read at a symposium on style run by R. P. Draper at the University of Leicester. I am grateful to Dr Draper for allowing me to use this paper when a substitute in the Browning section was required.

I owe particularly warm thanks to my colleague, Keith Walker, for his generous help with the manuscript during the last stages of this book.

CONTENTS

INTRODUCTION

The aims of this collection of essays can best be described by explaining why some Victorian poets—Meredith, Swinburne and the Rossettis, for instance—have not been discussed at all. These essays concentrate upon the poets whose reputations suffered from the great redirection of energy in English criticism initiated in this century by Eliot, Richards and Leavis. Whatever the differences of emphasis among these critics they were all alike in attempting to create and educate a public for twentieth-century poetry: their success is now one of the familiar facts in the history of criticism and so is one of its results—the renewal of interest in metaphysical and eighteenth-century poetry and a corresponding ebb of enthusiasm for Romantic poetry and for Victorian poetry in particular. This revaluation primarily affected Tennyson, Browning and Arnold. These, rather than Meredith, Swinburne and the Rossettis, were the poets singled out for discussion and 'Victorian poetry' was often equated with their poetry. In his essay on the meta-physical poets, written in 1921, T. S. Eliot recoiled from the crude sensibilities of Tennyson and Browning and ended his sweeping paragraph on the imbalance of thought and feeling in Romantic poetry with the dismissive 'and Tennyson and Browning ruminated'. Leavis saw mid-nineteenth-century poetry in very much the same way in *New Bearings in English Poetry* (1932), describing what he felt to be the debased 'poetical' tradition of Victorian Romanticism. Later, in *Revaluation* (1936) he talked of Arnold's 'dilute' Wordsworthianism and placed him as a precursor of the Georgian poets. Add to this Yeats's remark in his *Autobiographies* that the Victorians had 'filled their poetry with what I call "impurities", curiosities about politics, about science, about history, about religion': add F. W. Bateson's criticism of the language of Victorian poetry in *English Poetry and the English Language* (1934)—' . . . it was the words that suffered. The diction became as vague and

I

diffuse as the emotion.' It is clear that criticisms of the major Victorian poets earlier in this century were fundamental and comprehensive.

But these criticisms did not stop people writing about Victorian poetry, and anybody familiar with the great body of scholarly and critical work produced in the recent past might well ask why it should be necessary to return to the objections and generalisations of another generation of critics writing thirty and even forty years ago. People have gone on writing about Victorian poetry, certainly, but in the renewed discussion of the past fifteen years or so the objections I have described, voiced so authoritatively and apparently persuasively by critics like Eliot and Leavis, have been ignored rather than answered. Of course, it could always be allowed that such criticisms must be seen in the context of the history of criticism, that they had to be made so strongly in order that new kinds of poetic experience could be accepted and understood. Nevertheless, this is to disregard the force and importance of that revaluation of the Victorian poets. What these poets wrote about, the values they expressed, the form of their poems, the language they used, all these were examined and found wanting in some radical way. It is worth taking these criticisms as seriously as they were offered.

In recent years criticism has been much influenced by two impressive books on Victorian poetry, E. D. H. Johnson's *The Alien Vision of Victorian Poetry* (1952) and Robert Langbaum's *The Poetry of Experience* (1957). These have gone some way to suggesting fresh approaches to Victorian poetry. Johnson argues that Tennyson, Browning and Arnold expressed their deepest insights indirectly. Tennyson's fascination with the dream, for instance, or Browning's preoccupation with the psychology of the rebellious, anti-rational, intuitive mind, represent an implicit protest against the values of these poets' society and illustrate their relationship to it. Robert Langbaum looks at the peculiar possibilities of the dramatic monologue which is written in such a way that it creates a disequilibrium between the reader's sympathy and his judgment. Langbaum's interest in the dramatic monologue as a form arises from his belief that we see emerging in it a modern, 'relativist', or (though he does not use this word), ironic mode. These are subtle and exciting books but they do not attempt to answer the fundamental questions put by Eliot or by Leavis or by Bateson. In particular, it is not in their brief to consider the language of Victorian poetry. One might also wonder whether Johnson does not implicitly acknowledge the limitations of the poets he writes of, much as they were described by the earlier critics, simply presenting them in a more sympathetic and attractive way. Again, it must be asked how much we can genuinely rescue from mid-nineteenth century poetry if we see it in terms of the emergence of a modern, ironic mode.

Most of the essays in this book take as their starting point questions raised by the debate on Victorian poetry earlier in this century, or, where they are relevant to that debate, questions raised in more recent criticism. In this context it was obvious that the poetry of Tennyson, Browning and Arnold should be discussed. Clough, until recently forgotten about rather than misrepresented, is a poet whose stature must be acknowledged and in doing this one must reconsider some of the assumptions about Victorian poetry which I have mentioned. It was also appropriate, in a volume of essays which aims to achieve a clearer understanding of the nature of Victorian poetry, to include a piece on Hopkins because of (rather than in spite of) the fact that he is generally considered to be a modern poet.

In the main the method of the essays in this book is to discuss closely particular poems which raise important critical questions. Philip Drew, for instance, writes on Arnold's *The Scholar-Gipsy* and *Thyrsis* and Alan Sinfield on Tennyson's *In Memoriam*. Or, because generalisations about the nature of a poet's work and his achievement have often been based on a highly selective reading—intensive in some areas and perfunctory in others—some of the essays deal with works which have not been given much critical discussion. Michael Mason, for instance, writes on Browning's *Sordello* and Gabriel Pearson on Arnold's *Merope*. Some writers, however, have chosen to write on an aspect of a poet's work which demands examination rather than to concentrate on a single poem. Martin Dodsworth and Barbara Hardy have adopted this approach.

We have not set out to present a comprehensive account of each poet's work but rather to concentrate on those areas of his work where critical discussion seems most necessary. In the section on Tennyson, Martin Dodsworth deals with a general theme, Tennyson's morbidity, seeing it as the productive rather than the limiting mood of his work and relating it to the formal patterns of his poetry. Bernard Bergonzi's essay on *The Princess* examines how far the method Tennyson adopted to deal with a contemporary, public question is artistically successful and considers the ways in which the poem is still meaningful. Alan Sinfield's concern in his essay on *In Memoriam* is to demonstrate not only that the language of the poem stands up to close examination but also that the style of the poem is illuminated when it is related to its theme. A. S. Byatt redirects attention to the lyric elements of *Maud* (often seen exclusively as a dramatic monologue in the manner of Browning's poems) and shows how Arthur Hallam's description of Tennyson as a poet of 'sensation' rather than of 'reflection' is relevant to this poem and to the nature of Tennyson's lyricism.

Discussions of Browning have generally been based on his dramatic monologues and his lyrics—in effect, on a fraction of his work. I discuss some of these well-known poems in an essay which attempts to find a fruitful way of approaching Browning's style. The emphasis in this section, however, is on the re-evaluation of Browning's work by exploring areas of his poetry which have not been extensively discussed. It is useful to approach Browning in other ways than as the poet of the dramatic monologue. Michael Mason gives a detailed examination of *Sordello*, clarifying the theme of the poem and pointing to its importance as a formal and stylistic experiment. There are two essays on *The Ring and the Book* because of its strange status in Browning criticism. It is sometimes said to be his greatest achievement and sometimes seen as a sign of his decline as a poet. But whatever the position adopted, no one except Robert Langbaum has discussed the poem in much detail. John Killham's essay clarifies the way in which the poem should be interpreted. He rejects a relativist approach and places the poem firmly in its nineteenth-century context. My essay suggests an interpretation of the poem by approaching it through the question of Browning's prolixity, formal and stylistic, and offers a reading of the poem which makes its length an artistic necessity rather than a limitation.

In their discussions of Arnold, Philip Drew and Gabriel Pearson find that the most important critical issue resolves itself into the question of how far the so-called Romantic elements in his poetry are resilient and original rather than derivative and weak. Philip Drew explores this question through *The Scholar-Gipsy* and *Thyrsis*, seeing the poems as a single entity, an elegy on time. He argues that this new poem cannot be seen as a retreat, a declaration of withdrawal from the 'repeated shocks' of mid-nineteenth-century life. Gabriel Pearson approaches the problem through that seeming anomaly, the neo-classical *Merope*. He places this poem at the centre rather than on the periphery of Arnold's poetry and explores the implications of Arnold's neo-classicism.

Clough's poetry raises very different questions. Like Hopkins, he can be seen only too easily as a modern poet, defying the notions we usually hold about the poetry of the mid-nineteenth century. It is certainly fortunate that the poetry of Clough and Hopkins insists on making it difficult to produce happy generalisations about Victorian poetry; on the other hand, it would be hasty to recruit them as twentieth-century poets before their time and it is necessary to look closely at their work if it is not to be treated in this anachronistic way. To this end Barbara Hardy defines and isolates Clough's peculiarly self-conscious idiom, analysing the ways in which he uses what Arnold in another context called the 'dialogue of the mind with itself'. *Amours de Voyage* is accepted as Clough's most important poem but there has never been an extended discussion of it. John Goode repairs this omission and establishes the claims of this work as one of the major poems of the nineteenth century. A. R. Jones concludes this volume with an essay on Hopkins which places him as a Victorian poet and relates him to his contemporaries. Some elements of Hopkins' work, he suggests, look very different when he is seen in his proper context. Not only is his own work illuminated but we also gain an insight into the poetry of his contemporaries.

5

In discussions of Victorian poetry the epithet 'Victorian' is usually loaded with meaning—it signifies so much more than a body of work which falls into a definite period. Yet in spite of the knowledge that descriptive tags such as 'Romantic' or 'Victorian' may be misleading or meaningless when one is confronted with the variety of a literature at any given time people go on using them. They seem to be necessary if not useful to the critic, who is always divided between responding minutely to the stubborn uniqueness of a work of art and generalising about the things which relate the works of art to one another. Some generalisations may seem to be made rather arbitrarily, but on the whole it is no accident that notions about the characteristics of a period determine themselves or that people should want to determine them. It is necessary to evolve a shape, a pattern, a ghostly paradigm—however ghostly—if one is to see literature as more than a series of adventitious phenomena. And clearly it is as much the business of criticism to revise, alter and reformulate such generalisations as it is to construct them. These essays, by dealing with specific problems, aim to modify the kinds of generalisation made about Victorian poetry. At the same time it is to be hoped that they put some manageable notions in their place.

PATTERNS OF MORBIDITY:
REPETITION IN TENNYSON'S POETRY

Martin Dodsworth

'Everyone knows' that Tennyson is a master of technique, knows that he could judge the quantity of every vowel in the English language excepting the two in *scissors*. And yet this master of technique is an exceedingly repetitious poet. Phrases recur continually within poems and, as Christopher Ricks has shown in a recent British Academy lecture, they are frequently carried over from one poem to another in the course of years, so that a single line may appear in three different settings, that is, three different poems, before the poet at last has done with it. There is, too, another sense in which Tennyson is repetitious: no style is easier to recognise than his, and this is true *in spite of* the astonishing diversity of forms which he employed. In the rather discursive essay which follows, I wish to suggest that no satisfactory view of Tennyson's achievement can afford not to take this characteristic repetitiousness into account. It provides, for example, one answer to the very damaging criticism of Tennyson's style made by Bagehot. It is associated with the fundamental mysteries of Tennyson's personality, with his view of his own self and its relation to the world of external phenomena. The dazzling craftsmanship should be seen, I think, in relation to the basic sameness of Tennyson's subject-matter, which springs from the nature of the man himself; it serves as a means both of diversifying that sameness and of distancing the poet and his reader from it. Far from being superficial ('ornate', as Bagehot puts it), the Tennysonian style communicates a great and sometimes overwhelming intensity of feeling. Its repetitiousness acts as a constant reminder of the difficulty with which this poet turned his mind from the subjects of real concern to him. One thinks of the power of Arthur Hallam's

7

death to haunt his memory, or of Rosa Baring's rejection of him, if Professor Rader's hypotheses are correct.

There is perhaps no more satisfactory expression of the sense of something unchangeable and brooding at work in the mind and perceptible beneath the extravagant variety of means in Tennyson's poetry, than his own marvelling lines from *In Memoriam*:

> What words are these have fall'n from me?
>   Can calm despair and wild unrest
>   Be tenants of a single breast,
> Or sorrow such a changeling be?
>
> Or doth she only seem to take
>   The touch of change in calm or storm;
>   But knows no more of transient form
> In her deep self, than some dead lake
>
> That holds the shadow of a lark
> Hung in the shadow of a heaven?
>
> (XVI)

In his famous essay 'Wordsworth, Tennyson and Browning', Bagehot characterises Tennyson's poetry as 'ornate':

It works not by choice and selection, but by accumulation and aggregation. The idea is not, as in the pure style, presented with the least clothing which it will endure, but with the richest and most involved clothing that it will admit.

He says nothing of any intensity of feeling behind the verse; the words *accumulation and aggregation* imply, on the contrary, a weary and indifferent labour of composition. Repetition is not singled out as a special mark of Tennyson's kind of accumulation. Yet in no other poet has the full force of Wordsworth's remarks on repetition been so clearly demonstrated. In the 1800 note to 'The Thorn' Wordsworth justified his own use of the device in the following way:

There is a numerous class of readers who imagine that the same words cannot be repeated without tautology: this is a great error: virtual tautology is much oftener produced by using different words when the meaning is exactly the same . . . every man must know that an attempt is rarely made to communicate impassioned feelings without something of an accompanying consciousness of the inadequateness of our own powers, or the deficiencies of language. During such efforts there will be a craving in the mind, and as long as it is unsatisfied the speaker will cling to the same words, or words of the same character.

In other words, according to Wordsworth, repetition is the mark of an inability to progress from one state of feeling to another, and arises from a sense of inadequacy to express the strength of feeling experienced. His remarks make a perfect gloss to the impressive lines from *In Memoriam* quoted above, describing the dead lake of static emotions in terms of repetition:

> That holds the shadow of a lark
> Hung in the shadow of a heaven.

Tennyson's repetition is nearly always tied in this way to strong emotion; it is of the Wordsworthian kind.

Bagehot sees Tennyson's manner as springing from the attempt to dress up simple ideas so that they will seem grand. It is true that he is not an intellectual poet. But the metaphors of clothing and ornament will really not do as an account of what is going on in his verse. Bagehot quotes a long passage from *Enoch Arden* in order to demonstrate what he means by the term 'ornate'. There is no need to acclaim the poem as a masterpiece in order to show the weakness of his reading. His approach is sly and amusing. He praises the passage ('an absolute model of adorned art'; 'no expressive circumstance can be added to this description, no enhancing detail suggested') but makes it very plain that he dislikes it: Tennyson 'tells a great deal about the torrid zone which a rough sailor like Enoch Arden would not have perceived.' And again:

... what is absurd in Mr. Tennyson's description—absurd when we abstract it from the gorgeous additions and ornaments with which Mr. Tennyson distracts us—is, that his hero feels nothing else but these great splendours. We hear nothing of the physical ailments, the rough devices, the low superstitions, which really would have been the *first* things, the favourite and principal occupations of his mind.

There is no doubt that Bagehot prefers *Robinson Crusoe*. But

9

is he at all perceptive about *Enoch Arden*? The passage which he discusses is certainly gorgeous; but is the gorgeousness only there to distract us?

> The mountain wooded to the peak, the lawns
> And winding glades high up like ways to Heaven,
> The slender coco's drooping crown of plumes,
> The lightning flash of insect and of bird,
> The lustre of the long convolvuluses
> That coil'd around the stately stems, and ran
> Ev'n to the limit of the land, the glows
> And glories of the broad belt of the world,
> All these he saw; but what he fain had seen
> He could not see, the kindly human face,
> Nor ever hear a kindly voice, but heard
> The myriad shriek of wheeling ocean-fowl,
> The league-long roller thundering on the reef,
> The moving whisper of huge trees that branch'd
> And blossom'd in the zenith, or the sweep
> Of some precipitous rivulet to the wave,
> As down the shore he ranged, or all day long
> Sat often in the seaward-gazing gorge,
> A shipwrecked sailor, waiting for a sail:
> No sail from day to day, but every day
> The sunrise broken into scarlet shafts
> Among the palms and ferns and precipices;
> The blaze upon the waters to the east;
> The blaze upon his island overhead;
> The blaze upon the waters to the west;
> Then the great stars that globed themselves in Heaven,
> The hollower-bellowing ocean, and again
> The scarlet shafts of sunrise—but no sail.

Tennyson's point, which Bagehot misses, is that Enoch *feels* nothing of the splendours described; his attention is turned completely away from them. If they are enumerated at such length, it is in order to emphasise how truly remarkable is the want of interest in them that he shows:

> All these he saw; but what he fain had seen
> He could not see . . .

The idea of seeing is repeated in a way that suggests how *little* he sees of what is before him, and brings before us not only the intensity with which he scans the horizon for release but also the vacancy of his look when it is turned on the island's plenitude of objects, a plenitude which is reduced to monotony by Enoch's single desire to escape.

We can distinguish between two kinds of accumulation at work in this passage. The first is the accumulation of physical detail glowingly described—the mountain, the lawns and so on. The second kind is the accumulation of repeated words and phrases in relation to Enoch's subjective view of things. For *him* the scene is monotonous, and this monotony, together with its cause, the feeling of imprisonment, is suggested by lines like:

> The blaze upon the waters to the east;
> The blaze upon his island overhead;
> The blaze upon the waters to the west.

This *is* what Enoch sees, symbolically and literally. He sees that he is caught in a situation which is in essentials unchanging; and literally, the blaze upon the waters is all that he can see when looking out over the ocean. The two kinds of accumulation are used deliberately to present Enoch's situation dramatically by a contrast of the extravagantly diversified setting with the monotonous impression it makes on him.

Beneath this contrast, however, there is a level at which the two accumulative styles make *one* style. They realise a common identity, one beautifully conveyed by the poet when he describes the gorge in which Enoch sits as 'seaward-gazing'. It is Enoch who *gazes*; but the island does so too. Enoch cannot bear to be alone, and longs for 'the kindly human face' (*kindly* carrying with it notions of kinship as well as of kindness); but the island seems as frustrated as its prisoner. Despite the intense activity of the island as it is described by Tennyson, none of it produces a response. The aspects of the island touched on are all qualified by *in*transitive verbs; there is no sense in any of the frenzy suggested by *wheeling, thundering, winding* or *moving*, or by the nouns *flash, glows and glories, shriek, whisper, sweep,* that anything is ever going to change. Like the figure of the solitary shipwrecked sailor, the trees, birds, insects and so on proclaim their identities to an absence of response. No wonder the coco's plumes *droop*. The convolvuluses *coil* and seem to achieve release when they *run*—but they can only run to *the limit of the land*, which imprisons them as much as it does Enoch. Their shine is described as *lustre*; something of the Latin sense of *lustrum*—penitential purification, and measurement of time by five-year periods—creeps in, as well, perhaps, as a suggestion of lust, for there seems to be a repressed sexuality in the *glows and glories* too. The impression left by the passage as a whole is that both Enoch and the island are emptying themselves of themselves in the process of longingly proclaiming their identities to an unregarding world. The only change in that world seems to be that the ocean each night is *hollower-bellow-ing*; the word could apply with equal aptness to Enoch's perpetual, silent cry for help, for a sail.

It is hard to see that there is much justice in Bagehot's objections to this passage. The style is consistently Tennysonian, to be sure, but it most emphatically does not function simply as ornament or distraction. Its repetitions and accumulations, two aspects of a single view of things, are dramatically appropriate to the subject-matter, which, incidentally, is also highly characteristic of the poet. Whilst Tennyson dispenses with the verisimilitude of *Robinson Crusoe*, he creates a far more intense picture of his hero's spiritual isolation and (to use a favourite Tennysonian figure of speech) desperate hope.

Not that *Enoch Arden* as a whole succeeds. Bagehot could very reasonably object to the way in which the narrative is conducted once Enoch is off his desert island. He returns home after many years of exile to find that his impoverished wife has married again, on the assumption that he is dead; her new husband, Philip, is not only good and loving, but also able to provide for the family. This is a perplexing situation indeed; Enoch's answer is neither to retire from the scene altogether (for he continues to live in the same town as his wife) nor to declare his presence to her. This decidedly odd arrangement seems to have the author's approval. Enoch's definitive act of renunciation comes when he gazes through the window at the happiness of his family in their new home. They do not suspect his presence, and he has to repress

> a shrill and terrible cry
> Which in one moment, like the blast of doom,
> Would shatter all the happiness of the hearth.

To speak of 'the blast of doom' is not to see things in proportion; but then surely there is something wrong in the whole idea of going up to have a look at the wife you are painfully renouncing —is it not too masochistic, not to say suicidal? Tennyson evidently feels this when he sets out to describe the episode; Enoch is drawn by the light from Philip's cottage

> as the beacon-blaze allures
> The bird of passage, till he madly strikes
> Against it, and beats out his weary life.

By the time we come to the 'blast of doom', however, the madness of Enoch's action has become equivocal; it is hard to say whether the simile gives us only his view of the conse-quences of letting out the cry or the author's as well. There is no doubt that the author *does* share Enoch's point of view altogether, however, when we learn that

> His resolve
> Upbore him, and firm faith, and evermore
> Prayer from a living source within the will,
> And beating up thro' all the bitter world,
> Like fountains of sweet water in the sea,
> Kept him a living soul.

The trouble with *Enoch Arden* is that it wants to persuade us that very neurotic behaviour is really very good; it suffers, that is, not from the emotional thinness that Bagehot implies, but from an excess of emotion, which arises, one suspects, from the fact that Tennyson is more interested in the nobility of a man's refusal to reveal himself in all that he imagines to be his true horror, rather than in the question of what a man in Enoch's position *ought* to do. The conventional view of the poem's last lines is that they reveal Victorian vulgarity, which is impressed by costly funerals:

> So past the strong heroic soul away.
> And when they buried him the little port
> Had seldom seen a costlier funeral.

But the lines may just as well be a comment on the inadequacy of this gesture for a man who regards death as the only means of escape from his isolation ('"A sail! a sail!/I am saved"; and so fell back and spoke no more'). The real objection to the lines is a moral one—Enoch is neither strong nor heroic. Bagehot pretends to appove the morality of the poem ('It is true that he acts rightly; that he is very good. But such is human nature that it finds a little tameness in mere morality'), but his summary of the function of the ornate style in *Enoch Arden* is franker:

the dismal act of a squalid man needed many condiments to make it pleasant, and therefore Mr. Tennyson was right to mix them subtly and to use them freely.

It would be truer to say, I think, that the story of the poem was of such a nature that it encouraged an unwise and self-pitying identification with his hero on the part of the author. If the style has anything at all to do with this, its intensely dramatic nature may have been a contributory cause; but one might equally well argue that its quality of being a 'style' should have helped to distance the author from his work. In either case, Bagehot's account of its function seems false.

His essay is, however, an important one still for readers of Tennyson; the damaging account of the poet's technique as something that can easily be abstracted from the matter of his poems has not really been faced squarely by his advocates. Neither Nicolson's talk of 'mystical genius' nor Eliot's ascription of 'abundance, variety and complete competence' quite dispels the feeling that these eminent critics are defending what they know to be a lost cause. Eliot's subsequent remark that 'Tennyson's surface, his technical accomplishment, is intimate with his depths', seems only to confirm the impression of shallow brilliance given by the talk of 'variety and complete competence'. Almost certainly Eliot did not intend this.

One has to determine what 'technical accomplishment' means in relation to Tennyson. Are not all poets technically accomplished in so far as they write well? What other accomplishment is there than the matching of what is said to the manner of saying it so that it cannot be said better? It is a mark of Tennyson's failure that we are more impressed by the way he says things than by what he says; but even as we award him this second prize for creation, the one that goes to 'technical accomplishment' distinguished from the genuine poetic kind, we feel a certain reluctance. Reading Tennyson one is often moved by more than words, and not only on illegitimate occasions as in *Enoch Arden*; it is hard to believe the poet engaged with his work only at the level of verbal dexterity. On the contrary, Tennyson is a poet far too ready to let his feelings get out of control, as they do in poems like 'Locksley Hall Sixty Years After' or 'Happy: The Leper's Bride':

I loved you first when young and fair, but now I love you most;
   The fairest flesh at last is filth on which the worm will feast;
This poor rib-grated dungeon of the holy human ghost,
   This house with all its hateful needs no cleaner than the beast...

'Technical accomplishment' is of little use here, though this is characteristic Tennyson. Eliot assures us that Tennyson is a poet of great variety, but is this more than superficially true? His tones are as recognisable as any one's; the variety of form and subject-matter is not so great that we would not be able to identify most of his poems as his. *The Idylls of the King* and *In Memoriam* have much in common with 'Oenone' or 'St. Simeon Stylites'. The common element is an almost obsessive repetition of words and phrases: in 'St. Simeon Stylites', for example:

Yes, I can *heal* him. Power goes forth from me.
They say that they are *heal'd*. Ah, hark! *they shout*
'*St. Simeon* Stylites'. Why, *if so*,
God reaps a harvest in me. O my soul,
God reaps a harvest in thee. If this be,
Can I work miracles and not *be saved*?
This is not told of any. They were *saints*.
It cannot be but that I shall *be saved*;
Yea, crown'd *a saint. They shout*, 'Behold *a saint*!'
And lower voices *saint* me from above.
Courage, *St. Simeon!* This dull chrysalis
Cracks into shining wings, and hope ere death
Spreads *more and more and more*, that God hath now
Sponged and made blank of crimeful record all
My mortal archives.

15

'Browningesque before Browning,' says Jerome Buckley of this poem. Well, yes: but all the same, how close to *Enoch Arden*. Simeon's pillar takes the place of Enoch's island, but the sense of isolation amidst a crowd is common to both poems. I have suggested that there is irony in the allusion to the 'costly funeral' at the end of *Enoch Arden*, at the expense of the people of the little port, but it may also arise from doubts on the author's part as to whether Enoch's behaviour had been so heroic after all. Certainly the analogous situation of Simeon Stylites arouses grave doubts. Professor Buckley believes the poem to be, at least in part, a satire on the Evangelical preacher Charles Simeon, and he may have caught the intention of the poem perfectly. But the effect is not satiric, because it leaves the reader in too great a state of uncertainty. What is the effect of the repeated use of that word *saint*? It is at once emphatic and exhaustive of meaning. One of the sources for the poem is Gibbon, but Tennyson's position in regard to sainthood is not so clearly defined as the sceptical historian's. It is significant that the poem is in the form of a monologue, because the frankly subjective point of view can leave it altogether doubtful whether Simeon is a saint or not without the poet's offering his opinion at all. Simeon's own use of the word *saint* veers between two meanings; sometimes he hopes for exalted rank in Heaven, sometimes he merely wants to be saved (to be a *saint* in the sense of 'member of the elect'). His confusion on the issue is summed up in the brilliant line 'And lower voices saint me from above'— there is equivocation in the words *lower* and *above*, so that one is as baffled as Simeon to know whether the voices are illusory or not, devilish or angelic. The repetition of the word *saint* builds up our sense of the crucial importance of its meaning at the same time that that meaning is blurred by the variety of uses given it in the process of repetition.

In a note Gibbon comments on the ulcer on Simeon's thigh:

It has been reported that the Devil, assuming an angelic form, invited him to ascend, like Elijah, into a fiery chariot. The saint too hastily raised his foot, and Satan seized the moment of inflicting this chastisement on his vanity.

Tennyson's poem is written very much against the spirit of

Gibbon; it is as though he has asked himself: 'What if the invitation really had been divine? *Then* it would have been impossible to reply to it too hastily.' Simeon's situation is a perplexing one in more ways than Gibbon will admit, and Tennyson wants us to see this. How *can* the divine be distinguished from the devilish?

This question is the all-important one for Tennyson. He is a poet of passionate doubt, and this doubt is reflected in the continual anxious turning over of words and thoughts in the mind as well as on the page. He is as baffled as Simeon about sainthood, and this bafflement is reflected in the oddly perfunctory conclusion of the poem:

> I prophesy that I shall die to-night,
> A quarter before twelve.
> > But thou, O Lord,
> Aid all this foolish people; let them take
> Example, pattern: lead them to thy light.

'Let them take/Example, pattern' leaves us in as great a doubt as ever; should Simeon be the pattern for them or not? Tennyson can leave the matter hanging there because the reader is not being invited to take something *from* the poem—a moral, an attitude—but to put himself *in* it, to feel the pull of 'lower voices' sounding 'from above' himself. It is more important that he should have the experience offered by the poem than that he should moralise without it.

One would expect that Simeon's prophecy of his own death would conclude the poem emphatically, of course; but this is not the case. Tennyson's fundamental doubts about the nature of things, which reflect themselves in the passionate repetitions of his poems, also influence him in the kind of ending he employs. The characteristic Tennysonian conclusion is like that of 'St. Simeon Stylites'—superficially emphatic, actually inconclusive. Take the familiar last lines of the original 'Morte d'Arthur':

> Long stood Sir Bedivere
> Revolving many memories, till the hull
> Look'd one black dot against the verge of dawn,
> And on the mere the wailing died away.

The poem itself is full of repetition; an example at the simplest level would be the casting away of Excalibur, signifying a return to the state of affairs before Arthur acquired the sword. Bedivere only manages to cast the sword into the water at the third attempt. Arthur is carried off in the barge by the three queens, and the wailing dies away. The last line seems to bring the poem to a point of rest, as the idea of death itself dies away with the wailing. And yet Sir Bedivere is left 'revolving many memories'. There is plenty to think about—Arthur's own prophecy of change ('The old order changeth, yielding place to new') and his uncertainty about his destination ('For all my mind is clouded with a doubt'). Rehearsing these things in his memory, Sir Bedivere is left in a state of suspended animation, and a sense of this qualifies the conclusiveness of the last line. There is, too, a syntactic ambiguity about the wailing. The last line has all the appearance of being a main clause, but it might just as well be subordinate—'Bedivere stood until the wailing died away.' The uncertain status of the final clause softens its conclusiveness greatly. When Tennyson decided to continue the poem further for *The Idylls of the King*, and to give it a more optimistic ending ('And the new sun rose bringing the new year') he had no very difficult task, because the old ending had always left room for a continuation. Bedivere could go on reminiscing or he could take new action, and Arthur might or might not be dead. These alternatives are similar to those at the end of 'St. Simeon Stylites', where Simeon may or may not achieve sainthood. Is he humble and thinking solely of other people's welfare, hoping that they will be saved whether his life provides the pattern or not? Or is he vain, because he *does* think that he would be a good example for them? Tennyson does not make it possible for us to judge truly between these two possible interpretations. The forthright plea 'Lead them to thy light' concludes the poem satisfactorily without bringing the reader's own speculations to an end. Endings of this kind are consistent with the use of repetition, especially of impassioned repetition as in 'St. Simeon Stylites', because they also suggest the uncertainty underlying so many of the poems; and since they do not outrage our moral sense they are superior to the false resolution of *Enoch Arden*, where we are too well aware of the hero's ultimate heavenly destination.

Tennyson's repetition marks a reluctance or inability on his own part or on that of his *personae* to progress from one subject to another. He is always circling back; he is not a man who can easily reason himself out of a state of mind. When he does move on, the change is not gradual but, as in 'The Two Voices', instantaneous and beyond the bounds of reason:

> These three made unity so sweet,
> My frozen heart began to beat,
> Remembering its ancient heat.
>
> I blest them, and they wander'd on:
> I spoke, but answer came there none:
> The dull and bitter voice was gone.

The unreasoning instinct that leads Enoch Arden to repress his cry of recognition when he sees his wife is equally instantaneous. Tennyson almost habitually depicts himself or his imagined characters in states of mind that are self-enclosed—

> The doubt would rest, I dare not solve.
> In the same circle we revolve.
> Assurance only breeds resolve.

They are for the most part incapable of this assurance. They tread the same weary circle of thoughts, and as long as we read, we tread that circle with them, unless, like the speaker in 'The Two Voices', they can leap over the wall. We are drawn into the poems by repetitions which act as invocations, as pleas to us to listen; and once we are *in* the poem we are subject to it. The superficial emphasis of the conclusion is necessary to shake us back into our own life, as it were, and to confirm the enclosed nature of the poem's world, but it can rarely be finally conclusive because the poem exists as an entry into a state of mind without necessary end.

It is convenient in this respect to compare Tennyson's emphatically conclusive, covertly inconclusive endings with the *frankly* inconclusive ones of Arnold. Arnold blurs the margins of his poems so that they may fuse, as it were, with the reader's own process of thought. 'Tristram and Iseult', for example,

concludes by telling another story, supposed to be told by
Iseult of Brittany to her children. It is the story of Merlin and
Vivian—plainly offering Iseult's interpretation of Tristram's
enchantment by her rival, Iseult of Ireland. In taking another
story to comment on her own, she is acting as a model for us:
we can use her story to meditate on our own life. Arnold's
poem moves out of itself into the reader's world by this means;
it also shows itself aware of other modes of experiencing reality
than its own, as the self-enclosed poems of Tennyson do not.
Iseult's story of Merlin and Vivian ends Arnold's poem in this
way:

> Nine times she waved the fluttering wimple round,
> And made a little plot of magic ground.
> And in that daisied circle, as men say,
> Is Merlin prisoner till the judgement-day;
> But she herself whither she will can rove—
> For she was passing weary of his love.

It ends on a note of infinite suggestiveness. Tristram, like
Merlin, was a prisoner of the passion inspired by Iseult of
Ireland; Iseult of Brittany remains true to his memory; but
Vivian, the spirit of change and disaster in love, wanders out of
the poem into our own day. Such an ending is characteristic of
Arnold. It is of the same kind as the last stanzas of 'The Scholar-
Gipsy', or the conclusion to 'Sohrab and Rustum', where the
characters of the poem are left behind as the Oxus flows to the
sea and a new tranquillity. The reader's mind takes the course
of the Oxus also, and is led away from the scene of the narrative;
at the same time he can see a relationship between the father's
slaughter of his son and the final tranquillity which he may
ponder, and which he is left in a mood to ponder.

There is nothing like this in Tennyson. His aim is to draw
the reader *into* his imaginative world, and with his help to
encompass it. His beginnings and endings mark off the bounds
of the encompassed world of fantasy in such a way as to suggest
at once its discontinuity with the actual world and its continuity within itself. We have already glanced at the kind of
continuity implied by his endings; some illustration of the way in
which Tennyson establishes discontinuity may be helpful. One
might begin with his fondness for framing poems with pro-

logues and epilogues—'The Day-Dream', the original 'Morte d'Arthur', *The Princess*, or 'Tiresias'—or for giving introductions —'The Palace of Art', or 'Demeter and Persephone'. Such devices serve not only to close the poem off from the reader's world, but also to establish its independence from its maker. 'Demeter and Persephone', for example, is not merely a distinct object, for that would suggest a maker of the object; it is a plant which lives in itself:

> So may this legend for a while
> If greeted by your classic smile,
>   Tho' dead in its Trinacrian Enna,
> Blossom again on a colder isle.

The frame has a special attraction for Tennyson because it marks not merely the discontinuity of the poem with the world of everyday experience but also the inward nature of its subject matter. The poems tend to centre on states of mind or dramatic changes of heart, the action taking place within the speaker as much as outside him. The crucial moment in *In Memoriam* comes when the poet falls into a trance and imagines his own soul 'wound' in Hallam's. It is appropriate to the inward nature of this experience that it should be narrated within the framework of descriptions of the Somersby dusk and dawn, and in stanzas which themselves frame one couplet within another.

In the belief that these matters are inter-related, we have passed from repetition to the inconclusiveness of many Tennysonian endings, from there to the rhetorically conclusive nature of these inconclusive endings and to Tennyson's predilection for the frame as a setting for his poems. We are now approaching the central mystery of his poetry, and we shall do so by considering its 'morbidity'. Since the publication of Sir Harold Nicolson's book in 1923, Tennyson has come to be considered as primarily a *morbid* poet, and readers have not hesitated to relate his own talk of the 'black blood of the Tennysons' to such things as the inherited craziness of the narrator in *Maud*. Tennyson's fondness for the frame may reflect his anxiety that his poems should not be read in this way. It is hard to believe that he would care to be identified with Enoch Arden or

Simeon Stylites, although the way in which these *personae* are made over in a distinctively Tennysonian image makes it not unreasonable to see them as the poet's fantasy portraits of himself. Tennyson attempts to persuade readers that 'The Dead Prophet' is not about himself by subscribing the date '182–'; this *does* seem 'a deliberate attempt to mislead', as Professor Buckley suggests. Surely the poet's own fear of criticism and dislike of intrusion in his personal life are reflected in the savage, intensely imagined dismemberment of the once-revered prophet's body:

> She gabbled as she groped in the dead,
> And all the people were pleased;
> 'See, what a little heart', she said,
> 'And the liver is half-diseased!'

Tennyson's poetry *is* morbid, at least in the sense that it grows from morbid feelings in the poet himself. And yet it is surely not great *because* it is morbid, but because at its best it allows us to feel at once the poet's intense involvement with his subject-matter and at the same time his control over it. Tennyson's 'technique', that is, is not to be interpreted as idle display or decorative enrichment, but as a mark that the author *has* put himself to one side of his despair or spiritual sickness, and has found some release in the attempt to encompass it and to offer it to us for our meditation. The extent to which repetition is more than incidental to the success of a given poem may be indicative of the extent to which Tennyson has succeeded in distancing himself from his morbidity.

Repetition, after all, had a personal significance for Tennyson that cannot be overlooked. Its nature is clearly revealed in a crucial passage of Hallam Tennyson's *Memoir* of his father:

In some phases of thought and feeling his idealism tended more decidedly to mysticism. He wrote: 'A kind of waking trance I have frequently had, quite up from boyhood, when I have been all alone. This has generally come upon me thro' repeating my own name two or three times to myself silently, till all at once, as it were out of the intensity of the consciousness of individuality, the individuality itself seemed to dissolve and fade away into boundless being, and this not a confused state, but the clearest of the clearest, the surest of the surest, the weirdest of the weirdest, utterly beyond words, where death was an almost laughable impossibility, the loss of personality (if so it were) seeming no extinction but the only true life'. 'This might', he said, 'be the state which St. Paul describes, "Whether in the body I cannot tell, or whether out of the body I cannot tell".'

He continued: 'I am ashamed of my feeble description. Have I not said the state is utterly beyond words? But in a moment, when I come back to my normal state of "sanity", I am ready to fight for *mein liebes Ich*, and hold that it will last for aeons of aeons'.

It can hardly be said that this passage has gone unnoticed by commentators. Professor Arthur J. Carr says of it, for example, in a well-known essay, that 'if there is a definitive Tennysonian theme, this is it—a reiterated and dreamlike sense of loss that becomes idyllic self-assurance'; and more recently Mr. James Kissane has very sensitively explored the relation to his poetry of Tennyson's 'Passion of the Past', described in 'The Ancient Sage', and connected with the 'waking trance' by Hallam Tennyson in a note to the passage already quoted. Nevertheless, the experience itself remains obscure; and to link it with our own observations of the poetry may bring out its importance for Tennyson and his reader more clearly. Just as in the trance experience repetition of his own name produces a self-contradictory effect, at once denying and affirming the reality of personality, so in the poetry it weakens sense as it adds emphasis. The contradiction within the poems between the 'never-ending' nature of the states of mind represented and the rhetorically conclusive endings finds a parallel in the opposition between Tennyson's sense of 'boundless being' during the trance and the 'fight for *mein liebes Ich*' which follows it.

Again, if we take the early poem 'Armageddon' to be based on a similar experience, as seems most likely, then we find in it a more explicit account of the way in which elaborations of detail of the kind we considered in *Enoch Arden*, and which are by no means uncommon in the poetry, whilst seeming to provide variety actually create an effect of monotonous sameness. The speaker in this poem describes his vision as being one of extreme accuracy:

> I saw
> The smallest grain that dappled the dark Earth,
> The indistinctest atom in deep air . . .

This is associated with an escape from 'Time and Being and Place' into a 'victory of boundless thought'. Yet the 'victory' is soon reversed:

> An icy veil
> Of pale, weak, lifeless, thin, unnatural blue
> Wrapt up the rich variety of things
> In grim and ghastly sameness.

Tennyson seems to have been constantly aware of the possibility of such reversals of feeling as this. For him, things tremble on a balance; looking through the microscope he would say, according to Hallam Tennyson, 'Strange that these wonders should draw some men to God and repel others. No more reason in one than in the other'. Such a remark springs from the impulse which also caused him to write, in youth, two poems, one entitled 'All Things Will Die' and the other 'Nothing Will Die', and, in later life, two greetings for his new-born son, one viewing his arrival as part of the system of the physical universe, the other as part of a transcendent divine scheme. The two greetings are brought together under the one title 'De Profundis', with a concluding poem which again embodies Tennyson's vision of the doubleness of things:

> We feel we are nothing—for all is Thou and in Thee;
> We feel we are something—*that* also has come from Thee . . .

Doubleness provides the structural principle of poems spaced as far apart in Tennyson's career as 'The Two Voices' and 'The Ancient Sage'. It also lies behind Tennyson's partiality for the oxymoron—'faultily faultless' in *Maud*, or, from 'De Profundis':

> the pain
> Of this divisible-indivisible world
> Among the numerable-innumerable
> Sun, sun, and sun, thro' finite-infinite space
> In finite-infinite Time . . .

All Tennyson's uncertainty about the physical reality of the world comes through in these extraordinary lines.

MARTIN DODSWORTH

'Yet it appeared that he distinguished himself from external things', remarked Jowett. Evidently he did; but not without pain and anguish. He *had* to assert his own identity apart from other things to avoid a complete confusion of objective and subjective into the sameness of non-being. In 'The Two Voices', the 'still small voice' asks: 'Were it not better not to be?' The stuttering formulation (involving repetition) mimes the fall into meaninglessness that suicide, a permanent extinction of the self, would entail. 'Supposed Confessions of a Second-Rate Sensitive Mind' suggests that the poet was tempted by the idea of an existence without full consciousness like that of animals, though the idea is rejected, as in 'Morte d'Arthur':

> For what are men better than sheep or goats
> That nourish a blind life within the brain,
> If, knowing God, they lift not hands of prayer
> Both for themselves and those who call them friend?

This is not subject-matter which requires ornament, but it does need to be handled, like gelignite, with care. Tennyson's artistry can be seen as an assertion of his independence from the fantasies of timeless existence which lie behind his poetry. Much of his effort, in any case, is directed towards either a placing of his longings for an idealised timeless state as appropriate to the mad or foolish, or establishing what the true basis of things may be. Of Cyril, in *The Princess*, a poem which is as much as anything about the recognition of external reality, it is said that:

> These flashes on the surface are not he.
> He has a solid base of temperament . . .

That is true of Tennyson himself; though regarded as an artist of the superficial, he is always concerned with what lies beneath the surface. He sinks from the physical into the abyss of metaphysical speculation:

> For Knowledge is the swallow on the lake
> That sees and stirs the surface-shadow there
> But never yet hath dipt into the abysm,
> The Abysm of all Abysms, beneath, within
> The blue of sky and sea, the green of earth,

25

And in the million-millionth of a grain
Which cleft and cleft again for evermore,
And ever vanishing, never vanishes . . .

In the account of his 'metaphysical' trance-state, Tennyson says that it is 'utterly beyond words'; he uses language in such a way (and repetition is part of it) as to suggest what is incapable of direct expression. For example, the conclusion of 'Vastness' is an assertion of belief that is logically impossible; the last line can only be given meaning by imputing to it the force of feeling that we deduce in the poet, but which he cannot express:

What is it all if we all of us end but in being our own corpse-coffins at last,
Swallow'd in Vastness, lost in Silence, drown'd in the deeps of a meaningless Past?

What but a murmur of gnats in the gloom, or a moment's anger of bees in their hive?—

*   *   *

Peace, let it be! for I loved him, and love him for ever: the dead are not dead but alive.

Beneath the surface of Tennyson's poems lies the unspeakable: the unspeakable reality, which Tennyson regards with a mixture of horror and awe. In the beautiful poem 'To the Marquis of Dufferin and Ava' (who, as a family friend, had invited the young Lionel Tennyson out to India where he contracted a fatal illness) the word 'unspeakable' receives an almost impossible degree of emphasis:

Dying, 'Unspeakable' he wrote
'Their kindness', and he wrote no more . . .

It seems appropriate to place beside this the witty but profound dedicatory poem 'To Alfred Tennyson My Grandson':

Golden-hair'd Ally whose name is one with mine,
Crazy with laughter and babble and earth's new wine,
Now that the flower of a year and a half is thine,
O little blossom, O mine, and mine of mine,
Glorious poet who never hast written a line,
Laugh, for the name at the head of my verse is thine.
May'st thou never be wrong'd by the name that is mine!

The child is a 'glorious poet who never hast written a line'—
possibly *because* he has never written a line. The two Alfreds in a
characteristic Tennysonian coupling are being contrasted, after
all, and the curiously sombre last line suggests a distrust of
words themselves, for as a poet the old man would hardly
wrong his child consciously. A similar distrust appears in the
late dramatic monologue 'Romney's Remorse', where the
achievements of art are placed side by side with the pain which
it has caused in life. Romney in his final sickness repents of the
sacrifices he has demanded of his wife:

> O Mary, Mary!
> Vexing you with words!
> Words only, born of fever, or the fumes
> Of that dark opiate dose you gave me,—words,
> Wild babble. I have stumbled back again
> Into the common day, the sounder self.

Romney is talking about the words which escaped him in his
delirium, but he might also be disowning 'the Master's apo-
thegm' which 'lured' him from his family, and also 'that short
word' 'Art' which he can now 'so disrelish'. I believe that we
have here a late echo of a theme which appears in its fullest
form in *In Memoriam:*

> I sometimes hold it half a sin
> To put in words the grief I feel;
> For words, like Nature, half reveal
> And half conceal the Soul within.
>
> (v)

Poetry does not have its value for Tennyson in this mood
because it makes statements, but because Sorrow

> takes, when harsher moods remit,
> What slender shade of doubt may flit,
> And makes it vassal unto love:
>
> And hence, indeed, she sports with words,
> But better serves a wholesome law,
> And holds it sin and shame to draw
> The deepest measure from the chords:

        Nor dare she trust a larger lay,
           But rather loosens from the lip
           Short swallow-flights of song, that dip
        Their wings in tears, and skim away.

                                                  (XLVIII)

'For knowledge is the swallow on the lake'—and Poetry too, it
would seem. Passages like these suggest that Tennyson was well
enough aware of the sort of thing he was doing in his poems, that
he *was* in control as an artist, and that in his superficially
'ornate' use of such devices as repetition, as in his fondness for
bringing opposites into focus, he was adumbrating a deeper but
inexpressible unity to all things, a unity which nevertheless did
not deny their fundamental distinct and individual existences.
It is not necessary to confuse poetry with theology in order to
applaud this achievement, for surely the power of the mind to
imagine a unity beyond such diversity is basic to our ability to
deal with reality at all. Freud's essay 'The Antithetical Sense of
Primal Words' suggests the kind of unity 'beyond words', or at
least beyond the antitheses of language, which Tennyson
evokes in his best poetry.

        In words, like weeds, I'll wrap me o'er,
           Like coarsest clothes against the cold:
           But that large grief which these enfold
        Is given in outline and no more.

                                                  (v)

To his own mind at least, Tennyson's subject-matter was the
'Unnamable', the unknowable life after death and the un-
fathomable depth of self; and it is at these that the conspicuous
outlines of his poetry point.

   I have tried to show that Bagehot's account of Tennyson's
'ornate' style is unsatisfactory because he does not see how
appropriate it is both to the poems and to the mind of the man
who wrote them. In particular I have tried to hint at the range
of meaning that repetition had for Tennyson, and how far it
could satisfy contradictory impulses in his own nature. The kind
of evidence offered has been necessarily sketchy; Tennyson's
poetry by its very bulk presents any critic with great difficulties
of selection. I have quoted from as many different kinds of poem

and from as many different periods in the poet's development as I could, in order to emphasise what I believe to be the fundamental nature of the phenomena discussed, but I have also tried to be economical. A case has been set up, rather than proved. There is, however, one aspect of the poetry which needs fuller discussion and illustration, and that is the question of its value. It is not enough to show, in Tennyson's defence, that his deepest interests were engaged even when his style struck Bagehot as merely ornate. *Enoch Arden* fails precisely because Tennyson is too much involved in the story, His sympathy for Enoch leads him to an admiration for his hero which we cannot endorse. The elaboration of style can signify a distancing on the part of the author from his subject matter. It does so, for example, in 'Demeter and Persephone', where ideas of rising and falling are carefully repeated in the framework of an involved rhetoric invoking the continual struggle of shadow and light which Demeter would evade. It is the self-consciousness of this style that distances author and reader from the poem so that it may be considered as a whole:

> Faint as a climate-changing bird that flies
> All night across the darkness, and at dawn
> Falls on the threshold of her native land,
> And can no more, thou camest, O my child,
> Led upward by the God of ghosts and dreams,
> Who laid thee at Eleusis, dazed and dumb
> With passing thro' at once from state to state,
> Until I brought thee hither, that the day,
> When here thy hands let fall the gather'd flower,
> Might break thro' clouded memories once again
> On thy lost self.

The deliberate contrasts between *falls*, *laid thee*, and *let fall*, and *led upward*, *brought thee*, and *break thro'* are reflected in the variations of flow in the sentence, now shaping its clauses to the length of the line, now exceeding the limit which it sets. The opening sentence holds the rest of the poem in germ; and so does the conclusion, which characteristically looks forward to the time when there will no longer be fear of death, and yet in such a manner as to lay more emphasis on the actuality of that fear in its last lines:

and see no more
The Stone, the Wheel, the dimly-glimmering lawns
Of that Elysium, all the hateful fires
Of torment, and the shadowy warrior glide
Along the silent field of Asphodel.

Sisyphus and his stone, Ixion and his wheel are apt images for
Tennyson's own tormented fantasy of eternal doubt and the
self-enclosed worlds of his *personae*. 'Demeter and Persephone'
is a very fine poem, and one that is built around the favourite
theme of duality:

> 'The Bright one in the highest
> Is brother of the Dark one in the lowest,
> And Bright and Dark have sworn that I, the child
> Of thee, the great Earth-Mother, thee, the Power
> That lifts her buried life from gloom to bloom,
> Should be for ever and for evermore
> The Bride of Darkness'.

Tennyson's poem is surely the source of Lawrence's 'Bavarian
Gentians'; but it is not inferior to its derivative.

Tennyson's best poems are like 'Demeter and Persephone', I
think, in that they do not make statements but depict frames of
mind. They are ambiguous because they depict the confusion
of objective and subjective in our view of reality, but they are
also hearteningly direct, since the author himself perceives this
ambiguity and is to that extent free of it. The reader knows that
the ambiguity is perceived by the consistency and firmness with
which he delineates it. We have seen something of this process
in 'Demeter and Persephone' and also, I think, in 'St. Simeon
Stylites'; let us take for our final example a poem in which
repetition plays a more conspicuous part than in either of these,
one of Tennyson's masterpieces, 'Œnone'.

The refrain of Œnone', repeated nineteen times, establishes
the monotonous tone of the poem. Enoch Arden was trapped
on an island; Œnone is caught in her own frustrated passion.
The recurrence of her cry:

> 'O mother Ida, many-fountain'd Ida!
> Dear mother Ida, harken ere I die . . .'

emphasises her inability to move out of the present situation.

30

Her lament begins in the heat of noon, symbolically because she is at the mid-point of her career; she ends at sunset, foreseeing the end of the story and the end of her life ('I will not die alone, for fiery thoughts/Do shape themselves within me, more and more'); the story itself takes its origin in a dawn-scene. The whole day of Œnone's life seems to be blotted by her jilting by Paris. Here is morbidity, certainly! The monotony of the often-heard refrain is an equivalent for the excessive feelings to which Œnone gives expression.

The poem moves in a way appropriate to its subject-matter also; it expands into seemingly endless detail. The scene of the action is described, the speeches rehearsed, all at the same hypnotic rate, in sentences which grow and grow by an accumulation of adjectival phrases and clauses, by a simple multiplication of things described:

> 'I waited underneath the dawning hills,
> Aloft the mountain lawn was dewy-dark,
> And dewy dark aloft the mountain pine:
> Beautiful Paris, evil-hearted Paris,
> Leading a jet-black goat, white-horn'd, white-hooved,
> Came up from reedy Simois all alone.'

It is easy enough to suggest that Œnone is the means by which Tennyson gives vent to some of his own unhealthy feelings of isolation and despair. And yet surely this poem is very different in its total effect from a piece like *Enoch Arden*. I would say that the difference lies in the way that Tennyson *defines* Œnone's feelings by providing something in the poem, akin to the contrast of rising and falling in 'Demeter and Persephone', by which they may be measured:

> The swimming vapour slopes athwart the glen,
> Puts forth an arm, and creeps from pine to pine,
> And loiters, slowly drawn.

This is the substance and nature of Œnone's speech itself:

> 'Hear me, for I will speak, and build up all
> My sorrow with my song, as yonder walls
> Rose slowly to a music slowly breathed,
> A cloud that gather'd shape . . .'

Her sentences with their cumulative structure drift through the paragraphs of verse, hesitating and circling around certain subjects ('Beautiful Paris, evil-hearted Paris'), and giving an air of unreality to all that is related. Even Troy's walls seem cloud: but they seem to Œnone because she imposes her own feelings on them.

When the goddesses come to be judged by Paris:

> 'It was the deep midnoon: one silvery cloud
> Had lost his way between the piney sides
> Of this long glen. Then to the bower they came,
> Naked they came to that smooth-swarded bower,
> And at their feet the crocus brake like fire . . .'

The cloud and Œnone are both lost at this moment of the story. The cloud is out of its element in the fire of the sun, as Œnone is out of hers when Paris draws the fiery goddesses to him and so becomes precursor of the fire of war as he was formerly precursor of the day:

> 'white-breasted like a star
> Fronting the dawn he moved . . .'

Paris is associated with the fire that dances before the eyes of Cassandra, and he is the fire that surrounds and torments Œnone:

> 'Wheresoe'er I am by night and day
> All earth and air seem only burning fire'.

Eventually the fire enters the cloud of Œnone's sorrow:

> 'Fiery thoughts
> Do shape themselves within me . . .'

Paris becomes associated with fire; Œnone's element is water. She is 'the daughter of a River-God', she addresses 'many-fountain'd Ida' and her eyes are 'full of tears'. She recollects how Paris sealed his love for her with kisses, and 'water'd it with tears'. The opposition of fire and water is simple and yet not conspicuous, because Tennyson's aim is to represent a state in which, unnaturally, fire and water do *not* cancel one another out. Because Œnone loves Paris, she hates him. She is like a cloud, a cloud carrying fire, and devoted now to death, the specious rest foreshadowed in the description of her hair at the opening of the poem:

> . . . and round her neck
> Floated her hair or seem'd to float in rest.

The lines are recalled in the invocation of death: 'O death, death, death, thou ever-floating cloud . . .' In this way Tennyson presents a sick Œnone torn between her conflicting desires and cut off from the water that is love ('My eyes are full of tears, my heart of love . . . '). The very firmness with which the poet delineates this conflict by the use of images of fire and water is an assurance that he has distanced himself from the morbidity of his subject, and at the same time hints at forms of feeling beyond the control which he can exercise. It is significant that in the late, markedly inferior sequel 'The Death of Œnone' her suicide is depicted as an awakening of passion:

> The morning light of happy marriage broke
> Thro' all the clouded years of widowhood
> And muffling up her comely head, and crying
> 'Husband!' she leapt upon the funeral pile,
> And mixt herself with *him* and past in fire.

The last line is very different from that of 'Œnone' ('All earth and air seem only burning fire'); and the difference seems to lie in Œnone's acceptance of the fact of passion. It was this that she denied, and in the earlier poem the consequence of her denial was suffering. Fire is the symbol of war there. But in 'The Death of Œnone' it is transformed, symbolic now of the love that has forgiven Paris as he sought it from her. The images of cloud and fire are taken up again by the poet from the earlier poem and shown in a new light. Yet there is no disharmony. The excellence of 'Œnone' lies in the internal consistency that enables us even there to stand outside it and see the heroine for what she is.

Doubtless Tennyson's poetry often fails. But we do not help ourselves to appreciate its successes—and they are many—if we subscribe to the notions of 'ornate' style so seductively expressed by Bagehot. The truth is that he did not understand Tennyson at all well. Tennyson did not write in order to express ideas but in order to express states of mind which are of interest not so much for their own sake as for what they imply concerning the nature of reality itself. 'Spirit seems to me to be the reality of the world,' Tennyson once said. The proposition is not untenable, but it is perplexing. His poetry is about that perplexment.

NOTES

I have used the Oxford Standard Authors text of Tennyson and Kenneth Allott's edition (1965) of the poems of Matthew Arnold for my quotations. 'Armageddon' is quoted from Alfred Tennyson, *Unpublished Early Poems*, edited by Charles Tennyson, 1931.

I have referred to the following books: Hallam Tennyson, *Alfred Lord Tennyson: A Memoir*, 2 vols., 1897; Harold Nicolson, *Tennyson*, 1923; and Jerome Hamilton Buckley, *Tennyson: The Growth of a Poet*, Cambridge, Mass., 1960.

Walter Bagehot's essay, 'Wordsworth, Tennyson, and Browning; or, Pure, Ornate and Grotesque Art in English Poetry' was first published in 1864; I have quoted it from *English Critical Essays* (Nineteenth Century), selected and edited by Edmund D. Jones, 1916, reprint of 1924, in the World's Classics series. I have also referred to: T. S. Eliot, 'In Memoriam', in *Selected Essays*, 3rd enlarged edition, 1951, reprint of 1953; Arthur J. Carr, 'Tennyson as a Modern Poet', reprinted from the *University of Toronto Quarterly* in *Victorian Literature: Modern Essays in Criticism*, edited by Austin Wright, New York, 1961; James Kissane, 'Tennyson: The Passion of the Past and the Curse of Time', *E.L.H.*, XXXII, 1965, pp. 85–109; and Sigmund Freud, 'The Antithetical Sense of Primal Words', in *Collected Papers*, Vol. IV, 1925. Christopher Ricks's 1966 Chatterton Lecture, 'Tennyson's methods of Composition', has been published in *Proceedings of the British Academy*, Vol. LII. I owe the reference to Tennyson's exclamation over the microscope to Mr. Kissane.

My interest in Tennyson's repetitions was first aroused by an excellent critical study of 'The Two Voices' submitted for examination by Mr. P. A. F. Cooper, at that time (1965) a student at Borough Road Training College, Middlesex.

2

FEMINISM AND FEMININITY IN
THE PRINCESS

Bernard Bergonzi

Tennyson, despite Mr. Auden's notorious observation, was not
a stupid poet. Although, like most poets, he was not an original
thinker, he was certainly capable of thinking, as T. S. Eliot
once reluctantly admitted ('Tennyson and Browning are poets,
and they think . . .') : he was aware of the major ideas of his age,
and was excited and sometimes confused by them. Ideas got
into his poems, though not always to the advantage of the
poetry; one must admit that Eliot was right in saying that
Tennyson was not among the poets who 'feel their thought as
immediately as the odour of a rose', though one might also add
that the intellectual preoccupations of the Victorians were
possibly not of a kind to lend themselves to such attractively
immediate apprehension. *The Princess* is, I suppose, the strangest
of Tennyson's well-known poems, and it is also, in a literal
sense, one of his most thoughtful: ideas got into the poem more
successfully here than elsewhere, and I want to suggest that the
eccentricity of its form was dictated by Tennyson's desire to
entertain and contemplate ideas, some of them rather disturbing
ideas, to which he was not prepared to be formally committed.

In the opening lines of *The Princess* Tennyson unfolds a
substantial amount of information and shows that the poem's
subtitle—'A Medley'—is relevant from the very beginning.
The narrator is staying at Vivian Place, the mansion of Sir
Walter Vivian, together with five other young men, as the
guests of their fellow-student, Walter junior. Also in the party are
Walter's young sister, Lilia, and her maiden-aunt companion.
The occasion is a summer day when Sir Walter has thrown his
grounds open to the people of the district: his tenants and their
families, and the members of the local Mechanics' Institute. In

the second paragraph of the poem the narrator describes the interior of Vivian Place:

> And me that morning Walter show'd the house,
> Greek, set with busts: from vases in the hall
> Flowers of all heavens, and lovelier than their names,
> Grew side by side; and on the pavement lay
> Carved stones of the Abbey-ruin in the park,
> Huge Ammonites, and the first bones of Time;
> And on the tables every clime and age
> Jumbled together; celts and calumets,
> Claymore and snowshoe, toys in lava, fans
> Of sandal, amber, ancient rosaries,
> Laborious orient ivory sphere in sphere,
> The cursed Malayan crease, and battle-clubs
> From the isles of palm: and higher on the walls,
> Betwixt the monstrous horns of elk and deer,
> His own forefathers' arms and armour hung.

As description, this passage catches a particular moment in the development of early-Victorian taste. The architectural context may still be neo-classical—'Greek, set with busts'—but it has already been invaded by an energetically promiscuous connoisseurship, which ranges over the entire globe and back through time to prehistory in pursuit of cultural objects. The interior description is balanced by the succeeding fine account of the outdoor scene, where the working people in the park indulge in recreative pursuits that combine sober pleasure with scientific instruction, in a manner no less characteristic of the period. Within the poem itself, this veritable 'medley' looks forward to the fantastic adventures in the long central section, where every kind of exoticism is mingled with allusions to geometry, astronomy and paleontology.

The narrator goes on to look at the family portraits, and is shown an ancient chronicle which records the exploits in medieval times of the Vivians' illustrious ancestors. He is particularly struck by the account of a valiant lady knight who, in the manner of Boadicea or Joan of Arc, 'Had beat her foes with slaughter from her walls'. Here we are introduced to the theme of feminism which dominates the poem: it is amplified when, after the narrator and his host have joined the rest of the party at the nearby ruined Abbey, Lilia, despite the mockery of her brother and his friends, delivers herself of ardently feminist sentiments. Her ideas are to be given copious expression, both discursively and dramatically, in the succeeding section, but she focuses the debate in a single, vivid image when she ties her coloured scarf round a statue of one of the Vivian's sternest feudal ancestors, the knight Sir Ralph:

> and there was Ralph himself,
> A broken statue propt against the wall,
> As gay as any. Lilia, wild with sport,
> Half child half woman as she was, had wound
> A scarf of orange round the stony helm,
> And robed the shoulders in a rosy silk,
> That made the old warrior from his ivied nook
> Glow like a sunbeam.

A charming yet a disturbing picture, at least to those whose attitudes are rooted in traditional masculine attitudes: 'the feudal warrior lady-clad' provides an ideogrammatic juxta-position of opposed values, and hints at a time when the familiar differences between the sexes will be much less clear-cut, and may even vanish altogether. Modern readers of these lines may find echoing in their heads other, more recent phrases, where the splendours of a vanished past are symbolised by a broken statue or defaced hero: a 'broken Coriolanus' or 'two gross of broken statues'. *The Princess* is, in fact, a sur-prisingly modern poem: as Marshall McLuhan has shown, Tennyson often anticipates symbolist and post-symbolist techniques.[1] With this in mind, we may regard the lines about the interior of Vivian Place as more than just a piece of accurate descriptive verse: they have something of the quality of 'These fragments I have shored against my ruins', where the dis-located modern consciousness moves freely and uneasily amid the *disjecta membra* of cultural and historical relativism: 'every clime and age/Jumbled together'. Tennyson's 'first bones of Time' may present a more assured and hopeful picture than Eliot's 'withered stumps of time', but they seem to belong to the same universe. Such anticipations may look un-Tenny-sonian, but they are certainly not un-Victorian; whilst Tenny-son was working over the final version of *The Princess* Matthew

Arnold was making his brave and painful exploration of that most familiar of twentieth-century disorders, 'the dialogue of the mind with itself', and was lamenting:

> this strange disease of modern life,
> With its sick hurry, and divided aims.

Returning to the narrative of the opening section of *The Princess*, we move through the light-hearted badinage between Lilia and the youths concerning her scheme for a ladies' college, until we are ready for the transition to the central 'story' of the poem, which is to be improvised in turn by the seven young men. This narrative, when we come to it, reads as a kind of dream sequence, and Tennyson is remarkably explicit about the elements that will, as it were, compose its manifest content. Lilia is to be the Princess, of almost absurdly heroic stature: 'six feet high,/Grand, epic, homicidal', whilst the narrator is to be the Prince who will win her, thus suggesting that the flirtation and possible courtship of the two young people provides a sub-plot underneath the poem's more grandiose themes.

> Heroic seems our Princess as required—
> But something made to suit with Time and place,
> A Gothic ruin and a Grecian house,
> A talk of college and of ladies' rights,
> A feudal knight in silken masquerade,
> And, yonder, shrieks and strange experiments
> For which the good Sir Ralph had burnt them all—
> This *were* a medley! we should have him back
> Who told the 'Winter's tale' to do it for us.

These are the elements which, informed by the unfinished argument about women's rights and education, are transmuted into the lengthy fantastic narrative that is to follow. At this point, I shall refer to Mr. John Killham's admirable study of the sources and intellectual background of *The Princess*, from which I have greatly profited[2]. Among other points, Mr. Killham shows that the connection between the things mentioned in the opening of *The Princess* is less arbitrary than one might at first suppose; he points out, in particular, that there were close links between the feminist movement and the movements for the advancement and education of the working-class, so that the educative outing of a Mechanics' Institute is a not inappropriate background for a dramatic debate about the future of women. We can also consult Mr. Killham for a full account of the feminist movements of the 1840s, and the extent to which Tennyson was interested in them, although such knowledge is not essential for a basic understanding of the poem. But it is, I think, important to realise that its central narrative is a dream-transformation of a sober debate, and that many of its more singular characteristics arise from Tennyson's desire to make a full imaginative exploration of questions which, at the same time, are kept intellectually distanced. The transformation of Lilia into Princess Ida has something in common with Lewis Carroll's successive trans-formations of Alice, culminating in the 'Queen Alice' of *Through The Looking Glass*.

II

The central story, about the three young men—the Prince, Cyril, and Florian—who disguise themselves as girls in order to enroll in the ladies' university, has a fine air of *opera buffa* absurdity. After the dense social specificity of the opening of the poem we are immersed in a colourful but vague fairy-tale world, and the ladies' college is set in the kind of dream-landscape that tends to recur, though usually in more menacing forms, in Victorian poetry: one thinks of 'Childe Roland' or *The City of Dreadful Night*. The adventures of the three young men proceed energetically but smoothly, and one has to make a certain deliberate effort to recall that each section is sup-posedly improvised by one of the seven young men, whilst the songs—which Tennyson inserted into the final edition of the poem—are contributed by Lilia and her aunt. A suc-cessively improvised consciousness, such as the Prince's is supposed to be, can have little substantive reality, and we cannot be sure about the relation between the Prince's 'voice' and that of each of the seven successive narrators. In the 'Conclusion' of *The Princess*, however, Tennyson tries to resolve the difficulty by asserting that the story we have just read has,

in fact, been 'written up' by the narrator; he goes on to discuss
the difficulties he found in establishing consistency of tone.
Rarely can a poem have discussed with such frankness its own
process of composition:

> So closed our tale, of which I give you all
> The random scheme as wildly as it rose:
> The words are mostly mine; for when we ceased
> There came a minute's pause, and Walter said,
> 'I wish she had not yielded!' then to me,
> 'What, if you drest it up poetically!'
> So pray'd the men, the women: I gave assent:
> Yet how to bind the scatter'd scheme of seven
> Together in one sheaf? What style could suit?
> The men required that I should give throughout
> The sort of mock-heroic gigantesque,
> With which we banter'd little Lilia first:
> The women—and perhaps they felt their power,
> For something in the ballads which they sang,
> Or in their silent influence as they sat,
> Had ever seem'd to wrestle with burlesque,
> And drove us, last, to quite a solemn close—
> They hated banter, wish'd for something real,
> A gallant fight, a noble princess—why
> Not make her true-heroic—true-sublime?
> Or all, they said, as earnest as the close?
> Which yet with such a framework scarce could be.
> Then rose a little feud betwixt the two,
> Betwixt the mockers and the realists:
> And I, betwixt them both, to please them both,
> And yet to give the story as it rose,
> I moved as in a strange diagonal,
> And maybe neither pleased myself nor them.

Readers of Wayne C. Booth's *The Rhetoric of Fiction* will be
familiar with the idea that the 'implicit voice' of the author
will always be present in a novel, no matter how deliberately
impersonal and self-containedly dramatised; and what is true
of fiction is also true in many respects of Victorian narrative
poems. One problem in *The Princess* is to distinguish between
(*a*) Tennyson's own implicit voice; (*b*) that of the principal
narrator; (*c*) those of the six other narrators in the central

section; and (d) that of the Prince. Having raised this question, we can leave it; certainly there is no point in pursuing it with scholastic exactitude, since with such an avowedly 'random scheme' as *The Princess* one is hardly likely to discover any consistent distinctions. But such indirection in the narrative technique is, I think, another index of *The Princess*' modernity of form; it looks forward to the characteristic fictional complexity of Conrad and Ford.

In practice, this uncertainty about the relation between the various narrative levels, tends to heighten the sense of unreality that surrounds the Prince. And the unreality is emphasised in a fairly unsubtle way when we are shown the Prince falling, at regular intervals, in a cataleptic fit, in which all his surroundings become ghostly and insubstantial:

> On a sudden in the midst of men and day,
> And while I walk'd and talk'd as heretofore,
> I seem'd to move among a world of ghosts,
> And feel myself the shadow of a dream.

These periodic reminders of the potential insubstantiality, not only of the Prince but of those who surround him, prevent us from becoming too intently absorbed in the adventures of the Prince and his companions: unreality must remain unreality, and the profoundly serious is constantly held in check by the mock-heroic.

What is serious about the underlying debate, and what most involves Tennyson (or his narrator), is outlined in the preliminary exchange between Lilia and her brothers: are women fundamentally different—and in practice inferior—beings from men, or are the apparent differences simply the result of a long period of cultural and environmental conditioning? Lilia emphatically asserts the latter opinion: 'It is but bringing up; no more than that'. In our own day this position has been stated with greater rigour by such writers as Simone de Beauvoir and Betty Friedan, who see women as scarcely yet emancipated from the helotage of a male-dominated world; their position can be summed up in Simone de Beauvoir's phrase: 'One is not born, but becomes a woman'. Against this, one may set the traditional view of woman as the

41

Ewig-Weibliche, a biologically differentiated creature, whose child-bearing rôle makes her fundamentally different from men; as Freud put it: 'anatomy is a woman's destiny'. This is a fascinating debate, and one which is never likely to be resolved on the level of theory, since there is no possibility of common ground between the contestants, and not even a common terminology. And so far, the division has taken a predictable shape: almost all the professional opinion that sees women as an 'environmentally differentiated' being has come from women writers, and most (but by no means all) of the claims that she is 'biologically' different have been expressed by men.[3]

In practice, opinion tends to adopt various compromises, often not very rational ones, somewhere between the extremes represented by Freud and Simone de Beauvoir. A work such as Doris Lessing's *The Golden Notebook* shows, very movingly, how a modern woman can achieve a degree of intellectual, professional and sexual emancipation infinitely far beyond anything dreamed of by the young ladies of *The Princess*, and well in advance of the aspirations of the heroines of Ibsen and Shaw, and still remain a prey to her own emotions: to this extent she remains a victim of male exploitation.

In the central section of *The Princess* Tennyson uses the utterances of Princess Ida and her companions, and the reflections of the Prince, in order to examine some of the major possible attitudes to the 'position of women' question: at the same time, the dramatic working-out of his fantasy tends to undercut any easy repose in a purely intellectual solution. When Princess Ida welcomes the three supposed students to the college she sternly urges them to forget about men and thoughts of marriage. Not, indeed, for good (Ida avoids the pathological anti-masculinism of some of the later suffragettes), but for a long time to come:

> Some future time, if so indeed you will,
> You may with those self-styled our lords ally
> Your fortunes, justlier balanced, scale with scale.

One of the most traditional and extreme ways of seeing woman as a biologically differentiated creature is to regard her primarily as a sexual object, the plaything (or playmate) of the male. This position has always been rightly repudiated by feminists, and Ida refers to it only to dismiss it:

> Look, our hall!
> Our statues!—not of those that men desire,
> Sleek Odalisques, or oracles of mode,
> Nor stunted squaws of West or East . . .

The statues are, instead, of notable female warriors, rulers and builders of antiquity. The view of women as sexual objects · reappears in Section V, when the old king, the Princess' father, asserts it in lines whose terseness strikingly expresses the brutality of their sentiments:

> Man is the hunter; woman is his game:
> The sleek and shining creatures of the chase,
> We hunt them for the beauty of their skins;
> They love us for it, and we ride them down.

He goes on to emphasise the absolute opposition of sexual rôles in a series of crashing antitheses:

> Man for the field and woman for the hearth:
> Man for the sword and for the needle she:
> Man with the head and woman with the heart:
> Man to command and woman to obey;
> All else confusion.

It is, of course, a matter of everlasting annoyance to feminists that such sentiments are by no means confined to the male sex: for very many women, even today, they provide a perfectly acceptable self-image. And this attitude finds a certain support in a kind of sentimental Jungianism, which posits an absolute distinction between *animus* and *anima*, and sees woman only as a tender, complacent, yielding, maternal (and yet withal mysterious) creature, who is wholly complementary to man. That this over-simple dichotomy is false both to the facts of experience and literature is shown, not only by Ida's opinions, but by her rôle. The archetypes of the Good Angel and the Mother have always represented one aspect only of the feminine nature; against them one must set all the traditional images of woman as militant or destructive. The most extreme example is, perhaps, the black Hindu goddess Kali, the bloodthirsty wife of Shiva; one might equally mention Clytemnestra, or the various vampire figures beloved of the nineteenth-century Decadence. Of a more benign order there are such famous Old Testament heroines as Judith and Jael; the medieval St. Joan, and in Renaissance epic, Ariosto's Bradamante and Spenser's Britomart. (A debased version of the type is still in universal circulation as the Britannia of our coinage, complete with helmet, trident and shield.) Princess Ida sees herself, and is presented to us, as a figure in this tradition of the militant female.

The Prince does not share his father's brutally clear-cut sentiments; he is very sympathetic to the feminist cause, and throughout the narrative he responds rather like the worried, open-minded liberal who is such a common character in twentieth-century fiction. At the end of the narrative he is to suggest a possible evolutionary solution of the feminine dilemma. Meanwhile, after the Princess's introductory remarks, he and his friends listen to a lecture by the Lady Psyche, a young widow who has solved the problem of the working mother with enviable ease by letting her baby sleep beside her in the classroom. The lecture begins with a passage that shows the assurance with which Tennyson could transform scientific speculation into excellent poetry; at the same time, it dwells on the topic of evolution, which forms a major strand in the poem—appearing initially in the early reference to 'the first bones of Time'—and which recurs in such things as the nearby spectacle of 'the bones of some vast bulk that lived and roar'd/ Before man was' or the geological expedition.

> This world was once a fluid haze of light,
> Till toward the centre set the starry tides,
> And eddied into suns, that wheeling cast
> The planets: then the monster, then the man;
> Tattoo'd or woaded, winter-clad in skins,
> Raw from the prime, and crushing down his mate;
> As yet we find in barbarous isles, and here
> Among the lowest.

Psyche traces the rôle and treatment of women through the ages, and ends with a soaring vision of a possible future:

At last
She rose upon a wind of prophecy
Dilating on the future; 'everywhere
Two heads in council, two beside the hearth,
Two in the tangled business of the world,
Two in the liberal offices of life,
Two plummets dropt for one to sound the abyss
Of science, and the secrets of the mind:
Musician, painter, sculptor, critic, more:
And everywhere the broad and bounteous Earth
Should bear a double growth of those rare souls,
Poets, whose thoughts enrich the blood of the world.'

This presupposes a dual monarchy of the sexes, ruling as complementary equals. In its context, it is revolutionary enough;
but it stops short of according women total autonomy, inasmuch
as they are still supposed to exist in some kind of inescapable
relationship with man; they are still to be, literally, 'the
opposite sex'. The seeds of the problem that Lawrence was to
anatomise in *Women in Love* have been sown.

Shortly after this lecture, the male identity of the three
disguised intruders is made known, and the harmony of the
women's university is overthrown. Its equilibrium is seen to
have been indeed precarious, and its instability is shown in
such factors as the jealousy and bitchiness of the Lady Blanche,
and Psyche's deep maternal anguish about her child. We have
already been shown that many of the inmates of the college are
unhappy with their enforced seclusion:

others lay about the lawns,
Of the older sort, and murmur'd that their May
Was passing: what was learning unto them?
They wish'd to marry; they could rule a house;
Men hated learned women . . .

Ida's injunction that the women may marry one day, but that
they must wait until the female sex has been brought to a pitch
of true equality with the male is not, in the event, found very
helpful. *The Princess* is very much about the business of 'rôle-
playing', and a central topic is the fatal ease with which the
rôle of the *Ewig-Weibliche* thrusts aside the consciously pursued
goal of the woman who has overcome her cultural disabilities

45

and grown into the educated equal and companion of the male. This is clearly seen when, after the battle, the ladies of the college rapidly become ministering angels and tend the wounded men. Here one can only admit that Tennyson has focussed on an observable psychological truth, even though the radical feminist may deplore it.

The interpolated songs contain the most celebrated poetry of *The Princess;* although they are supposedly sung by Lilia and her aunt as interludes in the seven-part improvised narrative of Walter and his friends, they occur as anonymous outbursts of pure lyricism, moments of emotional stasis in the midst of the unruly narrative action. In 'Tears, idle tears', Tennyson's verse reaches one of its sublime heights, and its unalloyed lyrical seriousness almost destroys the mock-heroic setting into which it is inserted. The equally exquisite though less profound, 'Now sleeps the crimson petal', reflects, as Mr. Killham reminds us, Tennyson's interest in Persian poetry. Yet the songs provide more than a delightful anthology rather arbitrarily inserted into the narrative of *The Princess*. They are, I believe, reassurances to the reader that despite everything the *Ewig-Weibliche* will still dominate: their references to motherhood and erotic love provide familiar points of reference in a world seemingly disoriented by Princess Ida's pursuit of feminine equality. (Just as, in the preamble, Lilia, after her feminist outburst, is gently eased back into a more appropriate rôle by being asked to sing.) The songs themselves, with their intensity of feeling and static, self-contained quality, provide emblems of what the feminine nature is conventionally supposed to be.

But if Tennyson seemingly undermines the conceptions of feminism by showing the instability of an institution run according to its principles; and by setting against feminism the attractive and traditional femininity symbolised by the songs, the Prince takes a more sympathetic position. In his final address to the Princess he generously embraces her standpoint:

> Henceforth thou hast a helper, me, that know
> The woman's cause is man's: they rise or sink
> Together, dwarf'd or godlike, bond or free:

He develops his picture of the liberation of woman, though stressing the need to preserve her essential femininity: 'to live and learn and be/All that not harms distinctive womanhood'. He is being cautious here, for similar arguments were for a long time used to deny civic rights to women (and still are in Switzerland). The Prince, indeed, seems to be reasserting the traditional notion of biological differentiation:

> For woman is not undevelopt man,
> But diverse: could we make her as the man,
> Sweet Love were slain: his dearest bond is this,
> Not like to like, but like in difference.

But he continues with an interesting evolutionary speculation:

> Yet in the long years liker must they grow;
> The man be more of woman, she of man;
> He gain in sweetness and in moral height,
> Nor lose the wrestling thews that throw the world;
> She mental breadth, nor fail in childward care,
> Nor lose the childlike in the larger mind.

It is a beguiling picture, and one which is unlikely to be disturbing if simply confined to moral qualities. But its deeper implications seem to entertain the androgynous, a certain blurring of the sexes, which we have already had prefigured in the figure of the 'feudal warrior lady-clad'. It is indeed arguable that as civilisation continues to evolve, many traditional sexual attributes may become unnecessary, such as the aggressive masculinity of the old king, and that a mingling of sexual characteristics may become evident. According to some commentators this condition has already been reached: 'All around us, young males are beginning to retrieve for themselves the cavalier rôle once piously and class-consciously surrendered to women: *that of being beautiful and being loved*'.[4] Having allowed this possibility to present itself, the Prince concludes his speech with a stirring account of ideal marriage, in which questions of equality and inequality will not arise, and in which each sex will perfectly complement the other, until they become 'The single pure and perfect animal', almost as if the halves of the bi-sexual animal described in Plato's fable were reunited. It is a moving account, but an evasive one: we are not told whether

47

this process of evolutionary improvement is to involve any voluntary element, and whether the goal of intellectual and cultural equality with men that Ida worked for is to be regarded as a mistake, or at best unnecessary. In the last analysis, *The Princess* is a timid poem: Tennyson has raised implications that must necessarily have been upsetting to the habitual assumptions of many of his readers, even if the mock-heroic, spasmodic mode of treatment kept the pressure low; and he damps them down when they look like becoming too exigent. Nevertheless, the fact that they are raised at all places *The Princess* at the beginning of a line whose later exemplars include *The Doll's House*, *Women in Love*, and *The Golden Notebook*.

After the narrated adventures we return to the solidity of Vivian Place, and Lilia and the young men. The extravaganza is over, and the festivities in the park are also coming to an end: we meet Sir Walter, 'A great broad-shoulder'd genial English-man', a reassuring figure with both feet firmly on the gound, who makes an instant contrast to the Prince, with his frail consciousness and cataleptic tendencies. The party sit on in the gathering darkness, 'rapt in nameless reverie,/Perchance upon the future man'. Then, at last, Lilia removes the silk scarf from the statue of Sir Ralph, and they make their way home-ward.

III

It may reasonably be objected that in this discussion I have been too little concerned with *The Princess* as a poem, and too much with its intellectual content and its place in the history of ideas. If this charge has any validity, I can only reply that what is happening in the central part of the poem is a debate, in no matter how extravagant and oblique a form; and if we are not to read it as a mere extravaganza (and to do so, would I think, make *The Princess* a remarkably thin and boring work), then it is as well to have some concept of what the debate is about, and how the ideas, in whatever disguised or distorted form, work in the poem.

Considered as verse, *The Princess*, apart from a few of the songs, seems to me to refine on without strikingly developing the techniques of the 1842 *Poems*; and considered as a structure, it is open to all the faults of inconsistencies of tone, and shifts of direction, to which the poet disarmingly draws attention (and hopes to justify) in the passage which I have already quoted. If we are to read *The Princess* with any hope of grasping its essential qualities, then we have to read it in a deliberately *ad hoc* fashion, just as we do with that celebrated later 'medley', *The Waste Land*. If there are faults, they are to be found in the excessive *longueurs* of some of the discursive narrative passages; and, more interestingly, in Tennyson's failure adequately to characterise the Princess herself. A comparison with Spenser's Britomart will make the nature of this failure clear: there is simply too little of the militant female in Ida's make up; one can imagine her striking heroic gestures in a piece of Victorian alle-gorical statuary, but not plunging into a fight with the genuine relish of a Bradamante or Britomart. In this respect, Tennyson is part of his age; notoriously, with the exception of Becky Sharp (and she is not officially a heroine), the girls in Victorian fiction seem very lacking when compared with the vivacious heroines of Shakespeare's comedies: for whatever reason the Vic-torian consciousness had difficulty in imagining women who pos-sessed other than a narrow range of feminine qualities, and a reluctance to attribute sexual awareness to women clearly contri-buted to this difficulty. Beyond this, we can say the Victorian ideal of the feminine, as illustrated in pre-Raphaelite painting as well as in fiction, was too much fixated on a frail version of the *Ewig-Weibliche*, the passive, yielding, tender, feminine image, and was too little aware of the militant aspects of femininity. *The Princess*, though it undoubtedly suffers because of this fixation, may be regarded at the same time as an attempt to redress its deficiencies.

NOTES

[1] See H. M. McLuhan, 'Tennyson and Picturesque Poetry' in *Critical Essays on the Poetry of Tennyson*, ed. John Killham (1960).

[2] John Killham, *Tennyson and 'The Princess'* (1958).

[3] See Sidney Cornelia Callahan, *The Illusion of Eve* (New York, 1965).

[4] Leslie A. Fielder, 'The New Mutants', in *Innovations* ed. Bernard Bergonzi (1968).

MATTER-MOULDED FORMS OF SPEECH: TENNYSON'S USE OF LANGUAGE IN *IN MEMORIAM*

Alan Sinfield

'He was a natural stylist, with an inborn interest and instinct for words. And yet, with all his critical awareness, with all his charm and fluency, what a poor thing relatively Tennyson's style is! Slow, monotonous, overcoloured, over-musical, its essential diffuseness only emphasised by the niggling detail.'[1] F. W. Bateson here gives one of the more coherent accounts of what I suspect is a widely held view of Tennyson's style. He is often regarded as a great verbal artist, but the feeling seems to be that his facility with words is merely a façade, that he flatters and deceives his reader with the vague and 'poetical'. Some critics have discovered Tennyson writing some tight and compressed poems, but it is usually assumed that he did it by a happy chance and would be shocked if anyone had told him. Study of *In Memoriam* has convinced me that this crisis of critical confidence is unwarranted, and I propose to demonstrate this by looking at one area where Tennyson's achievement is impressive.

In Memoriam turns upon the poet's mystical experience in section xcv, where he 'came on that which is, and caught/The deep pulsations of the world'. Faced with the decay of faith and the discrediting of reason, the poet had no authority for choosing between the beliefs open to him. Until section xcv he oscillates from one idea or attitude to another; in section xli he fears he will be 'evermore a life behind', in xlvii he feels 'I shall know him when we meet', in lvi Nature cries, ' "The spirit does but mean the breath".' The general movement is towards a more optimistic outlook, but the poet has no way of judging the value of any view that may occur to him. Section xcv, through a visionary experience or trance, the experience of a power existing almost beyond man's apprehension and quite beyond his comprehension, gives the poet the authority he has been seeking. From this point on he is sure of Hallam's continuing existence and of the values to which he and his contemporaries must adhere. Section xcv is also the culmination of a series of attempts to trascend time and place, most notably through dream in sections LXVII–LXXI. It is through such a transcendance that the poet can regain a sense of contact with Hallam, and this is what he desires above all else. The dream provides only temporary satisfaction, however; the poet cannot dream of Hallam as dead, but the experience is backward-looking and its significance does not extend beyond itself: 'I wake, and I discern the truth' (LXVIII).

The fact that *In Memoriam* depends upon a visionary experience makes very special demands upon Tennyson's expressive powers. He was evidently perfectly conscious of the difficulty, as we can see from section xcv itself:

> Vague words! but ah, how hard to frame
> In matter-moulded forms of speech,
> Or ev'n for intellect to reach
> Thro' memory that which I became.

Language is, for the most part, best equipped for describing physical 'reality'; to explain and make actual something which is beyond material bounds—out of time and space—is plainly exceptionally difficult. Moreover, even as the nineteenth-century poet was faced with the problem of the credibility of traditional religion, so the language of Christianity, for centuries the natural way to present an awareness of mystical experience, was no longer fully appropriate. As soon as straightforward Christain terminology is introduced it tends to have a rigidifying effect, for the writer's individual outlook is swallowed up in the reader's immediate stock response to the familiar.

It is Tennyson's success in describing the mystical and making it actual to the reader of *In Memoriam* that I propose to discuss, first looking at several different ways in which he avails himself of the resources of the language and then treating at some length section XCV, the climax of visionary experience in the poem.

In section CXXII the poet refers to the vision of XCV, asking, 'Oh, wast thou with me, dearest, then?'—also alluding to section L, where he asked, 'Be near me when my light is low'; notice the change from 'near' to 'with', indicating how the experience of XCV involved a far closer relationship than the poet could have hoped for. In section CXXII the poet asks for a renewal of his vision, when

> all the breeze of Fancy blows,
> And every dew-drop paints a bow,
> The wizard lightnings deeply glow,
> And every thought breaks out a rose.

How does this account of transcendental experience work? Perhaps the most important way in which the breeze, the dew-drop and the rose are made to carry mystical significance is through their previous uses. The breeze has occurred several times in the poem. In section LXXXVI the evening air rolls on to the poet and away 'To where in yonder orient star/A hundred spirits whisper "Peace",' and at the end of section XCV it is associated even more strongly with the numinous. The rose is suggestive of the 'crimson cloud/That landlike slept along the deep' at the end of CIII, and both the rose and the rainbows in the dew-drops allude to Dante's vision of Paradise, again, as I shall show later, like section XCV:

> Two arches parallel, and trick'd alike,
> Span the thin cloud . . .
> And they who gaze, presageful call to mind
> The compact, made with Noah, of the world
> No more to be o'erflow'd; about us thus,
> Of sempiternal roses, bending, wreathed
> Those garlands twain.[2]

If the reader calls to mind Dante's 'Paradise', his understanding of the poet's experience is increased. The story of Noah has already been used in section XII. There the poet's mind flies out from the ark of his body like a dove, but finds no place to rest and can only circle in the air. In section CIII a dove flies in and brings a summons from the sea, calling the poet to a meeting with Hallam beyond the grave. The reference in section CXXII to God's promise that he would place the rainbow in the sky as a sign that he would not destroy the race again indicates that his visionary experience has provided the poet with a like conviction of the ultimate goodness of the universe. These relations to external systems of images and to other parts of *In Memoriam* build up associations behind the images of these four lines to suggest to the reader the poet's apprehension of mystical experience.

The reader's impression of the supra-natural experience is not derived from any one of these statements, but from the combination of all four. This is typical Tennysonian practice, specially when he is describing physical objects to suggest an inner condition. The fact that several images are needed to convey the meaning is itself part of that meaning, for it implies the extent to which the vision transcends the material world and baffles attempts to express it in 'matter-moulded forms of speech'. The experience cannot be presented in one piece through temporal and spatial language, so the reader makes a composite image from the details he is given. This process is assisted by the high degree of grammatical parallelism in the four clauses, which encourages the reader to abstract from the individual descriptions to what they have in common and to think of the four actions as simultaneous. Each line of the stanza corresponds to a clause, and each clause begins with a subject and an active verb, although Tennyson, with his usual discretion, avoids clumsiness by not allowing the parallelism to be exact beyond this point. All the clauses are of the same kind (they are temporal, ultimately controlled by 'Till', five lines earlier); the lack of grammatical subordination in the description indicates that the mystical experience is beyond rational examination. It is not amenable to analysis, and the poet can give only a series of metaphorical equivalents.

One might also observe that there is little attempt to create visually precise images in these lines. The descriptions are not there primarily to conjure up a picture from the natural world, but for their associations, both within and from outside the poem. Sharpness of visual detail is not in this case the main point—though Tennyson can produce it when required:

54

consider the storm of section xv where 'The rooks are blown about the skies'. Here the fact that the rooks have no control over their movements (and this is stressed by the use of the passive verb), when we normally expect to see them *flying through* the skies, brings out at once the force of the storm. But spiritual experience may be more adequately represented by language that is, as physical description, vague. In section lxx the poet is describing a dream consisting of a series of ghastly images. The manuscript of *In Memoriam* in the Usher Gallery, Lincoln,[3] shows that where the poem has 'Cloud-towers by ghostly masons wrought' Tennyson at first wrote 'A fort by ghostly masons wrought'. 'Cloud-towers', though less specific, is better in this context because it suggests the supra-natural by creating a sense of the mysterious, of something defying the language categories formed to deal with earthly phenomena.

A related point arises in connection with Tennyson's use of certain adjectives like 'wild', dark', 'deep', and 'dim', which are rather vague as descriptive terms. It would be wrong to assume, however, that they merely impart a 'poetical' shimmer to the language. Consider section lx, where a girl (like the poet) is pictured as

> Moving about the household ways,
> In that *dark* house where she was born.

'Dark' is imprecise as a description of a house, but that is not its only function. The house stands for the world as we know it, where the poet must live without his friend, and when we consider it from this point of view 'dark' also has the connotations 'little understood' and 'dominated by death' (in section xxxix the yew tree is 'darkening the dark graves of men'). This is characteristic of the way this group of adjectives operates: their strength comes from the fact that they can apply not only to physical phenomena, but also to ideas or states of mind. Something of the same nature happens in one of the lines I have already discussed from section cxxii: 'The wizard lightnings deeply glow'. Here the adverb physically applies to the colouring of the lightnings, but since the poet is talking about something which is largely in his mind, 'deeply' suggests also the fundamental character of the experience, that it springs from the depths of the soul.

'Deep', in fact, is important in all its forms to the movement between material phenomena and mental states, by which Tennyson conveys a state of mind through physical images. It is often used for the sea, for instance in sections XI, CIII, CXXIII, CXXIV and CXXV, and as such it smacks somewhat of 'poeticality'. But in section XLII it is used of the personality: 'And what delights can equal those/That stir the spirit's inner deeps?' and in LXIII of the spiritual world: 'The circuits of thine orbit round/A higher height, a deeper deep'. Adjectival uses of the word tend in the same direction, for section LXII has 'deeper eyes', and XLVI 'that deep dawn behind the tomb'. The two meanings (personality and ocean, an abstract and a physical sense) are linked almost overtly in section XVI, where the poet says that his sorrow 'knows no more of transient form/In her deep self, than some dead lake'. When we look again at sections CIII, CXXIV and CXXV we find a definite connection between the sea image and the depths of the personality:

> We steer'd her toward a crimson cloud
> That landlike slept along the deep;
>
> (CIII)

> And heard an ever-breaking shore
> That tumbled in the Godless deep;
>
> (CXXIV)

> Abiding with me till I sail
> To seek thee on the mystic deeps.
>
> (CXXV)

The ambiguity can be fruitfully carried over into the other sections which at first sight seem to be simply using a 'poetic' word for the sea. Spiritual connotations have become subtly attached to the image so that, as with the other ways I have described of moving between a physical and a mental state, the mystical sense arises almost imperceptibly out of the 'matter-moulded forms of speech'.

Apparently insignificant grammatical particles can also be of assistance to Tennyson in expressing an awareness of a supramundane event. The definite article often constitutes a plea for recognition and acceptance, and when contrasted with

less definite forms it can show the boundary between the known
and the not-known, the material and the spiritual.

> When on my bed the moonlight falls,
> I know that in thy place of rest
> By that broad water of the west,
> There comes a glory on the walls.

(LXVII)

This is the beginning of a section describing a strange experience
of contact with Hallam. In these lines the bed, the walls, the
moonlight and even Hallam's resting place have a definiteness
to the poet in comparison with '*a* glory'. The physical things
he knows about, but the strange nature of 'a glory' is something normally beyond man's comprehension, as the syntax
suggests. We find the same thing in the second stanza, where
there 'slowly steals *a* silver flame', but when the poet has
absorbed the experience and taken it into his personality, then
he can write, '*The* mystic glory swims away'. Tennyson uses
the smallest particles of language at first to bring out the
contrast between material things and the numinous, and then,
by switching articles, to suggest that the mystical has become
as real to him as the physical.

Tennyson's interest in effects of sound and rhythm in
language has often been regarded as merely a surface accomplishment, but these agents, divorced as they often are from the
material meanings of words, can assist in the expression of
mystical feeling.

> Known and unknown; human, divine;
> Sweet human hand and lips and eye;
> Dear heavenly friend that canst not die,
> Mine, mine, for ever, ever mine.

(CXXIX)

Here the poet is talking about his apprehension of Hallam as
absorbed in God and yet still present. The preponderance of the
sounds *m* and *n* is unique in the poem, and is the more startling
when one considers how similar they are, but this is by no means
just to make the stanza sound nice and poetical or 'significant'.
The section is about how the poet has come to 'mingle all the

world with thee', and the repetition of the same sounds suggests the oneness of all the vast universals mentioned in the stanza—and their further identity with the frail, physical human being.

The last line quoted is also remarkable for its rhythm. It is very unusual in *In Memoriam* to have three pauses within the line, and hardly anywhere else do they occur so determinedly off the beat. This seems to communicate the poet's excitement at the resolution of opposites he has achieved. The point can be demonstrated by comparison with the Trial Edition of early 1850, where the line reads, 'My friend, for ever, ever mine!' This line lacks completely the ecstasy expressed by the break in the first foot of the final version.

Once the importance of mystical experience in *In Memoriam* is appreciated, much of Tennyson's delicate skill becomes immediately accessible. The poet's highly individual experience is not amenable to the traditional language of the visionary, and Tennyson has to employ all the resources of poetry to come as close as he can to the communication of the spiritual through 'matter-moulded forms of speech'. A close look at section xcv, the climax of the poem, will display the same kinds of use of language as I have been describing, and will show how they work together within a section, and how they place that section within the context of the whole poem.

The section falls neatly into four groups of four stanzas each. Images from the fourth stanza are repeated in the thirteenth, and the eight stanzas in the middle are divided between reading Hallam's letters and the vision itself. The first four stanzas describe the setting for the mystical experience. The presence of the family, as throughout the poem, assists our sense of the poet's reality: the reader can see him as actually existing in a social group, with the family as well as the poet aware of and, initially at least, strongly affected by Hallam's death. Here they all join in in singing 'old songs', and this is reminiscent of gatherings during Hallam's life like that described in section LXXXIX where 'A guest, or happy sister, sung'. In section XXX the family sung 'A merry song we sang with him/Last year', and then a moment of exalted belief in 'The light that shone when Hope was born' followed. The opening of section xcv, therefore, recapitulates one of the poet's major forms of consolation up to this point, and it stands in contrast (through its ineffectuality and its backward-looking character) with the vision which is about to occur.

The main impression given by the landscape description in the opening stanzas is one of great peace:

> o'er the sky
> The silvery haze of summer drawn;

> And calm that let the tapers burn
> Unwavering: not a cricket chirr'd:
> The brook alone far-off was heard,
> And on the board the fluttering urn.

In the previous section the poet stated that spirits would come only when 'like them, thou too canst say,/My spirit is at peace with all'. The stillness at the beginning of section xcv is in the poet's mind. The sound helps build up the atmosphere, specially through the long vowels, often open, and the high proportion of continuant and voiced consonants in the first two stanzas. But the effect is by no means ponderous: there is a quality of lightness in the rhythm of these lines, proceeding in part from the use of words like 'genial', 'silvery', 'unwavering', and 'fluttering', which hover between having two and three syllables in speech, but are forced by the metre here to have two.

The lack of movement is also evoked by the verbs used (or not used). In all the statements quoted above verbs are played down in one way or another. The cricket is conspicuous by its absence; none of the objects mentioned is *doing* anything, except for the tapers which burn, and without wavering at that; passive or indirect verbal forms are used each time.

In stanzas three and four the description becomes rather more intense, and the reader becomes aware that this evening is to be different from others. The images display a peculiar combination of precision and imprecision—of 'ermine capes/ And woolly breasts and beaded eyes' and of 'filmy shapes'. Certain facts about these creatures are given in hypersensitive detail, but their overall outline is completely vague: they are just 'filmy shapes'. The result of this juxtaposition of uncanny detail and insubstantial vagueness is a peculiar feeling that the poet is, on this evening, specially sensitive, that something is about to happen. We remember that the previous group of sections was concerned with how Hallam's ghost might return to the poet, and we link the 'filmy shapes/That *haunt* the dusk' with this possibility.

The rhythm is also beginning to communicate a more agitated state. This becomes steadily more marked, with stanza four displaying determinedly run-on lines and unusual rhythms:

> The whíte kíne glímmer'd, and the trées
> Láid their dárk árms about the fíeld.

The strange description maintains our impression of the poet's preternatural sight on this evening. Moreover, the 'dark arms', because of such earlier lines as 'For all is dark where thou art not' (VIII) and 'Unused example from the grave/Reach out dead hands to comfort me' (LXXX), make us think of Hallam and the poet's desire for his return. 'Dark' is used like the vague and evocative adjectives I have already discussed, for it describes not only the visual appearance of the trees, but also the sense of the mysterious they arouse in the poet. The opening of section XCV is a very good example of Tennyson's power of using physical description to prepare the reader for a visionary experience.

The next four stanzas describe how the poet, left to himself in the darkness, reads Hallam's letters. Stanza five shows clearly how Tennyson builds up meaning during the course of the poem so that the most incidental expression becomes full of substance:

> But when those others, one by one,
> Withdrew themselves from me and night,
> And in the house light after light
> Went out, and I was all alone.

The first two lines mean literally that the other people went to bed and left the poet out in the dark, but 'me and night' is so phrased as to invite the reader to consider what the night and the poet have in common. Up to now in the poem night has usually been linked to the poet's grief, as in 'An infant crying in the night' (LIV) or 'Let darkness keep her raven gloss' (I). 'Me

and night' recalls the poet's abiding sense of loss, and leads into
the thoughts stimulated by the letters. A similar implication
underlies the remark 'and I was all alone'. In the context this
takes on the more general meaning that the poet is and has been
essentially alone since Hallam's death.

In stanza six he describes how he read

> In those fall'n leaves which kept their green,
> The noble letters of the dead.

Referring to the letters as 'leaves' neatly links the two halves of
the metaphor, for the word works literally ior sheets of paper.
The expression is also interesting because it shows that the
poet's attitude has changed since the image was last used.
In LXXV he said of Hallam, 'Thy leaf has perish'd in the green',
but now he finds that Hallam's influence remains fresh and
potent through the letters.

What he reads plainly has a very strong effect on the poet:

> And strangely on the silence broke
> The silent-speaking words, and strange
> Was love's dumb cry defying change
> To test his worth; and strangely . . .

The repetition of 'strange(ly)' is made supportable by the varied
relations of syntax to line-length, but the power of Hallam's
words is also indicated by the paradoxical expressions 'silent-
speaking' and 'dumb cry'. The words are silent not only
because they are written, but because Hallam is dead. He lives
on in some measure in these writings (the leaves have kept their
green) and this is evidence of the triumph of love over time and
change: it has not succumbed (as the poet feared in section I) to
the 'victor Hours'.

What the poet reads in the letters is relevant to his situation:
through the writings speaks 'The faith, the vigour, bold to
dwell/On doubts that drive the coward back'. The poet has
immediate need in this section of such firmness in the face of
doubt; in section XCVI his determination to hold by his vision is
given by analogy with one (plainly Hallam again) who was
beset by doubt, but eventually 'beat his music out' and came to
'find a stronger faith his own'. This is just what the poet has

done in *In Memoriam*, with the mystical experience of section xcv providing the ultimate assurance. Hallam's faith and vigour is an inspiration which helps to stimulate the vision, and afterwards it encourages the poet to accept fully its implications.

This revival of Hallam through his letters is itself quite an important step in the poet's path through his anxieties: like the memories aroused in the return to Cambridge (LXXXVII) it is a way of reliving life with Hallam, and the poet's ability to endure such reminders is evidence of his peace of mind. The placing of the letter reading here recapitulates the major form of consolation possessed by the poet up to this point, namely the memory of the 'four sweet years' (XXII). But although such memories may fortify the poet, they can be no answer to his deep need for Hallam's return and for eventual reunion with him. The past can provide no lasting consolation. What is required is something which will give a sense of immediate contact with Hallam. That is why the vision described in the next four stanzas is crucial to the poem: it arises in part from the sentimental reading of the letters, but its power is so great as to be in contrast with the benefit the poet derives from them.

> So word by word, and line by line,
> The dead man touch'd me from the past,
> And all at once it seem'd at last
> The living soul was flash'd on mine.

The change in name from 'The dead man' in the second line quoted to 'The living soul' in the fourth indicates the turning point of *In Memoriam*. The basic desire throughout the poem for Hallam's touch, for 'A hand that can be clasp'd no more' (VII), is here fulfilled. We now come up against the horny problem of the alteration from '*His* living soul', made in 1883. The change can be justified in terms of the poet's prayer in section XCI, where he first asks that Hallam will return in 'the form by which I know/Thy spirit in time', but then wishes for him 'beauteous in thine after form,/And like a finer light in light'. '*The* living soul' implies this second, fuller kind of vision. Tennyson's son writes in his note to the poem, 'He preferred, however, for fear of giving a wrong impression, the vaguer and more abstract reading.' The version we now have seems to me better because more mysterious, and the experience in question should certainly be that. Tennyson glossed, 'the Deity, maybe', and this is as far as one can go in understanding a vision of this kind. Presuming to specify more exactly would encourage the reader to question the poet's honesty. The mystical experience cannot be given one interpretation; it must surely seem to the person experiencing it absolutely inclusive. This is not the conventional ghost the poet had expected, but a revelation of the harmony underlying everything that is, and the vague diction is best here because it conveys this inclusiveness.

> And mine in this was wound, and whirl'd
>   About empyreal heights of thought,
>   And came on that which is, and caught
> The deep pulsations of the world,
>
> Æonian music measuring out
>   The steps of Time—the shocks of Chance—
> The blows of Death.

The nature of the vision is indicated by the passive verbal forms: this is not something the poet wishes upon himself, but a manifestation vouchsafed from outside. As in the lines from section CXXII, parallel syntax is used to build up the reader's notion of the experience, as 'that which is' is redefined first as 'The deep pulsations of the world' and then as 'Æonian music'. Several images must be used to convey that which is beyond earthly existence.

The winding and whirling described here relate this experience to others in the poem where images of circles are used. Until this point the main emphasis has been upon the separateness of the poet's circle, which confines him to the physical world, and Hallam's 'circle of the wise' (LXI): The circuits of thine orbit round/A higher height, a deeper deep' (LXIII). But in section XCV the poet transcends the boundaries of physical existence and the circles which had been distinct coalesce into one in a vision of a harmonious movement involving all creation. As well as drawing upon associations built up during the poem, the imagery alludes to Dante's *Divine Comedy*. At the beginning of Canto XII of the 'Paradise', for instance, we find:

> straight the holy mill
> Began to wheel; nor yet had once revolved,
> Or e'er another, circling, compass'd it,
> Motion to motion, song to song, conjoining.[4]

The reference to an established yet individual account of heaven helps Tennyson communicate the poet's sense of a spiritual world.

'Æonian music measuring out/The steps of Time' contains another example like 'fall'n leaves', which I discussed above, of a metaphor where one word applies literally to both halves. 'Measuring' refers both to the movement of a piece of music and to the dimensions of the paces taken by, or of the stairs of, Time. The music of the spheres heard by the poet here contrasts with the 'old songs' which the family sang in the fourth stanza: this music is vastly beyond the power of the other, for it is not old but timeless, and not backward-looking but transcending earthly categories. The unusual word 'Æonian' is also worth noting. In section xxxv the streams drew down 'Æonian hills', and there the word simply meant that the hills had been there a long time. But in section xcv the context suggests also the Platonic meaning, 'of a power existing from eternity, an emanation or phase of the supreme deity', and the change the poet makes in the use of this word reflects his change in outlook. The different uses of 'Æonian' act out the release from the bonds of time which the poet has achieved.

The trance comes to an end, but before allowing the reader to learn if the poet will accept its validity, he breaks off to comment on the difficulty of explaining such an experience in 'matter-moulded forms of speech'. The allusion to the beginning of Canto I of Dante's 'Paradise' is so marked that one suspects that Tennyson must have studied Cary's translation. Dante was

> Witness of things, which, to relate again,
> Surpasseth power of him who comes from thence;
> For that, so near approaching its desire,
> Our intellect is to such depth absorb'd,
> That memory cannot follow.[5]

The last four stanzas open with a description obviously parallel to that of stanza four. The dusk is 'doubtful' both because it is uncertain whether it is light or dark, and because the poet's doubts have begun to return as he comes out of his trance to an awareness of the external world; again Tennyson is able to use an adjective which combines physical and mental states. The parallel with the earlier dusk of evening—it is now morning—is a most extraordinary and startling way of communicating to the reader the fact that the poet's vision has lasted all night. It also suggests very clearly his return to the external material world, which is, at first sight at least, as he had left it. But yet it is not the same, for the poet is a changed person, and his experience does not remain cancelled by doubt. The last three stanzas seem to renew it, or to suggest the poet's renewed faith in its recent existence. The description of the knolls, kine and trees frames the poet's absence from the material world, but this world can now be transcended, the poet knows, and the new vitality he sees in all existence is exemplified in the last stanzas of the section.

> And suck'd from out the distant gloom
> A breeze began to tremble o'er
> The large leaves of the sycamore,
> And fluctuate all the still perfume.

This is a more than ordinary breeze—and Tennyson suggests as much through his unusual use of the words 'suck'd' (it is as if the fresh air were drawn in towards the poet) and 'fluctuate', which is rare as a transitive verb; the description seems as anxious to avoid the passive as it was to keep it at the opening of the section. The reader of *In Memoriam* has become accustomed to seeing something beyond the physical in an expression like 'distant gloom': in this context one is likely to think of the depths of the personality or of the Godhead.

> And gathering freshlier overhead,
> Rock'd the full-foliaged elms, and swung
> The heavy-folded rose, and flung
> The lillies to and fro, and said . . .

The intensity of the description encourages us to think that this breeze has a particular significance. The heavy swinging movement comes from the way the parallel syntax cuts across the line-lengths, with the pause in the same place in each line. It is also the product of the epithets 'full-foliaged' and 'heavy-folded', which work less by pictorial description than by the repetition of the notion of fulness and heaviness, which seems to correspond with the weightiness of the over-lengthy epithets themselves as well as with the rhythm. This wind arouses distinctly Pentecostal associations, and from henceforth the poet speaks to his age with a new confidence. The image is in complete contrast with the first 'dim dawn' of the anniversary of Hallam's death, where the storm made 'the rose/Pull sideways, and the daisy close/Her crimson fringes to the shower' (LXXII). The wind was then destructive, but after the experience of section XCV it spoke to the poet and said:

> 'The dawn, the dawn', and died away;
> And East and West, without a breath,
> Mixt their dim lights, like life and death,
> To broaden into boundless day.

This is the dawn of the poet's new life. At the start of *In Memoriam* the usual connotations of dawn as a time of freshness and joy and beauty were denied, for instance in section LXXII, or VII: 'And ghastly thro' the drizzling rain/On the bald street breaks the blank day'. But now the poet is in harmony with the world again. The 'dim lights' are presumably those of the sun and moon, though, as so often, the adjective suggests non-physical attributes too, implying 'dimly understood'. The sun is rising, bringing new life, and the moon is setting, dying its daily death, but both are mingled as the one light spreads across the sky, joining the two. Even so, in the moment of his vision, the poet found 'The steps of Time—the shocks of Chance—/The blows of Death' measured out and given their true proportions in the Æonian music.

Now he has emerged from his perplexity the poet is able to see the extremes of life and death as coalescing ultimately into one, and this is reflected in the sound of the lines. The predominant pattern in the stanza of *d* alliteration, which 'mixes' together two groups of words which have had contrary or ambiguous meanings in the poem: 'died, dim, death', and 'dawn, boundless day'. The opposites 'east, west' have their

66

sound link conveniently built in, but are not therefore to be overlooked, and they provide a connection through *s* and *t* to 'lights', which in turn is related to '*li*fe', and so to 'd*ie*d' and the *d* groups. In fact, everything is related to everything, and that is the theme of the stanza. There is, the poet now believes, a spiritual life of boundless day which transcends the limits of life and death as we know them in the physical world, and sound, like the other resources of language, is utilised to express such an exalted vision.

There is no reason to despise Tennyson's handling of his medium, language, in section xcv. Faced with the difficult task of expressing an awareness of mystical and visionary experience in 'matter-moulded forms of speech', he made use of the potentials of sound for linking words and of rhythm for expressing an abnormal state of excitement, exploited the vagueness in some words, specially adjectives, which enables them to imply an internal as well as a physical state, and developed the use of images for cross-reference within the poem and allusion beyond it in order to support his description or bring out changes in the poet's attitude. Like all great artists, Tennyson turned the restrictions of his medium so that they became not a drawback, but an advantage.

NOTES

[1] F. W. Bateson, *English Poetry and the English Language*, 2nd ed. (New York, 1961).

[2] Dante, *The Divine Comedy*, trans. Henry Francis Cary (first pub. 1814), ed. Edmund Gardner (Everyman's Library, large format: London, 1908), pp. 344–45 (beginning of Canto XII of 'Paradise').

[3] I am grateful to the authorities of the Usher Gallery for allowing me to inspect and use this manuscript.

[4] Trans. Cary, p. 344.

[5] Trans. Cary, p. 292.

THE LYRIC STRUCTURE OF TENNYSON'S
MAUD

A. S. Byatt

Tennyson described *Maud* as his 'little *Hamlet*'. W. H. Auden has pointed out that Tennyson became conscious in childhood of 'Hamlet's problem, the religious significance of his own existence'. *Maud*, however, is concerned not only with the general question 'Were it not better not to be?' but with the practical question of what it means to have sufficient identity to be capable of consistent and meaningful action—Hamlet's dramatic problem, and the dramatic problem of the hero of *Maud*. There are close parallels between their actions and thoughts. Both have a vision of the world morbidly coloured by treachery, violence, and the death of a father. Both shift between the temptations of complete inertia—insanity or suicide—and excessive violence. Both at moments of emotional release act wildly on impulse, committing murders which bring about the death, through grief, of the women they love. Both acquire the capacity to act purposefully only after this experience of pain and death. Both are convinced that there is a spreading corruption in society which is an image for, or a cause of, their own incapacity—both see society as inert through greed and sensuality, yet at the same time lawlessly destructive. Both, in this context, are right but extravagant—they have 'that species of grumbling that can only be evoked from high-souled natures', as Dr. Robert James Mann said of *Maud's* hero. Both idealise a vision of a heroic man, whose will is not paralysed. Hamlet speaks in praise of Fortinbras' certainty and decisiveness. The hero of *Maud* calls for

> a man with heart, head, hand,
> Like some of the simple great ones gone

> For ever and ever by,
> One still strong man in a blatant land . . .

And, like Hamlet, he adds

> And ah, for a man to arise in me
> That the man I am may cease to be!

Maud is centrally concerned with the process of creating such a 'man' through what A. H. Hallam called 'the energetic principle of love for the beautiful'. Dr. Mann, in his pamphlet *'Maud' Vindicated*, which was approved by Tennyson, said the poem was a 'statement that *the proper function of love is the ennobling and energizing of the human soul*'.[1] This theme subtly reflects a vague, but very general contemporary fear that the 'energy' of the 'individual' had in some way markedly declined. Coventry Patmore remarked that Tennyson reflected his age better when not overtly concerned with doing so, and it is arguable that if the attitudes to war and commerce in *Maud* do seem shrill and forced, the passion of the love story is related to them, and to general contemporary psychological views, at a much deeper level. J. S. Mill wrote in 1836: 'One of the effects of a high state of civilisation upon character is a relaxation of individual energy: or rather the concentration of it within the narrow sphere of the individual's money-getting pursuits'. In the same essay, *Civilisation: Signs of the Times*,[2] he deplores the growth of quackery and cheating, the decline of literary individualism, and the fact that 'the spectacle and even the very idea of pain' are kept from us. 'The evils are, that the individual is lost and becomes impotent in the crowd, and that the individual character itself becomes relaxed and enervated.' Carlyle complains that the age is an Age of Mechanism, 'a concentration on "the outward", "adapting means to ends" ' which 'even if for the time productive of many benefits must in the long run, by destroying Moral force, which is the parent of all other Force . . . prove pernicious'. 'In the management of external things we excel all other ages: while in whatever respects the pure moral nature, in true dignity of soul and character, we are perhaps inferior to most.'[3] The times are, he says, out of joint. Tennyson, who said that *Troilus and Cressida* might well be Shakespeare's best play, clearly learned a great deal from Shakespeare's imagery of the interaction of public and private degeneracy of ideals and strength. The loss of the heroic ideal and the ideal of courtly love in that play are behind the society in decay in *The Idylls of the King*, where love turns to lust, honour to pride, and courage to brutality. In the same way, but more subtly, the alternatives presented in *Hamlet*, moral inertia, or impulsive violence, are behind the human behaviour studied in *Maud*. In both *The Idylls* and *Maud* Tennyson attempts to go deeper than the location of contemporary social abuses or even the creation of individual character. He is trying to make an impersonal image of human nature itself. How far he succeeds depends, partly, at least, on the success of his use of the timeless and impersonal aspects of the lyric form.

The theme of the loss of sense of personal identity and value, owing to an experience of death, pain and grief, followed by the gain of a deeper sense of individuation, is central in *In Memoriam*, as in *Maud*. *Maud*, indeed, grew from the lyric 'O that 'twere possible' which was originally written about the death of Hallam. In *In Memoriam* XLV Tennyson describes what psychologists would call the individuation process.

> The baby new to earth and sky,
>   What time his tender palm is prest
>   Against the circle of the breast,
> Has never thought that 'this is I':
>
> But as he grows he gathers much
>   And learns the use of 'I', and 'me,'
>   And finds 'I am not what I see,
> And other than the things I touch.'
>
> So rounds he to a separate mind
>   From whence clear memory may begin,
>   As thro' the frame that binds him in
> His isolation grows defined.
>
> This use may lie in blood and breath,
>   Which else were fruitless of their due,
>   Had man to learn himself anew
> Beyond the second birth of Death.

It seems to me that the central experiences of *Maud* are concerned with the human being's capacity to discover his own identity, *through the use of his senses*, at precisely this basic level of experience. The hero of *Maud* is, psychologically, in many ways still a dependent child,[4] and possesses the infant's characteristic incapacity—described in the *In Memoriam* lyric—to differentiate himself from his surroundings. He has not really got a 'separate mind/From which clear memory may begin': he often confuses his childhood experiences with his adult ones, himself with his parents, the outside world with the world in his head. He confuses, also, Maud and his mother, Maud's brother and Maud's father, fears, wishes and real events. (This process is particularly clearly depicted in his melodramatic ravings after the duel.) Like the infant in *In Memoriam* and like all human beings he acquires a sense of his own isolation, of his own 'separate mind' and individuality, through his body—'the frame that binds him in' the 'use' that 'May lie in blood and breath'. In other words, his physical passion for Maud ennobles and energises his soul, as Dr. Mann describes it—and the flow of the blood is a major image in the poem. This theme of the achieving of individuality is, however, interwoven throughout the poem with the description of the opposite experience—the loss of self and identity in aesthetic and erotic contemplation. As an individual woman, Maud arouses the hero's sensual self and his moral self through his sensual self. But she is also, like many of Tennyson's women isolated in rich gardens, a symbol for 'the beautiful'. She represents the *aesthetic* experience of sensual beauty described in Hallam's phrase 'the energetic principle of love for the beautiful' (to which I shall return). Much has been written about Tennyson's capacity to substitute the description of landscape for the description of mood, to substitute sensory for emotional experience. *Maud* is the poem in which he most successfully brought sense and emotion together, and described their interaction, culminating in the achieved passion of the lyric 'I have led her home'. For the moment I want simply to suggest that one of the basic principles behind the organisation of *Maud* is the interplay, from lyric to lyric, between the painful learning of separate identity, through the 'use of blood and breath' which constitutes the drama, and the typical aesthetic and erotic experience that one *is* what one sees, and is *not* other than the things one touches, which informs the great lyrics. There is a sense quite different from the neurotic's, in which a return to the infant's undifferentiated world can be energising and illuminating.

'The peculiarity of this poem,' Tennyson said, 'is that different phases of passion in one person take the place of different characters'.[5] One could elaborate this by saying that the major tension in the poem is not between characters, or between events, but between the subtle variations of complete moods or feelings personal and impersonal, explored in the whole lyrics. It is difficult for modern critics to talk about lyrics: we have a critical language for assessing dramatic ironies, or locating points of view, but no terminology to describe the pure assent to feeling called up by a simple song ('Birds in the high Hall-garden'), or a flat lyric statement of wish and fear.

We cannot easily describe the universal *rightness* of

> O let the solid ground
>   Not fail beneath my feet
> Before my life has found
>   What some have found so sweet . . .

We can relate its imagery—the failing of solid stone, the idea of the seeking 'life',—to other uses of related imagery in the poem, but this is not the main reason why the expression of the particular feeling in this way is so memorable. C. Day Lewis praised *Modern Love* for its 'great, flashing transfigured platitudes' and it is arguable that *Maud* is a much greater lyric monodrama than *Modern Love* because of Tennyson's superior skill in orchestrating and expressing transfigured platitudes of this kind. With *Modern Love* one feels that the platitudes are selected to illustrate or intensify a drama organised by a good novelist. Its virtues lie in the dry wit of the characterisation, the insight into the moral impossibility of the dramatic situation. Meredith's moments of melodrama are irritating because they are uncouth: we resent the novelist's crudity in allowing the husband to see his wife with her lover whilst he is himself making love to his mistress. Tennyson's melodrama is more

73

blatant and more acceptable, and the characterless and unreal quality of Maud as a woman is unexceptionable, because they do not carry the real truths of the poem. The transfigured platitudes are, in *Maud*, themselves the most powerful actors in the monodrama. Beneath individual morbid actions and reactions, running sometimes with them and sometimes counter to them is a kind of impersonal emotional history of love and joy and pain and loss, a search for identity below individuality, deliberately worked through universally accepted images and readily recognisable rhythms and themes, which are then woven in and out of each other into a whole complex pattern of experience, so that a martial tune can be recalled in a context of doubt, a despairing cliché evoked in a moment of joy and transfigured, a Persian garden combined with a Victorian society dance and both with the hectic beat of the blood. It is possible that when Tennyson spoke of 'phases of passion' he meant by 'phases' the 'timeless moments' of the great lyrics where passion is explored in depth through image, rhythm and evocative platitude. The purely lyrical quality was more predominant in the first edition of *Maud:* it is significant that most of the changes Tennyson made in answer to criticism from reviewers were narrative elucidations. (He made explicit the hero's suicidal heritage, he added Maud's mother's distress over the feud, and Maud's assurance, for objectivity, that her brother was 'kind'). The lyric emphasis in *Maud* creates a drama like a *Hamlet* with much of the action pared away or reported, and other elements expanded—the universal reflective imagery of the soliloquies, the immediate pathos and beauty of Ophelia's songs. This generalising lyricism makes the story both more subjective and more universal at the same time.

Maud is not the only poem in which Tennyson deliberately created a tension between different kinds of lyrics, narrative or discursive and contemplative. E. D. H. Johnson has pointed out that the choric song of the lotos eaters is constructed as a conflict between alternate stanzas expressing different moods.

The odd stanzas, lyric and descriptive in quality, weave the spell of the lotos, while the even ones follow a rhetorical pattern suggestive of the conflict within the consciences of the speakers. Furthermore, the successive stanzas tend to increase in length as if to imply a growing recognition of all that is at stake.[6]

The moral conflict of the even stanzas is set against the 'dream-like state of irresponsibility' induced by the lotos in which 'time and space cease to have any meaning'. Tennyson's contrasted groups of images—sea, destruction, moral conflict and struggle against the 'garden' representing an undifferentiated sensuality outside time, space and moral stress recur in *Maud*, but in a much more complex form. In *Maud* there is a succession of lyric experiences of gardens, in which the feeling of being outside time and space and moral stress is achieved in differing degrees and with quite different values placed upon the experience. These are related with increasing complexity to the struggle of the narrative, until, again in 'I have led her home', what happens in the garden and the feeling of the drama are reconciled and unified, for a time.

Maud could also be compared structurally to *The Princess*, in which the movement of the lyrics is also orchestrated against the narrative movement. The stories have much in common. *The Princess* describes the relationship between a virginal princess retreated into contemplation in a landscape of oriental splendour and a prince given to fits of inertia and misty vision; they have, like Maud and the hero, been betrothed in infancy. In *The Princess* love is awakened after the duel with the brother, not before it, but the duel has the same paralysing effect on the Prince, who is awakened from his inert trance by the erotic and sensuous lyrics sung by Ida. These final lyrics—'Come down O maid' and 'Now sleeps the crimson petal', are, as John Killham[7] has pointed out, very close in their imagery to the great lyrics of the garden in *Maud* and describe the same kind of rich sensuous, timeless awakening to love, by means of substituting landscape description for the directly erotic. In *The Princess* the emotions of the lyrics are much more crudely and directly contrasted with the narrative before this erotic commingling. In the early part, when the prince is wooing and Ida is proudly and intellectually virginal, the lyrics are small songs about reconciliation in marriage, and children, either happy or dead—Tennyson does not attempt to weave them

75

into the story but leaves them to stand as comment on it. The lyrics of the central section of *The Princess* parallel those of *Maud* which precede Maud's acceptance of her lover. Again, they suggest *inactive* emotion. 'Tears, idle tears', 'The splendour falls' and 'O swallow, swallow' all concern a grief-stricken inactivity in which waiting for love could equally be waiting for death. Tennyson's 'passion for the past' evoked in 'The splendour falls' is associated by him with a falling away from richness of experience (*The Idylls* are based on this emotion and *Ulysses* appeals to it). In *In Memoriam* and *Maud* the 'passion for the past' is for past love, as in 'Tears, idle tears', and is again seen in terms of fear of death (the 'dying eyes' of 'Tears, idle tears') and nostalgia for past great men (Hallam as The English Gentleman, 'those simple great ones gone' in *Maud*). The lyric evocation of this whole mood of retrospective, death-wishing, fearful grief has, in Tennyson's work, certain recurrent images. I would mention two: in both *The Princess* lyrics and in *Maud*, ('Morning arises stormy and pale', 'Maud has a garden of roses') colours dying from a rich sky, and light glimmering in a square casement evoke this feeling which is related by further images to the whole complex. This could be elaborated: but my main point here is that, if it is compared to *The Princess*, *Maud* is structurally very much more closely woven and imagery and mood more subtly varied. In *The Princess* the lyrics are blocks of feeling, standing *against* a long and involved narrative, in direct contrast to it, operating at a depth of emotion it never reaches. In *Maud* there is very significantly less narrative; the lyrics are directly related to, and indeed part of, the history, which is a monodrama. Each 'phase of passion' uses the same images as earlier ones and elaborates them (whereas in *The Princess* each lyric was a separate exercise although the images can be seen to be related in Tennyson's mind by examining his other works). The work is thus much more unified. 'The excellence of the art' is here, as Keats said 'in its intensity'.

Keats' vision of 'the excellence of every art' being 'in its *intensity*' is directly relevant here, as I want to suggest, before going on to look at some details of the lyric organisation of *Maud*, that Tennyson's ability to use the lyric in this way, as well as the theme of the proper use of energy in his poem, depend upon his acceptance, and understanding of the views put forward by A. H. Hallam in his essay on 'picturesque' poetry, and on Tennyson's own work, in *The Englishman's Magazine* (1831)[8]. Hallam praised the 'Cockney school' in terms which showed that he would have understood all the implications of Keats' 'O for a life of sensations rather than thought'.

Much of Tennyson's poetry is like Hallam's thought, concerned with aesthetic *sensation* both as technique and as subject-matter. Since W. D. Paden wrote *Tennyson in Egypt* critics have been interested in Tennyson's capacity to use sensual response to landscape as a substitute for 'thought' about moral issues. Browning wrote of *The Idylls*:

We look at the object of art in poetry so differently! Here is an Idyll about a Knight being untrue to his friend and yielding to the temptation of that friend's mistress after having engaged to assist him in his suit. I should judge the conflict in the Knight's soul the proper thing to describe. Tennyson thinks he should describe the castle, and the effect of the moon on its bowers, and anything but the soul.[9]

It is arguable that Tennyson used his description of the moon *both* as an image for the conflict in the soul, and as an image for the displacement of his own interest from the moral to the sensual. In many early poems (*Mariana, Guenevere, Recollections of the Arabian Nights, The Palace of Art, The Lady of Shallott, The Daydream*) a solitary woman in a landscape represents, at the same time, unfulfilled erotic passion—the grief-stricken inactivity of the pre-erotic lyrics of *Maud* and *The Princess*—and the contemplating artist, living the life of sensation rather than thought, of aesthetic contemplation, that is, rather than moral action or moral reflection. If marriage made Tennyson able to achieve description of erotic satisfaction in *Maud*, it is Hallam's view that the 'life of sensation' can be *better* than the life of 'thought' which provides a rationale, in a moral age, for an intensely subjective lyric poem.

In his essay 'Tennyson and Picturesque Poetry'[10] H. M. McLuhan connects Hallam's view of Shelley and Keats as 'poets of sensation rather than reflection' who 'lived in a world of images; for the most important and extensive portion of their life consisted in those emotions which are immediately conversant with sensation . . .' with 'the Symbolist and Imagist doctrine that the place of ideas in poetry is not that of logical enunciation but of immediate sensation or experience'. McLuhan argues that Tennyson and the Romantic landscape poets were attempting to produce an aesthetic experience which fell short of, but was related to *le paysage intérieur*, which had to wait for Baudelaire, Laforgue, and Rimbaud and that 'Whereas in external landscape diverse things lie side by side, so in psychological landscape the juxtaposition of various things and experiences becomes a precise musical means of orchestrating that which could never be rendered by systematic discourse.' He calls symbolist vision a 'metaphysical breakthrough' and remarks that Tennyson and the Pre-Raphaelites 'were unable to achieve the intensity of contemplation' that led to it.

They remained picturesque. That is, they devoted themselves to the means of prolonging the moment of aesthetic emotion or of arrested experience, and failed to accept such moments as the thread through the labyrinth of cognition. They substituted immediate feeling and emotion for the process of 'retracing'.

It is perhaps worth asking, particularly in the context of *Maud*, why exploration of the labyrinth of cognition should be thought automatically so superior to 'immediate feeling and thought'. It is significant that it is Tennyson's early verse that McLuhan signals out for praise—*Mariana*, a landscape from the *Palace of Art*, in which landscape and emotion are coextensive, where, in Browning's example the castle *is*, precisely, the soul. But in *Maud*, I would suggest, Tennyson is doing something much more complex—by using the series of lyrics to describe a series of timeless moments, pure emotions, aesthetic contemplations and to relate them to each other and to a life with a moral structure, Tennyson is in fact fulfilling much more precisely the function that Hallam prescibed for the poet. For Hallam the landscape is not interior, but *exterior* and valued because it is therefore less likely to lead to introspection and inertia than is reflective thought. Beauty is energising.

This powerful tendency of the imagination to a life of immediate sympathy with the external universe is not nearly so liable to false views of art as the opposite disposition of purely intellectual contemplation. For where beauty is continually passing before 'that inward eye which is the bliss of solitude'; where the soul seeks it as a perpetual and necessary refreshment to the sources of activity and intuition; where all other sacred ideas of our nature, the idea of good, the idea of perfection, the idea of truth, are habitually contemplated through the medium of this predominant mood, so that they assume its colour and are subject to its peculiar laws— there is little danger that the ruling passion of the whole mind will cease to direct its creative operations, or the energetic principle of love for the beautiful sink, even for a brief period, to the level of a mere notion in the understanding. We do not deny that it is, on other accounts, dangerous for frail humanity to linger with fond attachment in the vicinity of sense.[11]

What Hallam is recommending here is not examination of the cognitive process: it is direct sensual response to exterior objects as a means to *relate* one's energy to the external world and thus release it. *Maud*, aesthetically and morally, is Tennyson's exploration of the states of mind on the way to and from this ideal—Maud is both individual woman and ideal beauty, an inhabitant of the sensual, the moral and of the dream world, and in one lyric ('I have led her home') all come triumphantly together and interact. It is surely significant that the landscape of *Maud* is that of Tennyson's own married home at Farringford, of the sexual emotion released by his own marriage: thus the landscapes can be expressions of more than wish, settings for emotion, rather than substitutes. In fact, Tennyson uses them as both, in *Maud*, which is part of its complexity. In this context, too, Tennyson is exploring the 'use' which may 'Lie in blood and breath'; the direct connection of sensual apprehension of what one touches and sees with the sense of identity.

II

The hero's incapacity to use his individual energy begins, dramatically, with his father's death, which Tennyson describes with more precision than any other *event* in the poem.

Tennyson is extremely skilful in showing how the hero's response to this event is woven into and confused with, his response to other events in the poem. The physical facts he remembers with such precision from the moment of this death—the broken body, the 'dead weight dragged', the mother's 'shrill-edged shriek'—recur in his responses at relevant and irrelevant moments. He talks of 'this dead body of hate', the 'dead weight' of 'that dead man at her heart and mine'. His social brooding on Timor-Mammon grinning on a pile of children's bones parallels his feelings that his father's bones (and his own) are being broken by the 'grey old wolf', Maud's father. When he dreams of his fear of loving Maud, which is also a fear of being rejected or damaged by Maud, he awakes to 'the scream of a madden'd beach dragg'd down by the wave'—here the scream, the madness, the dragging are responses projected on to the landscape by the memory of the shock of the death.

The effect of the death on him is imaged in terms of a paralysis of energy, a stopping of the *blood:* 'my pulses closed their gates with a shock on my heart'. With his heart stopped the hero's emotions remain at the childish level—he expresses both an overwhelming superficial need for love and a deep fear of it. He identifies himself with his father ('Must *I* too creep to the hollow and dash myself down and die?') and this fear of death and madness and annihilation arouses in him an immediate need for love as an assurance of life and identity.

'Would there be sorrow for me? There was *love* in the passionate shriek . . .' This impersonal childish cry for love re-echoes through the poem, always in association with the idea of death. The hero has lost both parents as a result of the catastrophe, and is asking the world (and Maud) to provide a substitute for the lost mother as well as an object of revenge for the death of the father. Thus even his responses to Maud's kindness carry a plaintive note from the past.

> Perhaps the smile and tender tone
> Came out of her pitying womanhood,
> For am I not, am I not, here alone
> So many a summer since she died,
> My mother, who was so gentle and good?

'Am I not, am I not' is childishly insistent in rhythm, and this passage is followed immediately by a self-pitying brooding passage, in which, in solitude, 'I hear the dead at mid-day moan'.

Thus the hero's responses to Maud herself are from the outset ambiguous—she is destined by association with his mother ('Maud the beloved of my mother'), by the childhood betrothal, to fulfil one set of needs. She is destined equally, because she is the child of her father, who caused the death, to destroy him, and to be the object of his destructive and violent impulses. Maud is destined by the hero's consciousness, before she appears, for a tragic end in the classic manner—they cannot escape past events, or the effect of the uncontrollable passions (almost like internalised Euripidean gods) set up in the hero by these events. And yet, through the impersonal drama of the lyric, Tennyson can show *both* the destructive passion and the real love which grows up for a time in response to Maud herself.

A man driven by violent and irrational passionate responses to a past event is the perfect subject for a series of dramatic lyrics, and Tennyson makes full use of his confusions in the early part of *Maud*. His virtuosity, from lyric to lyric, in describing the shifts in the hero's subjective vision of Maud herself, and rendering these as whole 'phases of passion' within the unity of each lyric, is remarkable. The hero fears Maud's violence, she is predatory, hunting game, a Cleopatra of a woman, and he fears she is cold, inert, unresponsive. He fears these qualities in himself, in fact, and projects them onto her, since at the beginning of the poem he can see blood and passion only as destructive, and inertia as a protection from violence. One's heart must be a stone, to prevent being hurt (or hurting) but this is tantamount to suicide, which turns out to be violent after all. Perhaps the best places to observe the operation of this colouring of dramatic mood are the two early lyrics 'Long have I sigh'd for a calm' and 'Cold and clear-cut face' and the later one 'Maud has a garden of roses'.

The first two illustrate clearly what Tennyson meant by 'phases of passion'. The first, dramatically, expresses deliberately unresponsive cynicism, inertia. Maud's face is 'splendidly null', 'dead perfection, no more'. The tone of the whole poem has a perfectly placed strained flippancy. The second poem, about a dream, reveals the real depth of response to this dead perfection. It reveals the hero's fear that both his cynicism and Maud's coldness may be forms of death—he may, by lack of response have killed Maud, *her* lack of response may be '*revenge* too deep for a transient wrong/Done but in thought to your beauty'. She is, as later, a ghost. He wakes to the scream of the beach, and the wording encloses his present preoccupations in his past ones.

In 'Maud has a garden of roses' the whole lyric expresses a complex ebb and flow of mood. The lover is now ready to hope, and Maud is seen, not as in the earlier poem, and later after the duel, as a revengeful ghost, but as a 'glorious ghost' who will glide to him from Heaven. But the thought of this ghost-like quality leads to the thought that she is 'kind/Only because she was cold' and this hint of a failure of response leads immediately to a vision of a landscape coloured by death and inertia.

> But I look'd, and round, all round the house I beheld
> The death-white curtain drawn;
> Felt a horror over me creep,
> Prickle my skin and catch my breath,
> Knew that the death-white curtain meant but sleep,
> Yet I shudder'd and thought like a fool of the sleep of death.

Here psychological drama and visual response are the same. The hero continues with the acute reflection that his 'dark mind' makes him dangerous, his love itself is dangerous.

> That if *I* be dear to someone else
> Then some one else may have much to fear;

Throughout these early stages of the drama sexual passion, the energetic rush of the blood in passion is seen as dangerous and destructive. 'Love' is mother-love. Both Maud and the hero are seen alternately as predator and victim—Maud is told that 'there is fatter game on the moor'; the hero sees love as a 'cruel madness' and Maud as 'a milk-white fawn' (Marvell's archetypal image of the bleeding victim of violence) who is 'all unmeet for a wife'. The vision is confused here too—there are victim and slayer, but the concepts have their roots in the past.

In the central, 'positive' lyrics, the vision changes. John Killham has described how Maud's martial song awakes the hero to the acceptance of death and destruction in life as well as to love; blood becomes warm, glowing, positive, blushing (in 'Go not happy day)' until in 'I have led her home' the hero can, for the length of the lyric, accept Maud, sexuality, and death all at once, and the flow of the blood is released towards an 'end' which is all of these. I intend to discuss this lyric elsewhere. In terms of the dramatic arrangement of the lyrics it is important to notice that between 'I have led her home' and the hectic, slightly hysterical dance-music of 'Come into the garden' lies a long passage of brooding on the feud, and old events, which are foreshadowed to be resuscitated in the complete confusion—presented not so much like a Romantic lyric as like Jacobean drama—between past and present events which again prevails after the duel, when all the deaths are the hero's, Maud's shriek is his mother's, the 'dead man' is linked by a Sultan of brutes to a 'spectral bride'. Maud is a ghost, and external drama, become intolerable, has been internalised into 'phases of passion' which bear only a fantastic relation to reality. This kind of truly insane confusion is dramatically studied in the lyrics of Part II.

III

The imagery of *Maud* has been studied at some length and much more could be written about its intricacy. In this context I want briefly to mention certain groups of images which provide continuity and unity between the narrative events, the expanded sick or maniacal vision of the narrator during the tragedy—the 'case history'—and those moments of *generalised* feeling which are presented almost impersonally in the great lyrics, and which give the poem its larger relevance.

There are various related groups of ideas, which grow out of each other. The contrast between red and white, rose and lily, passion and purity is related to imagery of the movement of blood in the body through things like Maud's blush or paleness, the roses which were 'not roses but blood', 'the red life spilt'. The imagery of the movement of the blood is related to various images of growth and the smooth flow of natural processes. There is imagery of the growth of light in darkness, and of the growth of plants through the seasons of the year, both connected to the idea of the natural uninterrupted flow of energy which, as I suggested earlier, the flow of blood is the basic symbol for. There is also imagery about the surface of the earth and the colour of the sky, concerned with contrasting coldness and warmth, emptiness and crushing weight, light and dark. The hero's passion for Maud, and the aesthetic intensity of the poem, culminate in a kind of reconciliation of opposites in 'I have led her home' when growth and decay, life and death, passion and purity, all run together in the one lyric.

Through the hero's sick vision 'red' is seen as blood spilt by violence, and 'white' as death or inertia. The feared deaths of his early ramblings carry these colours. The 'vitriol madness *flushes*' in the ruffian's head: 'chalk and alum and plaster' are *white* and death-dealing. Both suggest—what is true of the whole plot of the poem—that 'the spirit of murder works in the very means of life' (blood and bread). In moments of hope over Maud, a landscape coloured by wish will present the sunset 'burning' on 'blossom'd gable ends': in moments of despair it is 'a wannish light' in a 'stormy and pale' morning.

Blood is pervasive. The ledges of the hollow 'drip' with horror of it, the hero's family is 'flaccid and drain'd' whilst Maud's father, like a leech, 'dropt off gorged'. When Maud blushes in the church, red with warmth under the white stone angel, listening to the 'snowy-banded' priest, 'Suddenly, sweetly, my heart beat stronger/And thicker'. The 'energetic passion of love for the beautiful' causes the hero to be able to derive strength from Maud, and symbolically from the rose: 'And the soul of the rose went into my blood'—an assimilation of the landscape which is turned about in a ghastly way when the roses become blood because they are only flowers and have no fruit. It is a central image in 'I have led her home'.

Light images are used largely in terms of the growth of Maud's influence—stars in an empty sky, a candle in the dark, sunlight calling out flowers. Maud's whiteness is ambiguous—it can be the whiteness of death, ghostliness, or coldness, or even decay: it can be bridal, virginal and clean. The 'light' associated with her, and light in general, has the same ambiguous quality. She has a 'passionless pale-cold face/Star-sweet on a gloom profound': her smile is 'sunny as cold'. She passes in the garden, 'like a light', 'But sorrow seize me if ever that light be my leading star'. Throughout the poem the rhythm of the blood flowing and failing is paralleled by the rhythm of light growing, fading and glowing again, with all the intermediate stages of glimmer, spark and glare. Imagery of Maud as a precious stone tends to be also imagery of growing and glowing light. In the 'Persian' passages of 'Maud has a garden' and 'Come into the garden' as in 'Now sleeps the crimson petal', the beloved is 'a beam of the seventh Heaven', a 'silent meteor'. In these passages light is as sexual as blood. The light image recurs in 'See what a tiny shell' when the desolate hero sees a hope of regaining his identity, salvaging some energy. He will 'nurse in his dark heart' a 'spark of will/Not to be trampled out'.

Growth of plants, like blood and light is used sometimes to image sick vision (the 'flying gold' of ruined Autumn leaves), the overexcited heart which would leap under Maud's feet and 'blossom in purple and red'. The shining daffodil is like the pale-gold light of Maud's hair, a Spring growth, connected to the star-light of Orion. The roses hardly need elaboration. It might be remarked in passing that Tennyson's skill in making flowers both part of a Romantic, individualised landscape and part of a generally accepted, richly stiff structure of moral and erotic symbols is one example of the way in which *Maud* consistently works in the directions both of precise location of individual feelings and of general, timeless ones.

IV

It seems to me that the peculiar strength of *Maud* lies in this use of the lyric to combine the particular and the universal, and I should like, in conclusion, to examine a complete lyric—'I have led her home'—as an example of the perfect and intricate combination of particular dramatic propriety, the expansion of a single emotion into an 'eternal moment', a 'phase of passion' which is the main structural innovation of the poem, and of Tennyson's capacity to make universal assent to *feeling*—any reader's assent—an overriding consideration in a poem. The poem is, as it were, a perfect 'love poem' as well as the *right* poem in the sequence—just as 'Birds in the high Hall-garden', and 'O let the solid ground' are, much more simply, good 'love poems' in their own right.

I have said that Tennyson orchestrated the whole lyrics, as well as the images and ideas against each other, and 'I have led her home' gains greatly from the poems around it. 'Birds in the high Hall-garden' in rhythm and imagery expands the *English* simplicity and freshness of Maud herself—roses, lilies, and rosy daisies are purely English, the metre is that of a decorated ballad. 'Maud has a garden of roses' is a lyric I particularly admire for the poise with which it makes an *attempt* on the expansive and elaborate Persian passion of 'I have led her home', with imagery of passion-flower, jewel and star, and for the perfect control of its fall from assurance. 'Go not, happy day' which precedes 'I have led her home' has simple, jaunty crude assurance and a single image (red roses) which make the complexity of 'I have led her home' all the more striking: and again, Tennyson's form *allows* him to expand this crude as-surance within the 'moment' of the lyric so that that mood can be experienced for itself. In the same way the falling-off of assurance, the impatience, the slight lack of control of passion and blood in the next pure lyric—'Come into the garden'—create a vague uneasiness *after* the controlled flow of the earlier poem.

All these poems are poems about gardens. The garden is Maud's spring garden of budding roses and pure passion; it is the garden of Persian erotic poetry where the roses are identi-fied with the beloved; it is the forbidden garden of the Arabian nights, kept by a jealous Sultan, containing musks, spices, jewels and punishment, a garden where landscape is full of sexual menace, and action leads to sensual violence whilst inaction leads to swooning irresponsibility. It is the garden of the virgin in the Song of Songs. It is the garden of Eden where love and action are innocent and possible. It is, I would suggest also, the garden where Mary Magdalene found Christ after the resurrection. It becomes, finally, a garden where Hallam's energetic principle of love for the beautiful makes a contemplative sensuality not escapism, but a means, like love, of learning a defined isolation and energising the soul. The garden in 'I have led her home' combined all these at once.

Tennyson himself said of this poem 'Do any of the expressions "rapturous" "painful" "childish" however they may apply to some of the poems, fully characterise the 18th? is it not something deeper?'[11] In this poem the hero's assurance of his own identity *is* the impersonal assurance of the lyric and of the undifferentiated positive response of assimilation of the landscape and of union with the beloved. It opens and closes with a lack of self-assurance which is dramatically right and yet also has that impersonal simplicity of statement which is part of the power of a lyric and so hard to describe.

'I have led her home, *my love, my only friend*' is what any incredulous lover would say about his beloved: it is also what this loveless man would say in this context. The end of the lyric, on the other hand shades subtly away from universal emotion into case history.

> Blest, but for some dark undercurrent woe
> That seems to draw—but it shall not be so:
> Let all be well, be well.

Within the poem the repeated 'None like her, none' has the force again of the impersonal lyric appeal to universal undifferentiated emotion.

The imagery of other poems is, as I have said, drawn together here and made coherent. The roses here are the 'thornless' roses of the garden of Eden: the trees are both English, and eternal biblical symbols of richness and constancy. The perfumes and honey and spices of the Sultan's dangerous garden, the 'honey of poison-flowers', here all combine in imagery which combines sensuous and religious ecstasy. His life is a 'perfumed altar-flame' and if Love 'spices' his fair banquet with the dust of death, in this context life flows evenly and smoothly towards death which is an accepted and inevitable part of it. The blood here is released and identified with the river that flows from Maud's garden to his.

> And never yet so warmly ran my blood
> And sweetly, on and on
> Calming itself to the long-wish'd-for end,
> Full to the banks, close on the promised good.

The long-wish'd-for end is here death, but incorporated in love
and life—Tennyson is using the accepted sexual pun on 'die';
the river is the river of Paradise, the waters of life. Maud's
ghostly whiteness is innocence (*and* sexual nakedness): she is
'the snow-limbed Eve'. It is also bridal—'twelve sweet hours
that past in bridal white/And died to live, long as my pulses
play' thus combined with the sexual flow of the blood. Dreams
are not terror but 'fragments of the golden day'. The stars are a
bridal crown, the sky is not 'iron', Maud's 'passionless'
quality is transferred to the stars that blindly run—but in this
one lyric do not do so. The past, even, is incorporated in the
present, not something lost to be mourned—the cedars look
with delight like

> theirs of old, thy great
> *Forefathers* of the thornless garden. (my italics.)

In this lyric Tennyson has combined several techniques of
joining emotion to sense, and general to particular feeling.
If we look at 'Morning arises stormy and pale' and compare it
with 'Come into the garden' we can see two quite different
techniques of lyric landscape producing effects of intense
emotion. In the first, Tennyson echoes the kind of Romantic,
Shelleyan investment of the landscape with feeling through
natural description. One has precisely to visualise 'fold upon
fold of hueless cloud'. In 'Come into the garden', rose and lily
are heavily invested with personality in pseudo-Oriental
manner—visualisation of these flowers is difficult, the roses are
purely exterior symbols of interior feelings. In 'I have led her
home' tension between feeling and landscape are much more
complex. The 'pattering talk' of the laurels, the sway of the
branches, the whole sensual atmosphere of the poem demand
precise *sensual* imagination. The Biblical imagery, the generalisations about fate and love make the poem strictly sacramen-

tally symbolic. But the feeling of the whole poem follows Hallam's idea that the 'sacred *ideas* of our nature, the idea of good, the idea of perfection, the idea of truth' are intensified 'by being contemplated through this predominant mood' of 'immediate sympathy with the external universe'. It is, like the *Ode to a Nightingale*, the achievement of a timeless and spaceless contemplation of *an idea* (the idea of the annihilation of the battle between life and death, in love) and as an extension of an immediate sensual response to beauty. In Tennyson's earlier poems, and in parts of *Maud* itself, some guilt is to be felt about aesthetic contemplation in a garden—it leads to death in *The Lady of Shallott*, and in *The Palace of Art*. But in a series of lyrics, expressing phases of passion, in a tragedy which takes account of time, fate and morals, there is also room for an ideal vision of aesthetic and moral unity, like the song of the nightingale in Tennyson's *Recollections of The Arabian Nights*.

> Not he: but something which possess'd
> The darkness of the world, delight,
> Life, anguish, death, immortal love,
> Ceasing not, mingled, unrepress'd,
> Apart from place, withholding time.

But the sensual contemplation of truth and beauty does not hold against time and passion. Maud may be a Christ-figure, but the idea of 'atonement' calls up in the hero the old theme of vengeance—Tennyson's modulation from lyric unity to dramatic stress is masterly.

> My dream? do I dream of bliss?
> I have walk'd awhile with Truth.
> O when did a morning shine
> So rich in atonement as this
> For my dark-dawning youth,
> Darken'd watching a mother decline
> And that dead man at her heart and mine:

The vision of Truth is not an atonement, after all: blood must be paid. The idea of the dead father starts up the train of thought again.

89

V

In Part II Tennyson deliberately created a discord of all the
emotions and images he had woven together in Part I. Flowers
are 'plucked', the fires of Hell broke out of the 'dawn of Eden',
roses are blood, carriage wheels remembered from the party go
over the hero's dead, or mad, head. Maud is now a real ghost,
and a real accuser, and the confusion in the hero's head is not
Romantic morbidity but real dementia. It is brilliantly done
but slightly factitious.

'See what a lovely shell' stands out in two ways. It is a lyric
centred on a new image—read in the context of the whole of
Maud the contemplation of a small shell after the English
landscape and Persian garden is moving in a delicately bleak
way. And it continues the theme of the structure of one man's
individual energy and virtue through the lyric, through the
contemplation of the timeless moment. The shell is an image of
the will in solitude—it is a hard, finished, dead growth, but
durable. It is 'frail, but of force to withstand'. It is an object for
expanded sensual contemplation, a source of a kind of *secondary*
aesthetic energy—'a sharper sense/For a shell or a flower'.
It is dramatically moving that this dead shell recalls the
memory of the dead Sultan's ring—no jewel but his dead
mother's hair. Part II repeats, with a wild intensity, the emotion
kept at bay in Part I—the passion for the past, the will to die or
go mad in order to regain a beloved dead object. It is centred
on 'O that 'twere possible'—the germ of the poem, and a kind
of inchoate first version of the whole poem itself. I cannot feel,
however, that Part II really arouses the complex responses of
Part I, or has the same unity and assurance.

In Part III Tennyson is making, lucidly, the perfectly
egitimate point that a kind of grim individual courage to go
on in defeat, to live with life and the possibility of death, is all
we can hope for. Politically, this was what he celebrated: his
military poems, his historical drama celebrate courage in
apparent defeat. (*Harold* uses the *Maud* imagery—its final value
is simply Harold's courage for courage's sake, which Tennyson
apostrophises as 'O garden blossoming out of English blood!')

Part III of *Maud* brings together the disparate themes and images and attempts to direct them all towards the impersonal courage and use of energy in war. Maud is one with the stars, the cannon is 'the blood-red blossom of war' the 'passionate heart and morbid eye' are no longer diseased. But the poetic tension, the *lyric* unity, is, to my sense, completely lacking, although the intention can be read. This, for instance, is what happens to the complex of light images.

> And many a darkness into the light shall leap,
> And shine in the sudden making of splendid names,
> And noble thought be freer under the sun,
> And the heart of a people beat with one desire.

We have blood and light but only an ersatz energy.

VI

When Tennyson's contemporaries praised him for intellectual subtlety it was often this kind of complex exploration of shades of feeling, phases of passion, with a formal elaboration which is in itself another form of passion, that they meant. Matthew Arnold said 'the essential characteristic of his poetry is, it seems to me, an extreme subtlety and curious elaborateness of thought, and extreme subtlety and curious elaborateness of expression'. Gladstone, who had at first disliked *Maud*, questioned whether 'a poem should require from common men a good deal of effort in order to comprehend it' and whether *Maud* had 'Full moral equilibrium' but confessed that he had not only not done justice to the 'rich and copious beauties of detail' and 'great lyrical and metrical power' of *Maud*, but

what is worse, I have failed to comprehend rightly the relation between particular passages in the poem and its general scope. This is, I conceive, not to set forth any coherent strain, but to use for poetical ends all the moods and phases allowable under the laws of the art, in a special form of character, which is impassioned, fluctuating and ill-grounded. The design, which seems to resemble that of the Ecclesiastes in another sphere, is arduous; but Mr Tennyson's power of execution is probably nowhere greater.[12]

And Dr. James Mann argues that the stanzas of 'I have led her home' are marked by the highest and subtlest qualities of the Laureate's genius, and are, indeed, especially illustrative of the one leading characteristic of Tennysonian poetry, which is *intellectual elaboration*. Every image which Mr. Tennyson receives from external nature, or conjures up from the mysterious recesses of his fancy, he retains in his mental alembic, subjecting it again and again to the processes of reflective analysis, until he has at last extracted a material that is capable of being moulded into a form of severe perfection.[13]

These Victorians understood the formal complexity and the general scope of *Maud* better than we have recently been able to do, paradoxically because they were better able to respond to those elements which were not intellectual: the value of *feeling* in the lyric, and the value of immediate sensuous response in description, rhythm and imagery. The sensitivity of Hallam's essay shows that this, consciously, lay under their aesthetic: *Maud* is a piece of aesthetic writing as well as a love song and a drama, and one in which, as Hallam suggested, sensual beauty is 'a perpetual and necessary refreshment to the sources of activity and intuition'.

NOTES

[1] Robert James Mann, *Tennyson's 'Maud' Vindicated: An explanatory essay* [1856], p. 71.

[2] Reprinted in *The Victorian Consciousness*, ed. H. Levine (New York, 1967).

[3] Reprinted in *The Victorian Consciousness*.

[4] For a sensitive psychoanalytic study of *Maud's* hero see Roy P. Basler, *Sex, Symbolism and Psychology in Literature* (1948).

[5] Hallam Tennyson, *Alfred Lord Tennyson: A Memoir* (1897), vol. I, p. 396.

[6] E. D. H. Johnson, *The Alien Vision of Victorian Poetry* (Princeton, 1952), p. 10.

[7] John Killham, *Tennyson and 'The Princess'* (1958).

[8] Reprinted in *The Victorian Consciousness*.

[9] Robert Browning, *An Opinion on the Writings of Alfred Lord Tennyson* (privately printed, London, 1920).

[10] *Critical Essays on the Poetry of Tennyson*, ed. John Killham (1960).

[11] Hallam Tennyson, *Tennyson: A Memoir*, vol. I, p. 409.

[12] Ibid., p. 399.

[13] Mann, op. cit., p. 36.

5

BROWNING AND THE 'GROTESQUE' STYLE

Isobel Armstrong

Since Walter Bagehot called Browning's art 'grotesque' this has become an indispensable word in the discussion of Browning's style—there are so many things which are immediately and strikingly ugly.[1] Few poets create such an unease in the reader and few readers will feel that the poet is at ease with his language. The wrenching of metrical patterns, the heterogeneous vocabulary compounded of aggressive colloquialisms and highly literary fragments of poetic diction, these together have an eccentricity which it is appropriate to call grotesque. Effects are exaggerated to the point of extravaganza, whether it is the constant present tense or the habit of straining the syntax by omitting articles, relatives, verbs and auxiliaries. Ways of articulating the words are thrown out so that the language is left to hit one with the raw immediacy and obviousness of a sensation. And Browning's devices for doing this *are* obvious: the violence of his expletives and exclamations, the preference for extended simile and for strings of brute physical adjectives and compounds rather than metaphor, create a sort of verbal melodrama. Who, after all, says 'Grrr'? And 'Zooks!' is excessive even in the context of Fra Lippo Lippi's muscular aestheticism. Hopkins's description of Browning's style as a man talking loudly while chewing a mouthful of bread and cheese admirably captures the insistent, almost wilful, delight in inchoateness. There is a deliberate disowning of order, a refusal to structure language. This, I think, springs from a belief that experience cannot be structured and a scepticism about the capacity of language to express the true structure of our experience which I shall discuss. Meanwhile, it is enough to point out the centrifugal movement of Browning's poems; they throw words outwards, leaving a litter of linguistic wreckage for the reader to reconstruct, a wreckage which has a curious way of demanding more attention than it seems to deserve, even though one is tempted to call it the result of simple carelessness.

The element of exaggeration is always there even when Browning seems at his most idiomatic. I shall therefore take the aggressive bravado with which he uses, and even misuses, language as the starting point of this discussion. I shall not consider him as a 'colloquial' poet for although he can some-times create the illusion of a speaking voice there is no evidence that his style was based, or that he wanted to base it, upon the spoken idiom of his time. (And the term 'colloquial', in any case, begs too many questions about style.) The evidence about his intentions, in fact, is all the other way. If *Sordello* can be trusted as evidence of Browning's intentions, and I think it can, Browning thought of his style as something deliberately con-structed, an artificial language rather as we talk of Milton's style as artificial. The poet Sordello, whose problems with his poetic style seem so like what we find in Browning's poetry that one cannot doubt that Browning was exploring his own difficul-ties as well as those of the Italian poet, eventually evolves an entirely idiosyncratic language. He 're-wrought', 'melted' down and 'hammered' his language, welding his own invented words into the 'crude mass' of the vernacular and 'fusing' these with the 'Roman panoply' of his traditional poetic language (*Sordello*, Book Two, ll. 573–579). All these things have parallels in Browning's poetry and sound very like the 'grotesque' style which I have described. It is necessary to go into the reasons why he had to create an artificial language.

This consciously, even sophisticatedly, contrived grotesque style does not after all seem to have been the result either of carelessness or of ineptitude, yet it is primarily for his use of language that Browning has been described variously as a 'barbarian', a 'semantic stutterer' or, more frankly, as a 'vulgar' poet.[2] J. Hillis Miller in *The Disappearance of God* (1964), sees him as a kind of swamp poet wallowing in an almost pre-verbal state, a view which seems oddly to contradict the patently constructed and willed nature of Browning's style. I would argue that the sheer artifice of the style cannot be ignored; there is a good case for regarding Browning's style rather as one regards a convention with its own decorums, a convention which is capable of being handled skilfully or unskilfully. A literary convention requires an audience to be in collusion, as it were, with a selective and special way of using language or with a special range of stances and postures. One thinks of the conventions of poetic diction or of courtly love. I believe that Browning's melodramatic grotesque style requires the same kind of complicity and differs from a convention only in the extent, but not in the nature, of the complicity required. A style would scarcely make its effect if one were not conscious of its *being* a style, and in the case of the grotesque the violence and distortion of the manner draw particular attention to themselves and make really heavy demands on the reader. But they can establish a kind of decorum, even though this is a decorum of violation which is particularly prone to failure. The attention which this style draws to its theatrical excess is correspondingly large when the manner is misjudged. When Browning's style fails it does so not because it is grotesque—he does not always stop being vulgar even at his most successful—but because he loses control of the grotesque. When he is in control he can achieve a curious and complicated relationship with the reader and a style which creates rich and surprising effects, an odd mixture of brashness and subtlety. Perhaps this is why Bagehot slides from talking of Browning's style as grotesque because it is coarse and grotesque because it is complicated. It is certainly curious that such blunt weapons can achieve so much. There are times, for instance, when an archaic and a colloquial word achieve a dramatic collision. Or the lacunae in the syntax give such speed and liquidity to the language that one wants to use Browning's own description of it in the *Parleying, With Charles Avison* (1887)—running 'mercury into a mould like lead', shooting 'Liquidity into a mould'.

Of course, I recognise that I use the terms 'convention' and 'decorum' in a way perversely contrary to our understanding of them in, for instance, eighteenth-century literature. A privately evolved code, however consistent and specialised, is self-evidently different from a mode shared and recognised by a generation of writers and readers. Nevertheless it is helpful to retain these terms, used in this analogical way, for the same reason that I have used the terms 'theatrical' and 'parody' below in a loose and extended way. They are the best words for describing a style which manipulates language to such an extent that it has become a posture, a self-consciously exaggerated manner which depends to a large degree upon a kind of collusion between writer and reader.[3]

A good deal of the brashness of manner in Browning's poetry is caused by his strenuous attempts to alert the reader to his self-consciously projected rôle, a rôle projected half-ironically, sometimes with a full awareness of the efforts being made. Some writers have attributed this to his failure to find a proper poetic voice, to his uneasiness about and distrust of the reactions of his public, or to a lurking consciousness of the inadequacies of his own identity. These diagnoses are partly correct, I think, but there is a sort of tough confidence about his way of forcing himself on a reader, cajoling him, making him participate and involve himself, which suggests a more assured intention; I think they are devices to push the reader into a much more active and reciprocal response to the poem than he is used to. This is where the union of subtlety with brashness becomes important, for the rapid shifts, displacements and lacunae of Browning's style are so disorientating that they demand a real effort of reconstruction and synthesis from the reader before the meaning is extracted from the poem. In his impressive discussion, 'Two Styles in the Verse of Robert Browning', Robert Preyer argues that this style mimes 'the disorder, incompleteness, and puzzlement that clings to human activity', and constantly represents the ways 'by which we seek to complete and comprehend actions'.[4] I would agree that no poet could have been more aware, sadly, exasperatedly, of the fluid, messy, almost runny, nature of experience which continually evades the hard and resistant formulations of language, the 'abysmal bottom-growth, ambiguous thing/Unbroken of a branch, palpitating . . .' described in *Charles Avison*. On the other hand, I am not sure that Browning carries us to the brink of communication, or beyond communication, by confronting us with experiences which are 'logically unorderable' and 'incommunicable', for this seems to me a way of saying in a brilliant and courteous fashion that Browning simply could not communicate.

Certainly Browning was thoroughly sceptical about the power of language, the 'poet's word-mesh' as he calls it in *Avison*, to capture the half-wet 'liquidity', the evanescent 'mercury' of perceptual life and of the consciousness itself, but he does not retreat into nescience. On the contrary, his best poetry marvellously renders the structure of experience as a fluid, unfinished *process* on which we continually try to impose a shape, an order. Browning's poetry is unique in its attempt to force the reader to go through these unfinished processes and, indeed, to *create* them and their meaning as he reads. Like music (which, towards the end of his life, he began to prefer to language as a way of getting at the subtlety of experience) Browning's poems are really incomplete until they have been created, synthesised and interpreted in a reader's mind. A Tennyson poem is a burnished, meticulously finished object, demanding no more completion than it possesses; a Browning poem is organised so that the untidy, living immediacy of experience can be gone through and shaped as it is experienced.

Browning's abandonment of conventional modes of syntactic ordering becomes more and more important in a consideration of the methods of his style and I shall discuss his use of syntax in some detail later. What I would like to emphasise here is that his fascination with the language of inchoateness gives us a means of saying what his poetry is centrally 'about'; and Browning is so bafflingly odd, his work is so fragmented (the lyrics, for instance, seem unrelated to the monologues), and so elusive that one is always searching for an underlying preoccupation. His poetry does not represent an abandonment to the shapeless, anarchic flood of sensation as, perhaps, it would seem on a first acquaintance. At the same time as he establishes the living flux of experience he recognises the need, the necessity indeed, of creating order from it. In *Charles Avison* Browning acknowledges the need of the mind to order, to create a 'superstructure' of named and formulated constants; and yet the essential nature of life continually evades the 'Stability' of these structures with 'heaving sway and restless roll/This side and that'. It is possible to redeem this existence, however, but often at the cost of having it 'dead' or having art 'Construct' a fixed pattern rather than 'create' the living order of experience. But failure is not invariable; the structure of experience can be apprehended and an inherent order *discovered*. Running through Browning's poetry is a sharp antithesis between the meaning which is discovered and the meaning which is *constructed* along with an acknowledgement, half mocking, half sad, half exasperated, that our need to discover often compels us to construct, to force a shape upon experience. The double nature of Childe Roland's journey is a fine image of this dilemma. The journey is a journey of discovery and yet a journey can be preconceived; a hypothetical structure at least can be put upon it even though it is in the nature of a journey to be random, for its meaning and structure to become apparent only as and when it is undergone—'The tempest's mocking elf/Points to the shipman thus the unseen shelf/He strikes on only when the timbers start'. From the moment when he leaves 'safe road' for the 'ominous track' the knight's experience is that of successively abandoning pre-formed constructions about the nature of his journey and committing himself to the much more threatening and disordered process of discovery. The pre-conceived climatic moment of revelation never comes. Instead he discovers that the moment of insight is self-originated and that order and coherence must be derived from experience itself— 'This was the place! . . . Dotard . . . After a life spent training for the sight!' The blast on the horn is an acknowledgement of this, a recognition of a found order, at the same time as it is a willed and desperate refusal to be invaded by disorder.

People are right to feel that this poem, exceptional in Browning's poetry because it is overtly symbolic, is an important key to his work. So much of his poetry is about the ways in which we seek order or impose meaning, from the crudities of *Christmas-Eve and Easter-Day* to much more subtle works such as *Love in a Life*, *Two in the Campagna* and *By the Fire-side*. The baffled searching 'Room after room' for the just missed, scarcely defineable completeness, where all that can be defined is the sense of loss; the desire to control experience by holding fast to the ramifying thread of insight which is lost 'Just when I seemed about to learn!'; the need to find a significant order in the past accompanied by the realisation that the past is never complete until life is complete—there is an extraordinary consistency about Browning's lyrics. The variousness of the imagery—the maze-like house, the thread of the spider's web, the proliferating growth of a rambling hedge—has in common both the disorder and the unity of organic life. If the speakers of the lyrics discover, the speakers of the monologues construct meaning; whether it is Andrea del Sarto's careful, wan apologetics, a constructed identity made to make the past and the present bearable, or Caliban's attempt to construe the nature of the universe in terms of his own limited experience. The complication of the monologues is that though the speaker constructs an order the *reader* discovers the true nature of the experience. In the best of them Browning is able to make a subtle play between the construction and the discovery, between, for instance, del Sarto's self-pity and the reader's pity of his need to make such a structure out of his experience. It is no surprise that *The Ring and the Book* is a play with the multiform structures that can be made out of a single event.

In the following discussion of Browning's style I shall draw particular attention to the ways in which he alerts the reader to an unusually intense participation in the poem and especially to the ways in which he makes the reader aware of process and of the possibility of discovering that the process is meaningful. I shall examine a part of *Sordello* (1840), *By The Fire-side* (1855) and *Caliban upon Setebos* (1864) to discover the elements of Browning's style and the means by which he controls them. Then I shall suggest ways in which this kind of discussion can be extended to other of Browning's poems. *Sordello* is a good starting point because many of the features of his style are there in an exaggerated form. His experiments are at their most self-conscious and extreme and he has much to say that is illuminating about Sordello's difficulties in fashioning a poetic language. Of course, Browning's effects are never so concentrated in later poems and in taking *Sordello* as a type of the grotesque it is easy to ignore the considerable variations of his style, but there are habits common to much of his poetry which enable one to make comparisons between *Sordello* and other poems.

The following passage from Book One of *Sordello* produces the typical shocks of Browning's style. It describes the castle of Goito where the young poet Sordello grows up in isolation. The castle is made implicitly analogous with the labyrinthine complexities of Sordello's consciousness. The font here stands apparently for the source of his creative power—tainted and suspect as the unexpanded hint, 'contrived for sin', the mysterious dimness and garish eroticism suggest. It might be appropriate to call this kind of writing, as Bagehot did, distorted, but it is a controlled distortion, a controlled heterogeneity.

> Pass within.
> A maze of corridors contrived for sin,
> Dusk winding-stairs, dim galleries got past,
> You gain the inmost chambers, gain at last
> A maple-panelled room: that haze which seems
> Floating about the panel, if there gleams
> A sunbeam over it, will turn to gold
> And in light-graven characters unfold
> The Arab's wisdom everywhere; what shade
> Marred them a moment, those slim pillars made,
> Cut like a company of palms to prop
> The roof, each kissing top entwined with top,
> Leaning together; in the carver's mind
> Some knot of bacchanals, flushed cheek combined
> With straining forehead, shoulders purpled, hair
> Diffused between, who in a goat-skin bear
> A vintage; graceful sister-palms! But quick
> To the main wonder, now. A vault, see; thick
> Black shade about the ceiling, though fine slits
> Across the buttress suffer light by fits
> Upon a marvel in the midst. Nay, stoop—
> A dullish grey-streaked cumbrous font, a group
> Round it,—each side of it, where'er one sees,—
> Upholds it; shrinking Caryatides
> Of just-tinged marble like Eve's lilied flesh
> Beneath her maker's finger when the fresh
> First pulse of life shot brightening the snow.

(ll. 389–415)

The whole passage is a thoroughly good piece of theatre. The imperatives and exclamations are used very much as gestures insisting not only upon the immediacy of the reader's experience but also upon making him conscious of having it. They are in the nature of a public agreement made with the reader that he will assent to the mannered excess—Browning is never a private poet speaking to himself. Morbid excess is the norm in the strained and violent heterogeneity of the diction and the imagery, oriental, classical and biblical. The pillars, compared first with oriental palms, then with bacchanals, are eliminated from rather than illuminated by the simile and are buried lavishly in the things they are compared with. In the last biblical simile, not content with a conventional image, Browning galvanises the usual comparison by turning it upside down. Flesh is usually compared with marble, not marble with flesh, lilies and snow! The language seems to be modelled on the language which Sordello himself 're-wrought'. There is the odd juxtaposition of the archaic-sounding 'got past' (an attempt at an English ablative absolute) with the more colloquial 'You gain'. An extended, virtually metaphorical meaning is given to 'marred', where the verb means something like 'covered up'. In the bacchanal simile the shards of poetic diction—'purpled' 'diffused'—might be at home in an eighteenth century poem, but they are alongside the hectic 'flushed cheek' and 'straining forehead', which would certainly not.[5] The collision emphasises rather than diminishes the orgiastic quality of the simile. The metre likewise is handled with violence so that the basic pattern of the pentameter couplet is rarely allowed to emerge. No sentence ends where the line ends and heavy pauses chop the line into irregular fragments.[6] The language is so consciously manipulated that the final effect is of a kind of baroque virtuosity and display. Browning is so distanced from his set piece that one could never accuse him of a confused and romantic indulgence in it.

The extravagance of this passage leads one to expect a good deal of metaphoric language, but it is infrequent, or weak when it occurs. Browning relies on rather frenetic verbs of motion and on piling up adjectives. The explanation for this, I think, is that verbs and adjectives do direct attention to the raw immediacy, the 'thisness' of an experience, whereas metaphor can direct one away from it. Browning's ability to prevent monotony by using suffixes in a versatile way had already reached the point of virtuosity. 'A dullish grey-streaked cumbrous font' flanks a compound by adjectives formed with a native and a latinate suffix respectively.[7] He weights the lines with alliteration and assonance—it is the one thing which binds the disparate elements together.

These things, however, do not explain, though they collaborate with, the sense of being taken through a prolifically ramifying experience, and until one examines Browning's syntax it is not easy to account for the union of violence and complexity in this passage. The huge sentences are fractured into discrete units in such a way that the relationship each unit bears to another is concealed or ambiguous. The grammar, assisted by the breaks in the lines, constantly creates and dispels *illusions* of meaning and relationship and requires a continuous reorientation and adjustment to its direction. The second half of the first sentence, describing the gradual illumination of the maple-panelled room, is a good example. Two clauses intervene before the main verb picks up the sentence and the second clause, with its indefinite pronoun 'it'—'if there gleams/ A sunbeam over it'—might refer either to the haze or to the panel or to both and floats ambiguously between them, like the sunbeam itself, making the part of the sentence before the verb merge and mingle. The same shifting process is at work in 'A dullish grey-streaked cumbrous font, a group . . .' where the line-break encourages a reading of the font and the group as joint subjects. But then follows 'Round it' in the next line and then a dislocating parenthesis and the font re-arranges itself as a subordinate part of the sentence. It could even be said that the font plays a double function, first as a subject (for one reads it momentarily as a subject) and then, like a palimpsest, imposes itself as a free-floating appositional phrase. The different ways of describing the phrases testify to the hallucinatory effect of these sentences.

I have already said that this truncated syntax and the shifts and lacunae created by it are an important element in Browning's grotesque style; *Sordello* provides a good deal of evidence for regarding syntax as crucially significant. Of course, the

grammar here is mimetic in that it could be said to enact the
experience syntactically of feeling one's way through a maze; on
the other hand, the language of *Sordello* works like this most of
the time and when there is no such dramatic necessity for it to
do so.[8] It forces one to be aware of the elementary process of
perceiving, which is usually automatic. The processes of discovering a meaning and of discovering what it is like to discover are
as important as the meaning itself. In Book Two Browning
actually describes Sordello's audience (referred to rather
haughtily as the 'crowd') being forced to 'clutch/And reconstruct' his language—'painfully it tacks/Thought to thought . . .'
(ll. 569–599). The explanation he gives is that Sordello's
experience is not orderable by the conventional structure of
language. Sordello apprehends experience in 'perceptions
whole', that is, with a kind of all-at-onceness, grasping everything instantaneously. Perception, he explains, is quite alien to
'thought' which makes language its vehicle and is never more
than a representation of perception, a translation into entirely
different terms. Thought is sequential; it breaks experiences
down and spreads them out, replacing 'the whole/By parts, the
simultaneous and the sole/By the successive and the many'
(ll. 593–595). Language would obviously have to defy itself if it
were required to convey the immediacy and the irreducible
all-at-onceness of Sordello's perceptions; and in despair he
attempted to exploit the sequential nature of language while
forcing his audience to be aware that the nature of experience is
different from the order of language. This explicit preoccupation with the nature of experience and perception would
account (I am identifying Browning with Sordello here and the
evidence is the style of the poem itself) for the particularly
shifting, amorphous grammar of this poem—but there is a
sense in which the important things that go on in all Browning's
poems happen outside it as the reader is forced through the
processes of inference and discovery.

On the other hand, compelled though he is to exploit
sequence, language nevertheless comes very close indeed to
defying itself in Browning's poetry. The 'parts', the 'successive
and the many', cannot achieve simultaneity, the wholeness and
indivisible flux of experience, but they can suggest syntactic

equivalents of it. This is what Browning seems to be trying to do in *Sordello* and in a more modified way elsewhere in his poetry. In the passage above, for instance, the prolific colons coil up sentences within one another in circular fashion. Everything is done to obscure the grammatical precedence that one part of a sentence takes over another—destroying precedence stands as the equivalent of destroying sequence. Parentheses and disjunctions, inversions and omissions, these are the obvious ways in which this is achieved. Not so obvious is the way in which participles create self-contained, free-floating units all on a grammatical level with one another (the bacchanal simile) or prepositions stand in for verbs so that groups of phrases are run together with an effect of grammatical foreshortening (the Eve simile). Most important of all, though the word order is arranged to convey the successive order of the visual experience, the grammatical relationships perpetually strain against this visual order and cut across it. The description of the font, to which I have already referred, is an example. The first sentence is another.

> A maze of corridors contrived for sin,
> Dusk winding-stairs, dim galleries got past,
> You gain the inmost chambers, gain at last
> A maple-panelled room:

The initial participle phrases seem to mark off a succession of experiences, suggesting . . . and then . . . and then . . ., but these are telescoped when 'got past' collects them all together. When in the third line the main verb asserts itself and the tense shifts from past to present the first two lines are firmly collapsed into subordinate parts of the sentence. Grammatically speaking, you might say, the experience is over before you've begun. The same process is at work in the following co-ordinate clauses— 'You gain . . . gain . . .' The co-ordinate clauses, grammatically static and parallel, seem to be trying to bond together successive actions, or successive actions seem to be asserting themselves against a grammatical equation. 'Room', leaping to another stage in the journey through the castle, is not a synonymous amplification of 'chambers' as the clausal parallelism leads one to expect. How different if Browning had written 'rooms'. It is as if two kinds of order are made to react upon one another, a 'logical' or perceptual order and a grammatical order. This goes on, of course, whenever we read, but here, by encouraging and deviating from the reader's expectations and forcing him, to correct the false analogies suggested to him, Browning intensifies the process until it becomes virtually the meaning of the passage.

This syntax requires a drastic reduction of the ways of putting a sentence together and can be monotonous. But in this passage the complexity of response created by the attempt at all-at-onceness makes one feel that the poem is enriched rather than impoverished by Browning's grammer. The syntactical sur-prises, inducing the sense and process of discovery, co-operate with the general flamboyance of the style. This is another way, like the attitudinising gestures I began by discussing, of making the reader absolutely conscious of the demands being made on him and of encouraging through this consciousness an assent to the need to discover an order in the poem.

The danger of the grotesque style is its tendency to fall into strained and clumsy heterogeneity and spasmodic incoherence. This, in my opinion, happens in *By the Fire-side*, that flawed and brilliant poem, which I shall discuss next. Perhaps the success of the monologues is partly a result of the decorum they impose on the language by forcing it to express a consistent persona. For this reason I shall conclude my discussion of particular passages by looking briefly at the first lines of *Caliban upon Setebos*, the poem Bagehot discussed as an example of the grotesque.

By the Fire-side does not ever quite match the subtlety of its conception. It is two accounts of the same memory or two overlapping memories of the same experience, built up by alternating a series of reveries in the present with the memories of the past. The situation is complicated by the fact that the speaker begins in the hypothetical future, imagining himself as an old man imagining the past (stanzas 1–5). Then follows an account of what is actually past, the autumn walk which he and his wife took as lovers to a deserted church in the Italian mountains. This account is interrupted and concluded by reverie spoken in the present (stanzas 21–30; 47–53). Haunting as this interleaving of past with present, reverie with memory often is, Browning's style does not easily encompass the transitions between future, present and past and the voices of the old, young and (presumably) middle-aged man. The autumnal simile towards the end of the poem, for instance, (stanzas 41–43) is a clumsy attempt to relate the sections by picking up detail from the preceding description of autumn and expresses the speaker's tentative caution in cheerful proverbs—' "Hold the last fast!" runs the rhyme'. The jocular old man of the beginning reasserts himself in place of the meditative speaker of the last reverie. As I shall suggest later on, this is probably intentional, but it is very doubtful whether it is successful.

At two points in the poem (stanzas 4 and 30) Browning tells us how we should read it but these promise more than the poem finally achieves. We are to read the first account of the past as the process of a groping rediscovery of experience.

> Greek puts already on either side
> Such a branch-work forth as soon extends
> To a vista opening far and wide,
> And I pass out where it ends.

The Greek buds a proliferation of thoughts and associations creating a passage or a vista of memory and the speaker goes *forward* into memory discovering the experience of the past as it creates itself in front of him (most people think of looking back on the past—this is a splendid way of putting the self-generating immediacy of memory). The characteristic lacunae work to suggest the rapidity of the experience. As in the *Sordello* passage, co-ordinate clauses keep parallel what are successive actions— 'Greek puts already . . . a branch-work forth . . . And I [simultaneously] pass out where it ends'. The speaker seems both to be keeping pace with and jumping ahead of his experience.[9] The image suggests that we must read what follows both as the discoveries of a straying eye (the abrupt movement from open prospect to sharp detail, for instance) but also as the action of a straying mind discovering a past—an exquisite and subtle doubleness. One should know that with Browning a poem is often as much about the way the mind works as what it works upon.

But even with this in mind it is difficult to defend the following stanzas.

(11)

Oh the sense of the yellow mountain-flowers,
    And thorny balls, each three in one,
The chestnuts throw on our path in showers!
    For the drop of the woodland fruit's begun,
These early November hours,

(12)

That crimson the creeper's leaf across
    Like a splash of blood, intense, abrupt,
O'er a shield else gold from rim to boss,
    And lay it for show on the fairy-cupped
Elf-needled mat of moss,

(13)

By the rose-flesh mushrooms, undivulged
    Last evening—nay, in today's first dew
Yon sudden coral nipple bulged,
    Where a freaked fawn-coloured flaky crew
Of toadstools peep indulged.

In the first edition of the poem these stanzas were all one
sentence and it is still something of a triumph to have made the
final trimeter of the quintain bridge the stanzas to match the
unbroken continuum of the visual experience. With the same
virtuosity Browning exploits the duple-triple measure to convey
sudden jerks of surprise. And yet what a jumble of crudity and
complexity this is. It begins well: the impressionistic mountain
flowers suddenly displaced by the tactile immediacy of the
chestnut shells (the oddly eighteenth-century peripharsis
enables Browning to give you the thing before the name and
the impression before the formulation), the parts of the sentence
merging together and encouraging the effect of a simultaneous
bombardment of sensation—there is no main verb and no part
of the sentence takes precedence over another. But with the
image of the leaf as a blood-splashed shield on the fairy-cupped
elf-needled floor of the wood (it is surprising how often
Browning can produce feeble compounds) the intense abruptness ceases. The grotesque becomes coy. The reader is asked

as in the *Sordello* piece, to see the whole thing as a contrived and theatrical spectacle, but the difference is that here the language becomes over-indulgent and self-conscious. The joke rhymes of the last stanza—'undivulged', 'bulged', 'indulged'—convert the sensuality of the description into jocular eroticism. The inventiveness of the compound bringing rose, flesh and mushrooms into the closest relationship, and the immediacy of 'coral nipple' are destroyed in the indiscriminate piling up of words. The syntax, far from enriching the passage, simply jams discrepant adjectives violently together. Milton's 'freaked', used in the pastoral set-piece of flowers in *Lycidas*, appears in an almost slangy fashion as an epithet for the unpastoral 'flaky crew' (another fragment derived from the eighteenth-century apparatus of language of natural description) of toadstools indulging themselves by peeping at the mushrooms. 'Peep' has babyish overtones quite out of keeping with the eroticism of the passage. The heterogeneousness of Browning's style jars here as it does not jar in the *Sordello* piece and brashness takes command. It is clear that he wants to suggest a bursting, troubled, repressed sexuality but in trying to hedge the sexuality of the description Browning loses control of the extravagant artifice of this set-piece and comes near to parodying poetic diction.[10]

At stanza 21, the memory breaks off suddenly and the speaker returns to the present and celebrates his love for his wife. There is no explanation of the significance of the walk—the past, in fact, is explicitly repudiated in favour of the present. But after this mediation there is again an abrupt transition. From stanza 31 the speaker rearranges and continues with his memory, recapitulating his account of the church and describing it in much more emotive detail. The event and the experience are the same, but the mood of the memory has changed. He returns to the past in order to evaluate his experience—'Let us lean and love it over again', the speaker says,

> Let us now forget and now recall,
>   Break the rosary in a pearly rain,
>   And gather what we let fall!

Past events have not the order and sequence of actual experience but like beads on a rosary can be broken and gathered up in different sequences, rearranged and reformulated, and one can continually subtract from and add to their significance. The two images of growing branch and rosary beautifully suggest the difference between discovering and shaping experience. The rest of the poem shows how succeeding experience has amplified the significance of the past. And the past is continually open to reassessment; the poem ends by asserting the openness of the past which becomes, indeed, part of one's future growth, not completed until death. But again, paradoxically, the conception is more subtle than the words of the poem.

This is how the speaker comes to assess an unlooked-for moment of harmony, cancelled almost instantaneously, but recreated by a triumphant effort of will.

(49)
How the world is made for each of us!
How all we perceive and know in it
Tends to some moment's product thus,
When a soul declares itself—to wit,
By its fruit, the thing it does!

(50)
Be hate that fruit or love that fruit,
It forwards the general deed of man,
And each of the Many helps to recruit
The life of the race by a general plan;
Each living his own, to boot.

It is not surprising that commentators have thought that the speaker is saying his love is part of a predestined plan for humanity—all we know about the world convinces us that these things are inevitable.[11] The thumping lines, the gawky antitheses, behave as if they are Browning's *Essay on Man* and hint at an attempt to introduce an eighteenth-century strength into the aphoristic generalisations. In fact it means something rather different, but the condensed syntax, particularly of the third line of stanza 49, obscures this. Only the involuntary moment is 'given'; the product of the moment is determined by each individual alone and by all that he has done with his past experience. All that we have done to see and grasp the world prepares us for the way in which we respond to the given moment and determines whether we shall use the opportunity it offers creatively or not. Actions are the fruit of our whole lives, not of a single moment. They are the visible signs of growth. The 'general plan' of life is merely the totality of each individual's attempt to live his own life, whether he lives it well or ill. Browning is trying to emphasise the wholeness of experience. Every part of it counts in our growth.

The meaning of these stanzas is not as objectionable as it seems on a first impression, but Browning disguises this by the crippled symmetry of the language and by the attempt to give it the finality of a universal statement. His style destroys the possiblity of achieving the beautifully poised explicitness and generalisation of eighteenth-century poetry; the impressionistic word order, the fragmentation of the sentences, above all the inherent tendency to extravagant verbal poses, provide no basis on which to build such a style.

The failures of *By the Fire-side* are the result of local uncertainties of style.[12] There is so much that is impressive about it—the flashes of lyricism, the play with layers of time, the subtle way in which memory is seen as a dynamic part of our existence, the musing account of the church to which the lovers go, a visible embodiment of the dead husk which their own relationship could have become, even the sheer energy with which Browning goes wrong. And yet it is a strained work on the whole. Perhaps the verbal strain occurs because of the difficulty of writing what might be called an anti-romantic romantic poem; the infinite moment, the emotional climax to which the whole poem leads, is not intended to be the real centre of the poem; the much less exciting business of shaping one's life with a good deal of hard work to achieve spiritual contentment in marriage has to be made to seem of equal importance. Everything is done, formally and verbally, to contradict the lyrical climax. The structure of the poem, besides representing formally the interweaving of past, present and future, enables Browning to cut across the lyrical mood by introducing different and disruptive tones of voice. The reader is always denied a complete assent to the lyricism. It is a poem full of surprises and complexity, but with most of the complexity left out of the words.

A brief look at the introductory passage of *Caliban upon Setebos* shows how the need to establish a consistent persona disciplines Browning's style although, curiously enough, one would never want to argue that the monologues are invariably his best poems. The usual habits are present but this time all co-operate to construct a highly artificial 'primitive' language. Though less extreme than in *Sordello* the fragmented sentences are there, and so are the present tense and the grammatical foreshortening and lacunae. Here they work to suggest that Caliban uses a language of essentials, juxtaposing rather than articulating, avoiding all but the most straightforward relationships. (He avoids the passive throughout the poem, for instance, and backs away from the past tense—'He hated that He cannot change . . .' (l. 32).) Bagehot called this poem 'nasty and gross' and so in a fashion it is, but the language creates in a stylised way an elementary, hardly articulate, consciousness and demands more than admiration of its virtuosity.

> Will sprawl, now that the heat of day is best,
> Flat on his belly in the pit's much mire,
> With elbows wide, fists clenched to prop his chin.
> And, while he kicks both feet in the cool slush,
> And feels about his spine small eft-things course,
> Run in and out each arm, and make him laugh:
> And while above his head a pompion-plant,
> Coating the cave-top as a brow its eye,
> Creeps down to touch and tickle hair and beard,
> And now a flower drops with a bee inside,
> And now a fruit to snap at, catch and crunch,—
> He looks out o'er yon sea which sunbeams cross
> And recross till they weave a spider-web
> (Meshes of fire, some great fish breaks at times)
> And talks to his own self, howe'er he please,
> Touching that other, whom his dam called God.
>
> (ll. 1–16)

These lines establish the movement of the poem, a creature attempting to rehearse to itself a rudimentary sense of its own identity and intellect in order to construct a meaning of the world—'He looks out o'er yon sea . . . And talks to his own self . . .'—but constantly invaded by its arbitrary sensory life. The third person pronoun does what the imperatives and demonstratives do in the rest of the poem—they assert Caliban's self-consciousness. But what he feels comes before what he does or thinks. In the second sentence the main verb 'He looks' is thrown to the ninth line and the orgiastic physical sensation takes over in the series of parallel co-ordinate clauses which precede it and seem to hold in simultaneity all the pullulating life going on over and around Caliban. The subjects of these clauses shift from Caliban to a part of the natural world and because the verbs endow the world with emphatically anthropomorphic characteristics (the plant *creeps* down) Caliban's nature and that of the mindlessly cruel and goading world of plants and insects around him seem analogous and interchangeable. The same kind of effect is achieved by the verb in 'small eft-things course'. Blood courses through veins, too, and the creatures seem part of his physical being. Browning's experiments in 'all-at-onceness' gave him a means of conveying here the sense of laborious thought and involuntary sensation going on together.

It is hardly necessary to emphasise the appropriateness of the child-like alliteration (sometimes merely childish in *By the Fire-side*) and strange 'gross'-sounding words. Whereas the use of compounds with a superfluous element and unfamiliar terms for ordinary things seem gratuitously affected in *By the Fire-side* ('boulder-stones' (stanza 10), 'chrysolite' (stanza 37)) they are fitting here. 'Things' tacked on to 'eft', which is adequate on its own as a generic term for crawling creature, looks in this context like a rudimentary attempt to categorise, as does 'plant' in 'pompion-plant'. And pompion for pumpkin contributes to the exotic strangeness of Caliban's environment. The compounds are for the most part unremarkable—'cave-top', 'spider-web', 'winter-time'—but they do suggest a language being built up by discrete units brought into juxtaposition rather than related. Later on there are 'fire-eye' and 'sleek-wet' and the outstanding example of Browning's amazing control of adjectives, 'green-dense and dim-delicious'. The adjectives bring together the qualities of the water and the nature of Caliban's response to it—first its colour and consistency, then 'dim' with its suggestion of transparency half-counteracting 'dense', then 'delicious' evaluating the preceding words but bringing with it the suggestion of taste. The sheer clumsiness of this language has an extraordinary immediacy, and Caliban emerges from it gross, pathetic and strangely admirable in his naive efforts to make something of his experience.

The decorum imposed on Browning by this dramatic monologue is of the same kind as that created in most of the monologues. Because they portray characters trapped within the limits of their own consciousnesses they impose a series of consistent distortions upon Browning himself. Caliban, rejoicing in and yet tormented by the cruelty and energy of the universe, is trapped because he construes his god in its distorted terms. In conceiving the sun as a spider weaving meshes of fire round him he is imprisoned in his own teeming sensory life and is like the fish which he sees trying to leap from the water, its element, through the web of light. Distortions of feeling, distortions in thinking, situations neither tragic nor comic and too gross for the subtleties of irony—these are the things for which the grotesque achieves consistency and decorum. Browning is at his best dealing with the response which holds a latent excess or deviation from the norm. And the style is so assumed, so consciously projected, that by drawing attention to its distortions it manages to carry with it a suggestion of the mean or proportion from which it deviates. It reminds you (I quote Bagehot again) 'of the perfect image, by showing you the distorted and imperfect image'.

Caliban, of course, is a poem where the grotesque is so appropriate that there can be no question about its decorum. It is like poems such as *Porphyria's Lover* (1836), *The Laboratory* (1844) and *The Bishop orders his Tomb at St. Praxted's Church* (1845), where the situations and the extremes of feeling—these are all poems about sexual or aesthetic feeling, where a desire for the fullest possible possession of an object, the fullest possession of life, has gone wrong—require the style. In the same way the threatening, distorted psychological landscape of *Childe Roland* (1855) necessitates the grotesque style. And even by putting these poems together it is possible to see what range it is capable of achieving. Yet the most interesting poems are those where the grotesque does not seem immediately appropriate or where it is manipulated in a particularly subtle way and I shall discuss some of the larger effects of the style in this sort of poem to extend the particular points I have made so far.

To take first a minor example of a poem where the style does not seem immediately dramatically necessary, the last lines of *Too Late* (1864) come as a surprise. The speaker is talking of the death of the girl he never married and who married someone else and he goes through a number of different emotions—a pitiable sense of the girl deserted in her grave ('Needs help in her grave . . . Wants warmth from the heart . . .' (ll. 11–12)), envy of the husband, despair, affectionate and familiar recollection. The poem ends with the speaker imagining her present and being treated by him with royal adoration.

> There you stand,
> Warm too, and white too: would this wine
> Had washed all over that body of yours,
> Ere I drank it, and you down with it, thus!
>
> (ll. 141–144)

This sudden lunge into excess—he wants to bathe her in his wine and swallow her down with it—looks with its erotic cannibalism, not to speak of blasphemous undertones, like a piece of misjudged extravaganza, but I do not find it mistaken. In the first place it alerts one to the latent violence and hysteria of the speaker (the stabbing pulse in his cheek, for instance) which is just concealed until this moment and it involves a retrospective recognition of, and adjustment to, this element in the poem. Also (for it would be wrong to give this coda heavier implications that it can bear) it *is* an extravaganza, a way of expressing a delight which wants to gorge itself upon its object, so that the poem ends on a note of half-fantastic, half-serious fulfilment and warmth. The death of the girl has a terrible finality with its insistence on incomplete and deprived experience and yet paradoxically the finality of death opens up possiblities for fulfilment and completeness in fantasy. The emotional range of the poem is large and unexpected—lament and celebration, violence and pity, erotic extravagance and fond recollection.

In a Gondola (1842), the poem written when Browning heard of Maclise's painting, *The Serenade*, is a more complicated poem which is often dismissed as a macabre melodrama—and it is obviously intended to be. There is a Venetian violence about the situation—a pair of clandestine lovers pursued by the mysterious 'Three' who finally overtake and stab the man—and there is a more than usually rich sensuality about the style. But Browning manages to manipulate the style so that it becomes a criticism of itself and the excess becomes its own corrective. The ending has the effect almost of parody. 'Care' says the lover.

> Only to put aside thy beauteous hair
> My blood will hurt! The Three, I do not scorn
> To death, because they never lived: but I
> Have lived indeed, and so—(yet one more kiss)—can die!
>
> (ll. 227–231)

The absurd aestheticism of this death makes the man's claim that he has 'lived indeed' oddly suspicious. The whole thing is bloodless and mannered. Up to this point, certainly, the feelings of the lovers are full-bodied and felt to excess and yet by their very extremity they become sterile: the indulgent delight in secrecy, the fascination with the thought of death, the fantasies of abasement to a destructive sexuality, are powerful and at the same time disinfected of reality. The man thinks of the coiled hair of the girls as the snakes which Roman girls twisted over their breasts to cool themselves. The girl thinks of herself as a flower shattered by the bee which penetrates it. The eroticism, restricted and rarefied by its extremity, is very different from the feeling of *Too Late*:

> . . . so all is rendered up,
> And passively its shattered cup
> Over your head to sleep I bow.
>
> (ll. 60–62)

The surprising quality of the poem is its power to command an assent to its emotions at the same time as it forces a criticism of them. The speakers construct; the reader discovers, and the style invites collusion as well as criticism so that the melodrama is used in a serio-comic way. The closed, heavy emotional world of the pair is powerful and yet, for this very reason, almost absurd.

The double evaluation which the stance of *In a Gondola* invites is required, as I have said, by the dramatic monologues, poems where the grotesque is at its most obvious but also where it is often most puzzling. The difficulty of a style which can take two attitudes at once is to know whether and when it is to be taken at its face value. Are we asked to accept the buffooning gusto of Fra Filippo Lippi straight or not? Or are the worldly casuistries of Bishop Blougram unpleasant but inescapable? These difficulties are increased by the nature of the dramatic monologue: it is not only a performance in the sense that the words are spoken by somebody other than the poet; it is also a performance because the speaker is directing his words to somebody other than the reader. The reader has an indirect relationship to the poem. He is at three removes from it and there are innumerable opportunities for the distortion of what is already distorted. In the dramatic monologues Browning sets up a model of the devious processes of communication and interpretation. Nevertheless, the consistent distortions built into the language of the monologues do become a guide to their meaning. It is possible, as the monologue evolves, to see how the grotesque is being manipulated and to arrive at a reading of the poem—I do not believe that the monologues are open poems capable of several interpretations; we must accept that there is a reading which is approximately 'right'.

The examples of Blougram and Lippi (1855) are interesting because what they say is so frequently assumed to represent Browning's position, however oddly it masquerades. These lines make one uncomfortable because the same sense appears so frequently in his poetry and it really does look as though Browning believed them too.

No, when the fight begins within himself,
A man's worth something. God stoops o'er his head,
Satan looks up between his feet—both tug—
He's left, himself, I' the middle: the soul wakes
And grows. Prolong that battle through his life!

(ll. 693–697)

In actual fact the situation need not be complicated by the
knowledge that in all probability this *was* Browning's position:
the important thing to be aware of is the quality of feeling
created by the words; the notion of self-development through
suffering and conflict—the perfectly acceptable belief that life
is a vale of soul-making—is conveyed through eager military
rhythms, and the farcical tug-of-war image, in spite of a lurid
appropriateness, works to pull the idea into the shape of a
comic game, a virile gambol in moral athletics. It is not so
much that the Bishop's position is implausible—the difficulty,
after all, is that it is a religious view eminently possible to
hold—but the coarsening undergone in this thin and facile
formulation makes it impossible to accept what the words
create of it. This is what the poem is about. The emphasis all the
way through is on the quality of the Bishop's belief and not on
the truth of what he says. The emotional and moral feeling
from which he creates his structure of the world is inadequate.
The evolution of the monologue suggests that the nature of
belief depends, not on a series of isolated choices, but involves
the whole nature of a man's being, moral, emotional, intellectual, and the language he uses will show precisely what this
is. Here, distorting, but distorting only so much as to make the
position still momentarily plausible, the words reveal the
poverty of the bishop's response to the problem. The same
thing happens in the gross corollary, 'Up with the Immaculate
conception, then—/On to the rack with faith!' (ll. 704–705).
Here again excess is its own corrective and acts as a comic
control directing the reader's response. It is both subtle and
robust because the enormity is comic as well as vicious. The
same process is at work in the earlier comparison between the
stimulant of doubt and the effects of taking snuff—'I need the
excitation of a pinch/Threatening the torpor of the inside
nose . . .' (ll. 670–671). The notion is trivialised by being

117

translated into sensation so that doubt becomes a minor irritant. Browning was fascinated by what can happen to an idea or an emotion when it is formulated and reformulated—the same preoccupation, differently explored, is in *By the Fire-side*—and in what happens when different words make a different idea or a different emotion.

In *Fra Lippo Lippi* the grotesque is controlled more by the external situation than by an inner tendency to self-exposure and this is probably why it is difficult to see the direction of the poem. Until Lippi's circumstances are taken into account it is difficult to see why such a richly satisfying view of art as a celebration of the world should be put across with such simple-minded buffoonery. The situation is that the painter has to gain the sympathy of his hearers by persuading them that he is like them, a common man bitten by the same old Adam—'I saw the proper twinkle in your eye' . . . (l. 42). At the same time the commonness has to be exaggerated so that his listeners can feel complacently superior, but not too much exaggerated so as to provoke the severe moral condemnation which will lead to his arrest. One of the results is that Lippi's sexuality is made to seem ridiculously harmless (rabbits and mice—see ll. 9–11; 58–59—are not compelling images of animalism) in spite of his boasts. Mixed up with these compromising antics is a genuine anxiety to assert his freedom as an artist and to communicate the dignity and passion which art can possess for everybody. But all this is hedged round with an awkwardly defensive exhibitionism because the painter is so uncertain of the reactions of his audience, particularly to art. He is divided between making himself seem innocuous and important and talks down to the philistines. His account of himself is consistently distorted for this purpose. Hence the brute cheeriness, the ingratiating verbal nudges and the final impression of an embarrassingly undignified performance. Like so many of the monorogues this poem dramatises the problems of communicating the expedients, postures and uncertainties imposed by a listener. Browning has contrived the discomfort and divided impulses of the man who is suddenly confronted with the audience he is painting for.

Discomfort is never very far away from this style. One can

never underestimate Browning's aggressive delight in calculating confusions and disorientations for the reader. It is all a
part of his poetic stance. This is why the lyrical poetry presents
very real difficulties. Either one is constantly being deflected
from an assent to the lyrical feeling, as in *By the Fire-side*, or the
feeling itself becomes distasteful as it does in the pounding
emphases of *Saul*. Browning's lyrics, *Misconceptions* and *A Pretty
Woman*, for instance, often sound like parodies of the lyric. But
though as a rule the short lyric cannot hold the discomforts of his
style there are some poems where it almost comes off. *Love
among the Ruins* (1855 but rearranged in 1863) exploits with
deliberate awkwardness the friction of two modes, the pastoral
and the heroic, so that each can contradict and evaluate the
other. In the first stanza, for instance, although the spreading
anapaestic lines are very different from Gray's, the echoes of
the *Elegy in a Country Churchyard* are immediately recognisable (a
manuscript draft of the poem is entitled 'Sicilian Pastoral'), and
yet it becomes almost immediately a parody of the pastoral.[13]
The staccato trisyllabic line cuts in alternately with a flippant
martial drum beat and disrupts the mood of the long line.

> Where the quiet-coloured end of evening smiles,
> > Miles and miles
> On the solitary pastures where our sheep
> > Half-asleep
> Tinkle homeward through the twighlight, stray or stop
> > As they crop—
> Was the site once of a city great and gay,
> > (So they say) . . .

As far as the sense and syntax is concerned the whole stanza
could be read without the short lines. They are flagrant in-
trusions, impurities lodged in the stanza only by the rhyme.
Their function is to contradict and mock the usual associations
of the pastoral making it seem barren and empty of energy
and fulfilment in contrast to the historic past and the life of the
city which once stood where the sheep graze. Browning's
rearrangement of the stanzas from fourteen six-line stanzas to
seven of twelve lines was presumably done to make this contrast more acute. The heroic city superimposes itself on the

quiet landscape, and the oppositions developed as the poem goes on—love, war, solitude, social involvement, contemplation, action—are created by the collision of two styles. One extreme is continually balanced out by the other until the poem turns back on itself with the final statement, 'Love is best,' and the pastoral, as a criticism of the barbarity of the past civilisation, reasserts its traditional place. War should seem as crude at the end as the pastoral seems barren at the beginning. The trouble with the poem is that it is too short for either of these extremes to be fully qualified by this method of dramatic juxtaposition so that the final line cannot carry complete conviction. Browning needs space.

I have concentrated on the larger effects of Browning's style in the final part of my discussion to suggest that though the grotesque is so obviously recognisable the ways in which it is managed are not. Its range is wider and its effects are more complicated and more varied than at first looks possible. But it is variety within limits. More important than the objection to its vulgarity is one's feeling that it is ultimately tiring because of its limits. It is posturing; it depends upon the knowing, dramatic projection of a manner and this creates a more than usually exacting relationship with the reader. Like Byron's, but more violently, it is a rhetoric which asks for the reader's assent even while it seeks to outrage or disconcert. I have mentioned more than once the sense of parody in Browning's poetry, the manner without the material of the parodist, and it is to this genre that his poetry tends. It shares its possibilities as well as its limitations—the self-consciously exaggerated stance, too enlarged for irony, more complicated than melodrama or farce, the distortions which carry along with them the norm from which they deviate, and finally, the recognition of the power of language to pull a concept into a different and startling shape by reformulation (the innumerable gradations of repetition in *The Ring and the Book* come to seem almost inevitable in this context). Parody of the highest and most serious form, dense with concentration and energy—obviously, to describe Browning's poetry like this is to stretch the meaning of the word beyond permissible limits, but it can stand at least as an illuminating comparison. Taken further it suggests an explanation for Browning's badness. If you mimic a shoddy idea or feeling there is every likelihood that you will write a shoddy poem. *Rabbi Ben Ezra* and *Holy Cross Day* are failures of this kind and their effect on Browning's reputation is out of all proportion to their importance. But if the comparison helps to explain why these poems are bad it may also explain why other poems are not. And the analogy with parody does at any rate suggest where an examination of Browning's style must begin—with the sheer flagrance of the rhetoric, and with the uses rather than the limitations of the grotesque manner.

NOTES

Quotations from Browning's poetry are from *The Works of Robert Browning*, ed. Frederic George Kenyon, 10 vols. (London, 1912). Dates are the first date of publication.

[1] Walter Bagehot, 'Wordsworth, Tennyson and Browning; or Pure, Ornate, and Grotesque Art in English Poetry', *National Review*, XIX (1864), pp. 27–67.

[2] See George Santayana, *Interpretations of Poetry and Religion*, Torchbook Series (New York, 1957), pp. 118–216; S. W. Holmes, 'Browning: Semantic Stutterer', *P.M.L.A.*, LX (1945), pp. 231–255; Robert Graves, *Mammon and the Black Goddess* (London, 1965), 56–58.

[3] There are obvious dangers in loosening the sense of these terms but discussions of nineteenth-century literature seem to be in need of a vocabulary which will convey something like their meaning. R. Garis, for instance, in *The Dickens Theatre* (1965), emphasises the virtuoso display of Dicken's theatrical manner and J. Loofbourow in *Thackeray and the Form of Fiction* (Princeton, 1964) sees Thackeray as a parodist sporting with conventions. These are both attempts to look at the curious relationship set up between writer and reader by the manipulation of style. The Victorian writer was faced with the problem of creating an identifiably public voice, for an audience whose reactions he was by no means certain of, in a post-romantic literature which provided him with no acknowledged means for doing this. I think that the current use—not always satisfactory—of the terms I have mentioned results from an attempt to describe what this public voice, or voices, are like.

[4] *E.L.H.*, XXXII (1965), p. 75. I have not made Preyer's

distinction between two styles in the poetry because both seem to me to be inextricably involved with one another. Isn't the simple style just Browning at his worst anyway?

5 The heterogeneity of Browning's diction is discussed by Bernard Groom, *On the Diction of Tennyson, Browning and Arnold*, S.P.E. Tract, No. 40 (London, 1939). Groom's conclusions have been modified by WilliamW. Ryan, 'The Classification of Browning's "Difficult Vocabulary" ', *S. P.*, LX (1963), pp. 542–548. His analysis shows that Browning's use of nonce words, rare, archaic and obsolete vocabulary is not excessive though the proportion of unfamiliar words is high. This is no doubt statistically the case, but the effect of Browning's vocabulary is produced by odd juxtaposition and by the context in which the words appear and this is much more difficult to analyse by statistical methods. There are some revealing discussions of Browning's vocabulary in P. Honan, *Browning's Characters* (New Haven, 1961), pp. 207–232.

6 H. H. Hatcher, *The Versification of Robert Browning*, Ohio State University Studies, Graduate School Series No. 5 (1928), p. 6, finds the constant principle of Browning's versification is to collapse the metrical pattern and to impose a new pattern of his own above it.

7 'His metaphoric vision is poor, so that he does not exploit syntax for metaphoric expression. He uses the most ready-to-hand formulae, and even with verbs he prefers the more obvious relationships.' Christine Brooke-Rose, *A Grammar of Metaphor* (London, 1958), p. 312. This conclusion is clearly justifiable, but it ignores in the first place Browning's amazing control of adjectives as a substitute for metaphor and secondly his experiments with breaking down conventional syntax altogether in order to achieve shifting, amorphous relationships. The loss in one direction is a gain in another.

8 The consistency of Browning's grammar in *Sordello* is analysed by Henri Hovelaque, *Browning's English in Sordello* (Paris, 1933).

9 At first sight this image seems to have an affinity with metaphysical poetry and with Donne in particular. Clearly Browning learned a good deal from Donne in the way of the handling of metre, colloquialisms and violent changes of tone, but the resemblances are superficial. See Joseph E. Duncan, 'The Intellectual Kinship of John Donne and Robert Browning', *S.P.*, L (1953), pp. 81–100.

10 I do not find myself worried whether 'this syntactical pattern acts out a train of feeling significant to the burden of the whole', like Donald Davie, *Articulate Energy* (London, 1955), p. 74. The

straying eye and the straying memory are enough to account for it. It is not the syntax but the *manner* which is so objectionable.

[11] Santayana, op. cit., p. 202.

[12] A recent critic of Browning's lyrics has suggested that they should be described as 'anti-lyrics', and that the movement of his poems deliberately sets itself against the movement of lyrical feeling. I am sure that this is what goes on in *By the Fire-side*, but even the anti-lyric cannot excuse the failures of the style. See William Cadbury, 'Lyric and Anti-Lyric forms: A Method for Judging Browning', *U.T.Q.*, XXXIV (1964), pp. 49–67.

[13] See W. C. De Vane, *A Browning Handbook*, second edition (New York, 1955), p. 212.

THE IMPORTANCE OF *SORDELLO*

Michael Mason

It is hard enough to know which of those two equally intractable topics—the technique of *Sordello* or its content—to take as a starting-point, but even harder to keep the two distinct. The difficulty arises because quite a lot of the poem is about a poet and his ideas on poetry, and in no simple fashion. Not only does Browning describe in *Sordello* habits that are actually exhibited in the fabric of the poem, it is also a specimen literary growth that has been cultivated in the interests of a special theory of literary evolution. It is, in rather a grandiose way, the poem it is about. It is also, it can be shown, the poem that a good deal of contemporary chat on literature, especially in journals, was about. Whether the 'importance' of the poem lies in any of the things that have just been said is a matter of opinion. For my part this importance does lie in the poem's being a grand technical experiment, and one that ventured single-handed to confirm hypotheses about literature that were current in the 1830s—but at the same time I would like to approach this seamless fabric unargumentatively, simply expounding and placing the poem.

One of the first facts to be grasped about *Sordello* is the structure of its narrative. The fulcrum of the story is one evening in Verona, the evening with which the poem opens. Although the span of the narrative is something over thirty years, the 'present' time of the poem only runs from this evening onwards for about three days, the whole of the rest of the period being covered retrospectively. In fact this evening is, in Browning's view, a watershed between the two main areas of Sordello's life—those thirty years in which he was budding and actual poet, and those three days in which he toyed with the rôle of politician. From this opening in Verona we survey the past

125

thirty years, learn in what way Sordello abandoned poetry, and see how he has come to Verona at the request of Palma to try his hand in the complicated politics of the day. This brings us to the beginning of Book Three, and back to the crucial evening, though now in its proper place temporally.

At this point Browning, having brought one half of his story full circle, breaks off to give us an account of his thoughts while in Venice in June 1838—actually the date at which he had almost completed three books of the poem.[1] This amazingly illegitimate digression is a dense reservoir of clues to the meaning and application of the rest of the poem. The last three books take us through the few days of Sordello's fastidious shadow-boxing with politics, culminating in his death.

The most striking fact about this arrangement is how ill-balanced, in terms of narrative content, these roughly equal parts of the poem are. The explanation is, of course, that their equality is thematic;[2] the components of contemplation and action, poetry and politics, balance, even if exhibited over thirty years and three days respectively. This is our first example of something we will encounter a lot—the massive subordination of history to theme.

Is it true that the poem effectively falls apart into these two halves? This is a difficult question; external and internal evidence (mainly the latter) shows that the last three books stem substantially, if not wholly, from after the *volta* experienced in Venice, though external and internal evidence (of a less clear kind) also shows that the first three books were quite deeply revised at the same time. There are obvious technical differences between the two halves; Books 4–6 confine themselves to Ferrara, and their burden is massive abstract discussion in a typical Browning vein; Books 1–2½ have various settings, and more concreteness. Nevertheless the two parts have their calculated symmetries. The major one is the pair of verbal frontis-pieces occupying 1. 389–427 and 4. 138–169. The first, the account of the sensuous 'maple-panelled room' and the adjacent ascetic 'vault' at Goito prefigures the whole opposition of themes in the poem, but with a special emphasis in the vault's caryatides on the agony of Sordello as poet, the material of the first three books. Their posture is suffering, suffering because of a rejected and unresolved contact with real experience; carved in 'just-tinged marble'. they are like vestals 'Penanced for ever' after 'sin impure'. The statuary on Taurello's terraces, the second initiating emblem, is 'meant to look/ Like'

> A certain font with caryatides
> Since cloistered at Goito; only, these
> Are up and doing

because this is the 'up and doing' part of the poem. The apex of the hierarchy of statues is the Fighter, superbly described, and the Slave. The first is Sordello, pitting himself in a hopeless fight; the second is Palma, losing herself in devotion to her hero.

This big fact of *Sordello's* two-part structure is heuristically good; it helps us to organise the randomness of the story's material. Also important is the business of sites in the poem. The first half is Goito and Mantua; the second is Ferrara; Verona is transitional. Browning relies quite heavily on how he locates the story in one of these four North Italian theatres. Nothing happens to Sordello other than in one of these places, and nothing of what does happen is inappropriate to its particular background as indicated by the author. The link between these sites and the kind of action they enshrine is so strong that the names alone can be used as a king of shorthand: 'Ferrara's reached, Goito's left behind' (5. 238).

Goito, the cradle of Sordello's youthful imagination, is a compelling blend of the vague and the ravishingly vivid, at least in its first appearance (1. 374–962). In its second appearance (2. 948–1003), for Sordello's return in disillusion from his career as poet in Mantua, there is a studied effect of disenchantment in all the features that Sordello's imagination wrought on in the first account: the trees ('A querulous fraternity'), the vines ('leafless and grovelling'), the castle ('dwindled . . . gone to ruin'), the maple-room, now seen at night. Mantua (2. 473–934) is physically featureless, being the context for theoretical issues. This is the most completely literary part of the poem, where literary questions are canvassed. What does characterise Mantua is a group of figures (Naddo, Eglamor and others) that represent, with more or less complexity, talking-points in this section's debate about poetry.

Ferrara stands very much in contrast to Goito. Because of the poem's epistemological bent Browning can use changed ways of seeing to indicate modulations in theme. The scales have fallen from Sordello's eyes in his passing from the life of poetic imagination to that of political empiricism, a fact indicated by the gruesome realism of the account of war-torn Ferrara (4. 1–107). Facts assert themselves despite the viewer, or so the angular, obtrusive quality of the description of the implements of siege suggests:

> The lazy engines of outlandish birth,
> Couched like a king each on its bank of earth—
> Arbalist, manganel and catapult

But because of the argumentative, discursive character of the last three books objects in the world tend to get tied down in a mechanical, limited way to certain values in the discussion—conforming in fact to Browning's typical use of imagery in his later work. A good example is the starry sky and its reflection in the river (6. 11–16, 565–70). At Goito such images are allowed to be less applied, more suggestive: for instance, the flooded Mincio (2. 26–33).

Verona, of all these sites, is the one of which it is least true to say that the action is significantly localised. Still, there are important changes in the manner in which the same events at Verona are described on the two occasions (1. 311–45, 3. 260–592). In the first account the emphasis tends to rest on activity that, suspended or terminated, remains enigmatic—the noise of political argument in the market-place is smothered, Palma has just left. In the second (with the recognition that this political scuffle means no less than the 'cheer or detriment' of 'Christendom', with Palma present, in physical contact with Sordello and expounding his situation at length) the implications of these activities are fully articulated.

This is no place for a detailed account of the poem's matter, but something about the main contours should be said. The first book is the best-known portion of a little-known poem—partly because not many readers get beyond it, and partly because it is about a familiar topic that is easily assimilated to that of some long romantic poems, the growth of the poet. The second is a poor motive. *Sordello* is about much more than 'the poet'; indeed one of the points of the poem is to put poetry firmly in its (not very dignified) place. More than that, comparison with, say, *Alastor*, is a short-cut to explanation that simplifies and distorts what is a remarkably complicated and fresh analysis of poethood. Characteristic of this first book is the constant undercutting by the author of Sordello's overweening solipsism, either by wry asides, or by reminding us how very undistinguished the Goito landscape is (1. 381–382) or how innerly sinister (1. 389–391), or in the delicate sarcasm behind Sordello's finding even the dragonfly's life a flattering contrast to his own (1. 980–910). The main labour of Book One is in fact to indicate the nature of Sordello's hyper-sensitive solipsistic imagination, and what this imagination makes of its surroundings, while simultaneously contriving to imply the real facts of the case, geographical and historical.

Unfortunately Browning uses for his analysis an array of rather grandiose and ill-formed concepts, expressed in an ambiguous terminology such as 'soul', 'body', 'Will'. In fact the main problem of interpretation throughout the poem lies in this direction, the problem of attaching the right range of values at the right places in a specially fashioned vocabulary. Clearly the whole business is highly stylised (especially in the first two books or so), with a use of concepts such as thought and action that is misleading if taken at face value. What Browning is trying to convey in this stylised and simplified form is the relation of imagination to the outer world, to identify the tendency of a gifted, sensitive and highly imaginative personality to gratify its appetite for a multifarious life in various experiments poetical and political. What is impressive is the meticulous fidelity to experience in this palpable groping for elusive aspects of personality. There is seldom a trace in *Sordello* of a second-hand psychology; instead one senses the pressure of the actual, even if clumsily responded to, throughout Browning's anatomy of his hero.

Not only Book One but, in a general way, the whole of the story depends on the analysis of the two types of poet/beauty-lover/imaginative man ('the regal class . . . framed for pleasure') that occupies 1. 462–567. This is a complicated and rather unfamiliar kind of distinction of types. Browning finds as common ground the tendency to project human qualities into the experienced world, but whereas the first type simply loses itself in rapt contemplation of these imaginative creations, the second retains a degree of almost sceptical awareness of the mind's part in this activity. Unfortunately the consequent 'homage' to self will lead either to reluctance for real action (because of great resources of imaginary, vicarious action) or to extravagant plans for making a mark in the world; both alternatives are likely to be disastrous.

Sordello belongs to the second type (1. 567), and his career in the poem exhibits just these over-negative and over-positive phases in his relations with mankind. The first application of this analysis does not come until, the reader having learnt how Sordello in his earliest years projected life into objects around him indiscriminately but gradually perceived them to be inanimate, the hero realises his need for something to act on, a 'crowd' to make respond. The first type of imaginative man, absorbed and humble in his own world of fantasies, is indifferent to such a response; Sordello's type, because of its self-awareness, needs this kind of assurance (1. 730–747). So, by an original paradox, the true poet (for the analysis, despite its ironies, is weighted in favour of Sordello) is temperamentally most at the mercy of his audience, most dubious of his own powers, and most agnostic about his own fictions. A corollary will be that the greatest poetry is that in which the audience does most work. We leave Sordello at Goito eagerly awaiting this 'crowd' to act upon.

At Mantua the whole issue becomes a purely literary one. We meet not only Eglamor, representative of the first type, but also Naddo, publicity-agent and low-level theorist of poetry. Just as for Eglamor the life of the imagination is a 'temple-worhsip', so Naddo has a boundless obsequiousness to 'Genius', to the 'tetchy race' of poets and their whims. One of the most attractive aspects of Browning's treatment of poethood is how he cuts it down to size, though not to a familiar shape. Naddo and Eglamor are pretty contemptuous of the rest of mankind; the poet is 'a man apart/From men' (2. 220–221). So Eglamor's interest is nature rather than mankind, the pastoral rather than the urban. But there is a paradox here, for this emphasis on the poetic psychology means that actual poetry and its effectiveness is not very important (2. 819–820). The poet gives the audience what it expects, even if this means a diet of shabby conventionalisms, empty of thought (3. 255–259, 2. 788–790). So here Naddo and his kind, oddly, are at one with mankind: 'Build on the human heart!'

Sordello's position embodies a contradiction that is the pure reverse of this. His temperament is such that he relies on the audience, and his real concern in his poetry is humanity deeply and truthfully analysed (2. 850–867). But because of his regal arrogance, based on an inner life of universal vicarious activity, he rejects both action and the ideals that stimulate it, in fact any common concern with humanity (2. 352–415). While impatient with the dead wood of poetic convention his experimentalism drives him *away* from human life; 'each joy must he abjure/Even for love of it' (2. 554–555). His sensitivity and acute sense of identity constitue both his greatness and the cause of his failure. While potentially more deeply committed to mankind than the superficially chummy and unalarming Naddos and Eglamors he cannot realise this commitment in merely using men as a sounding-board. It is in disgust at the failure of this project that he escapes back to Goito at the age of twenty-nine.

When Palma's summons to Verona reaches Sordello at Goito he is ready for it. His interval of hermetic passivity has given way to a resolve to throw himself actively on the world. The last three books deal with the effect of this resolve and Sordello's progressive recognition of his social responsibilities. The stages of this progression are not as clearly indicated as those at Goito and Mantua—where the phases are almost too explicitly signposted. Owing to the poem's idiosyncratic evaluative terms the reader may be deceived about the purport of some of the developments at Ferrara, until a subsequent recognition puts them in perspective. Partly Browning is restricted because Sordello's Ferrarese mistakes don't spring so much, like those at Goito, from a peculiar epistemology, and no ironic contrast is available. But Sordello's development now is more a descent through successive illusions, a stripping of false assumptions, than at Goito and Mantua, where it took the form of a set of false assumptions that were explored in their various branches until their sudden partial destruction at the end of Book Two. If each of Sordello's formulae at Ferrara seems at first to be the right one, this reflects the movement of his mind.

What passes at Ferrara is much too complicated to go into in detail, but there are a couple of main themes. One of these is Sordello's gradually learning to settle for less and less in the way of immediate impact on society. He arrives at Ferrara apparently expecting politics to be a glamorous affair, but even on the way there, surveying the crowds, realises that it is really grotesquely inegalitarian, with drab multitudes of 'mouths and eyes' (4. 189–240). Not too put out, he decides to establish a 'mighty equilibrium'. This is a step in the right direction, but still a mere preliminary in his mind to imposing his personality on society. He can't even get the first utopian scheme off the ground, as his interview with Taurello (4. 330–333) and his subsequent observation of Ferrara's inhabitants (5. 1–21) persuades him. The ideal is still there, though he is forced to approach it pragmatically, considering what little can be done to initiate a gradual process of reform (5. 21–303). A feasible project is to persuade Taurello to take up the Guelf cause (why Sordello favours the Guelfs will be explained in a minute) but to his horror not only does Taurello offer him the *Ghibbelin* leadership, but Palma effectively endorses the offer by revealing his secret kinship to the latter. So here is a test case for Sordello's new conviction that he should modestly do what he can towards reform within the limits of his situation—a practical opportunity for influence which ideologically puts him on the wrong side. This dilemma introduces the long debate of Book Six.

At this point the two themes of Ferrara come together. Just as Sordello as poet had Eglamor for counterpart, as politican he has Taurello, *de facto* Ghibbelin leader. Taurello is the pure representative of the active phase of the story, a man for whom thought and action, even in connection with culture and human relations (4. 598–619), are indistinguishable. We are invited to suppose that the soliloquy and musing that exhibit this in Book Four are themselves an aberration. But this active phase, though it remains a more or less featureless alternative to Goito during the first part of the poem, is now shown to be flawed. Taurello's special faults are an inadequate response to emotion (shown in connection with his dead wife and lost son), and a kind of pathological need to be second string, exhibited throughout his political career. He is a Warwick; Sordello is the true 'lord' (5. 472–473).

Kingmakers are necessarily monarchists, and Taurello is no exception (4. 762–769). This is a crucial part of Browning's characterisation of the whole Ghibbelin position, and there is good reason to suppose that it had a contemporary application for him. As well as being the poem's major historical fact the Guelf-Ghibbelin opposition takes on more and more meaning in these last books. The Ghibbelins (lead by Taurello but chiefly emblematised by Charlemagne, who has all the former's qualities 5. 131–140) stand for a society that is hierarchical, authoritarian, and expedient. The Guelfs (the figurehead is Hildebrand) offer egalitarianism and political idealism. In fact we can see a good example of the poem's fascinating assimilation of historical background to theme—to be discussed later—in the amazing thoroughness with which the metaphor of Church and State has penetrated the story. It is even in these terms that Eglamor and his 'temple-worship' is distinguished from Sordello, self-styled 'Monarch of the World'.

It is practical opportunity plus ideological repugnance that causes Sordello such distress in Book Six. This book is largely trying to show us the dilemma of the altruist, divided between the claims of the long and the short view, and apparently hamstrung if he acknowledges either. Too generalised an idealism would let Sordello out of his instinctively felt loyalty to one group, the Guelfs ('all service . . . rates/Alike' (6. 127–128)), but having granted that hazy benevolence must be replaced by actual loyalties and attention to actual conditions he can pursue this in the opposite direction to conclude that such conditions shouldn't be tampered with in the interests of an ill-defined progress (6. 201–230). In fact, he goes on to inquire, isn't the evil in the world not only attractive, not only the thing that his feeling for the people is based on, but an essential condition of happiness' being a convincing ideal (6. 235–291)? So the natural outcome of pragmatism seems to be selfish hedonism.

Sordello can't see his way through these problems of political faith, so acutely analysed by Browning, because of his lack of principle, a point many times anticipated in the poem in the accounts of the flexibility of response his imagination permitted him. This theme reaches a climax with that bold and, for its day, amazingly searching cry of Sordello's 'Where's abstract Right for me?' (6. 477). The conjectural picture of a morally relativistic universe that follows still leaves the question, what does one do here and now? Doesn't the perception of this relativism wither the stimulus to action (6. 554–579)?

The answer would seem to be 'No', since Sordello does, for undefined reasons, reject the Ghibelin badge of office in dying, and there is vague talk of a 'Power' in terms that loosely suggest Christ's incarnation (it is a mistake, by the way, to assume that this idealism that Sordello needs is the same as Eglamor's, as an attentive reading of 6. 603–609 shows). But perhaps Browning needn't be too explicit. What he has done is to lay bare in great detail the pre-conditions of a moral choice He shows in particular the frightening booby-traps there are in any profession of political faith, especially one conceived in the absence of a notion of ultimate value. What is really striking is the scrupulousness of this enquiry, its resistance to glibness despite the corollaries, and the prophetic nature of some of its insights.

So much for what *Sordello* is about. There remains a more than usually uncomfortable inkling that this is not good enough, that the real character of the poem has not been approached. The many interesting questions concerning *Sordello's* style cannot all be dealt with here; among those I shall leave out are the planned use of a varying idiom of lyrical and rhetorical styles, and the emergence in this poem of a typically Browning manner of proceeding from point to point in both narrative and argument. I shall deal with a couple of topics that seem to demand attention: one of them being prominent in the poem's own discussion of poetic style—'simultaneity', and the other being that elusive oddness of manner which has always attracted and exasperated readers.

Sordello finds that 'perceptions whole' (which is what he strives to express) are broken up by the linear medium of language: 'the simultaneous and the sole/By the successive and the many' (2. 594–595). This is perhaps Browning's most unashamed bit of poetical autobiography via Sordello, for such a notion of an attempted 'simultaneity' (though there is a chicken and egg difficulty here) is unmistakeably connected with certain important habits of syntax and arrangement of material exhibited in *Sordello*.

One of the great causes of obscurity in the poem is its subtle subversion of correct syntax, or refusal to take advantage of correct syntax even though it is always present. Sentences are so long that normal short-term memory of their structure is baffled. Time and again the really functional elements of sense appear in a syntactically deceptively subordinate position. There is heavy reliance on a kind of para-grammar of interjections and parentheses.[3] On a small scale a license with syntax permits such 'simultaneous' descriptive effects as this semi-onomatopaeic syzygy of consonants and monosyllables that accompanies Taurello's pacing: 'As shows its corpse the world's end some split tomb' (5. 935), or the keeping of two topics in play at once which is exhibited in the interleaving of Eglamor's funeral and the analysis of some of Sordello's early attitudes (2. 192–195).

But the weakening of syntax has a more important effect in that sentences step down in favour of paragraphs. The typical unit of the poem is a long verse paragraph with a neutral or irrelevant syntax that is held together by associations of sense (often very local ones) across the sentences that form it. This long unit is effective both descriptively and rhetorically. A standard effect in description is an uninterrupted passing from, or penetration from, general impressions to successively clearer and more intimate contacts with the subject. Of several instances in the early part of the poem perhaps the most striking is the return to Goito (2. 978–991), a passage that passes by gradations from the distant, unspecific 'slim castle' to two simple sensory experiences of smell and hearing. Alternatively the tree-like structure of a ramified sentence (the poem is a 'transcendental platan') makes the accounts of the Fighter and the Slave monolithic.

More general is the use of the large 'simultaneous' unit as a way of precipitating in close conjunction associated topics in argument. Browning's passages of argument, despite the appearance of sequence, are really better regarded as static series of linked, mutually illuminating statements. This is connected with a persistent vagueness of terms which, though irritating, is genuinely countered by the use of collateral statements which narrow these initially vague meanings (e.g. 2. 47–53, 4. 290–297). Nor is it just vagueness that is at issue here, for part of the need for this kind of parallel reading arises because a term will be deliberately allowed only *some* of its possible meaning, or one of its possible bearings, on each occurence.

What this lopsidedness boils down to, in less abstract terms, is the slight but pervasive mental attitudinising, a kind of gentle dramatising, that runs through practically all Browning's passages of argument. An obscure passage like 2. 659–689, for example, can only be disentangled by sensing the alternating voices of 'Poet' and 'Man'; the reader must be alert to the persuasive colourings in such signal-words as 'forsooth', 'notime', 'astounding'—a skill that is in fact the initiation to a reading of most of Browning's poetry.

Finally, there is a kind of narrative simultaneity. Some of the most striking uses of the verse paragraph are to summarise enormous sections of surrounding narrative (e.g. 2. 905–923, 6. 644–673), and this hanging of so much narrative material in one parcel from one hook is simply the poem's whole plot technique writ small. In other words, the final instance of simultaneity in *Sordello* is its arrangement in two parts around the evening that separates Sordello the poet from Sordello the politician, and this of course is the means of a more significant selection and juxtaposition of elements than serial narrative would permit. Just as the early paragraph of invocation to Dante (1. 345–373) falls together with the delayed mention of

Dante's name, so the details of the initial scene at Verona are finally clarified at 3. 273 *et seq*.

There are obviously more problems in the poem's narrative technique than can be explained by this formula, and this leads us straight on to what I can only call its 'oddness'. The story of *Sordello* is astonishingly thorough. Not only does it bristle with authentic historical detail but, as a causal chain, it is meticulous and complicated; there is not one dangling motive. This is not strange in itself, but it is strange in view of one's strongest impressions of the poem. The whole work is tinged by a sense of unreality, such that it comes almost as a shock to recognise how elaborate, realistic, and consistent is the plot. It is in this tension between matter and tone, history and fantasy, reality and unreality, that the poem's special oddness is to be sought. It is worth making the point, however, that this pervasive modifying tone is not used uniformly. Some of the accounts of Verona and Ferrara have an unusual immediacy, instances of how the varying opacity, as it were, depends on theme. Even the degree of causal consistency and authenticity in the plot varies according to theme, by the way. These are qualities connected particularly with Taurello and Adelaide, representatives of action and expediency. Naddo and Eglamor, for example, are scarcely anchored in the sequence of events at all.

One important way in which the actual situation in *Sordello* is obscured, or only partially realised, lies in the strong superficial uniformity of the poem's terms, and not just through repetition. Direct speech, for instance, is rarely mimetic; the fact of speaking seems to set up no special linguistic conditions. Indeed some phrases have a kind of diplomatic immunity, and appear freely in speech, thought, or description in a way that no facts of the story can explain (e.g. 1. 429, 5. 797, 6. 11–16, 6. 565–570). These are cases where actual speech approximates to a plain undramatised form, but the same levelling of the contours of reality takes place from the other direction; mere description tends to appear in the form of apparently dramatic utterance without a mouth to speak it (e.g. 3. 303). Of course the situation was significantly worse in the 1840 edition, which had virtually no quotation marks. They were only used, interestingly, to indicate quotation of the written word by the poet—either from another part of the text, or from some contemporary writing, imaginary or otherwise. This has the very important effect of blurring discriminations in the imagined situation, but of drawing attention to distinctions that are nearer to the actual writing of the poem.

This blurring is tied up with a general indeterminacy about the provenance of comment and description. In the 1863 revisions Browning did try to associate parts of the poem more firmly with one character by turning them into direct speech, sometimes very unconvincingly (e.g. 3. 424–427), or else giving them a source in one person's consciousness. Though a particular consciousness will be used sporadically to engineer a description (e.g. 5. 891–1009), no simple explanation of *Sordello's* method lies in this direction. Browning's technique is a flexible and varying assimilation of external things to theme. But what we do find a lot is an ill-defined point of awareness partly in the poem and partly outside it. Many remarks seem to occupy this territory between author and fiction, eliminating, as it were, the gap of history; how do we apply the pronouns in 'nature's and his youth gone,/They left the world to you, and wish you joy' (3. 82–83)?

As I said, the first revisions try to tie many of these ambiguous phrases to individual consciousnesses, especially by eliminating such equivocal personal pronouns. The general effect is to give the narrative more autonomy, to set it more firmly in the past, though we are still left with that unusual sense of the thirteenth-century world spilling over into the nineteenth. The most striking examples of this lie in the appearance of some characters both in the fiction and in Browning's theorising about poetry at Venice (e.g. 'Plara' 2. 769 and 3. 881–900, 'Lucio' 2. 538 and 3. 904–905, and, the extremest case, though eliminated in 1863, 'Elys' at 3. 879). To get a notion of the oddity at issue here the reader will really have to look these references up for himself.

What we have here is the practise of a writer who is deeply involved in the issues raised by his story, and who is in consequence strikingly unable to contain the narrative within its limits. Instead he constantly implies its more extensive ranges of meaning. As a result there are persistent mischievous failures in realism. I think the doctrinal emphasis I am suggesting here is indicated by, for example, the way many of these distancing revisions affect political statements (e.g. 4. 1025, 5. 12, 6. 230, 6. 847). There is no space to set out the evidence here, but there is plenty of reason to suppose that the Browning of 1840 would have been far from discouraging the inclination to mistake Sordello's most radical sentiments for his own, what-ever his more Pilate-like attitude twenty years later. There is little doubt that Browning saw *Sordello* as the unique poetic statement of a fairly extreme radicalism.

The minor characters like Plara are not the only ones to ignore the rules of the narrative, but they provide the key to the rather similar behaviour of more important figures like Naddo and Eglamor. These are summoned or recalled on several occasions (e.g. 1. 693, 2. 10, 4. 230) in a way that has nothing to do with their place in the plot, but does show very clearly their usefulness as representatives of certain points of view. Like Palma (5. 995–996) they are dismissed at the end into some sort of extra-narrative dimension (5. 1011–1012, 6. 797–818). Connected with these characters is a strange license with the probabilities of time and space that contributes strongly to the sense of a dreamlike unreality. This is exhibited in the coincidence of Eglamor's funeral-train stopping by Sordello's hiding-place, or the suddenness of Naddo's arrival at Goito. Of course the whole status of human personality in *Sordello* is rather bizarre. We find that varying realism in characterisation suitable for theme that I mentioned, but also a more or less general sense of deadness about human contact. Conversation, for example, sometimes comes in long direct speeches, but more often the living voice is muffled by an oblique report.

The explanation of all this really has two aspects, literary-theoretical and psychological. Running through *Sordello*, but enunciated particularly at 3. 862–915 (in Browning's own person) and 5. 580–620, is a theory of literary progress. Literature becomes more humane and inward as it evolves, though in the first of the three stages of development that Browning distinguishes (represented mainly by Dante) it employs only the simplest and most exaggerated moral dis-criminations (shown in some of Sordello's Mantuan poetry

2. 521–531). This is the phase, according to the 1863 headline, of the 'epoist'.

The next phase is that of 'dramatist' or 'analyst'. Now the poet penetrates beyond simple moral categories to psychological ones, imaginatively constructing the circumstances that will 'conduct/Each nature to its farthest'.[4] This will be a relativistic view of man that will simultaneously have its effect in a new political egalitarianism (3. 787–804, 6. 245–248). Now man is to be seen not in terms of his conformity to a single mode of behaviour, but in his inner, subjective aspect, relative to the special conditions of his existence and his 'own conceit of truth'. A man in love is not merely 'sad'; within the limits of his aspiration to love he may be 'gay'. On this view 'love' and 'lust' are no longer opposites; they are even irrelevant, 'colourless', except insofar as they define the scope of a relativistic judgement in terms of 'triumph' and 'defeat'. Instances of personality judged within its conditions are the specimen sketches of the lover in prison and of the pastoral poet whose background was uncompromisingly urban.

The culminating period is a 'synthesist' one, to which Browning's 1863 interpolation at 5. 620 gaily indicates that *Sordello* belongs. This means abandoning the machinery of circumstances that assisted 'analysis' in order to penetrate to the 'inmost life'. This seems to be a 'synthesis' because it has transcendental implications (3. 914–915); certainly in *Sordello* itself the penetration in Book Six to 'the mid-deep yearnings' of the hero's personality (6. 461) is accompanied by the outward movement of 'his expanding soul' (6. 468), leading to final epiphany. Whether a new analytical relativistic poetry could be succeeded by a fresh moral synthesis was an abiding preoccupation of Browning's.

In at least two ways we can see in these passages how Sordello's temperament as described earlier, rather than Eglamor's, is appropriate for this kind of literary progress. To start with, the emphasis is very much on humanity, better and better understood and rendered. Secondly, there is mention at each stage of the poet's relation to the audience, whether displaying himself in the work and guiding the audience explicitly (in the first and last phases—and, indeed, in Book Three), or, as 'dramatist', taking a back seat. But most important for our purposes, in trying to explain the technique of the poem, is what these passages have to say about 'external things'. In a general way it is clear enough how a 'synthesist' license with externals is exhibited in some of the things I have pointed out in *Sordello's* handling of its matter. But the notion of an 'inmost life' dominating externals is not yet precise, and to explain this involves the psychological aspect I mentioned before.

The feeling will grow on any reader, and will be confirmed in Book Six, that one of the keys to the odd treatment of externals is a strange continuity between the inner world of Sordello's mind and the outer world of thirteenth-century things and events. A typical phenomenon in reading the poem is a sense that a word like 'crowd', in two appearances, has passed unannounced from one sphere to the other, from denoting a collection of people to representing a certain value in Sordello's thoughts. This effect operates on several elements in the story (e.g. Sordello's origins 2. 315–352, or the Guelf-Ghibbelin opposition) but 'crowd' is perhaps the most complicated instance. It not only blends in a curious way the notion of 'audience' and 'society', but at 6. 327–391 becomes something within the hero, something like his moral sense. The crowd do not symbolise Sordello's moral life; rather, they are contained by it, indistinguishable from it, for certain purposes.

Internal things are becoming externals; what are the internals that are left, if any? Browning has some firm but rather vague notions about this. At 6. 492–549 he uses a Body-Soul distinction that passes in a typical fashion from a conventional application to rather an odd one. He seems to have in mind an opposition of the earthbound, realistic, morally myopic aspects of man to the 'spirit's absoluteness' or 'Mind', from which, in its dying vision of moral relativism, no values can be derived. Likewise he lists the conventionally incommensurable 'Virtue, Good, Beauty' together not because he is a neo-platonist, but because he wants to discriminate between the monad of 'Soul' and *all* mundane qualities inanimate or animate, visible or invisible, outward or inward.

As a synthesist the poet cast away external things 'once more'. These two words are easy to overlook, but they are crucial, for the only previous stage at which this had happened, according to Browning's account, was in the landscape of the *Divine Comedy* (5. 583–599). The epistemology of *Sordello* is Browning's attempt to use the world, in a manner akin to Dante's, only as an adjunct to an inner or moral situation.[5] Sordello's landscape is different, of course, because this situation is greatly refined from the simple moral alternatives of Dante; it is the bringing of this irreducible, atomic 'Mind' or 'Soul' to bear in *any* way whatsoever. So action and thought are equivalent in the last resort. This may seem to contradict the story's outlines, but in fact whether Sordello actually puts his ideals into practice is not at issue. Ferrara is preferred to Goito, but not Taurello to Sordello.

Browning is really interested in dispositions to activity, and above all in each individual's need to commit himself firmly and intelligently to one of these, whether it issues in action or thought. *Sordello* tells of the difficulties encountered by a person of unusual self-awareness and sensitivity in fulfilling this requirement. In examining possible attitudes or dispositions certain priorities about politics and poetry are expressed, but it is towards that naked business that the poem moves. The basic situation is that of 'take the single course'; because the poem is only concerned with 'where descry the Love that shall select/That course' (6. 585–586) the perceived world remains an interior landscape.

With a poem as rich in content as *Sordello* it seems inappropriate to concentrate on one topic, but from the historical point of view, which I want to adopt for the last part of this discussion, it is as a poem about poetry that *Sordello* is most significant. How does this very original poem, and its attendant theory of literary evolution, fit with its immediate environment? This, by the way, is a question that is too seldom asked of Browning's work in general.

Browning, in his veiled way, does acknowledge one influence in the poem, that of Walter Savage Landor (3. 950–966), a writer whom he praises constantly and to the highest degree in his letters.[6] For me this connection with the author of the *Imaginary Conversations* endorses the poem's whole emphasis on a sophisticated philosophical and humanist literature. In Book Three the new relativist poet has to provide a 'speech . . . in proof' (a typically Browning notion) for his 'incarcerated youth', who is dwelling in memory on his sweetheart Zanze. Not only is the general situation like that of Tasso and Leonora, the subject of an *Imaginary Conversation*, 'Tasso and Cornelia', that Browning was later to admire,[7] but there may be close verbal echoes. Landor's Tasso exclaims, under the influence of an hallucinatory memory of Leonora, 'I smell the lemon-blossoms. Beware of the old wilding that bears them; it may catch your veil'; Browning's lover warns: 'Stoop, else the strings of blossom, where the nuts/O 'erarch, will blind thee!' (3. 873–874). If there is a direct link at this very significant juncture it would confirm one's feeling that Browning's admiration for Landor rested particularly on his technique of vivid sympathetic entry into human predicaments, enhanced by a wealth of authenticating detail. Whether conscious or unconscious such an echo at such a point, plus the quasi-dedication, would suggest that Browning saw Landor as a leading innovator in the new literature.

What of Browning's unacknowledged debts in his theory of poetry? The whole notion of literary progress in *Sordello* speaks sharply and consistently of the kind of German romantic view that is best expressed in Schiller's 'Über naive und sentimen-talische dichtung'. According to this view literature is an increasingly subtle instrument of perception, moving from the plain description of physical appearances in classical times to a Christian and romantic inwardness, a concern with the human soul and with the outer world only as perceived and modified by that soul.

This, in various forms, was also a commonplace of English romantic thinking, but it appears in such a fresh and vigorous form in *Sordello* that I think we are justified in looking for ways in which Browning could have been directly re-fertilised by it.[8] Browning's German was pretty rudimentary even a few years later, but he may have read some of the remarks in the opening lecture of A. W. Schlegel's *A Course of Lectures on the Dramatic Art and Literature* (1815) or in the twelfth of F. Schlegel's *Lectures on the History of Literature, Ancient and Modern* (1818), which shares with *Sordello* the important distinction between an analytical and an interpretive modernism. Schiller himself was probably untranslated at this date.[9] As far as indirect contact with this element in German idealist aesthetics is concerned, Browning might have known Mme. Stael's *L'Alle-magne*[10] but a more likely source is a few of the English popularisers of the Germans who for one reason or another could have come to Browning's attention in the thirties.

Perhaps the most remarkable of these reasons applies to the last of Crabb Robinson's articles on 'Goethe's Works' in the *Monthly Repository* of 1833,[11] for it starts less than ten pages after W. J. Fox's review of *Pauline*. Indeed this fact is of general interest for Browning's thinking about poetry, because Robinson stressed the terms 'objective' and 'subjective'. Here is a classic restatement of the theory of increasing inwardness in poetry:

The epic is marked by this character of style,—that the poet presents his *object* immediately and directly, with a total disregard of his own personality . . . The opposite class of poetry is the *lyric*, in which the poet gives mainly objects as they are reflected in the mirror of his own individuality.

Coleridge is another writer who could well have attracted Browning's notice at the time of the composition of *Sordello*, for his death in 1834 was followed by the publication of *Specimens of Table Talk* (1835), part of Allsop's *Letters, Conversations and Recollections* (1836), and *The Literary Remains* (1836–1839). There are several suggestive remarks about ancient/modern, objective/subjective in these writings, but most important for our purposes is the record of the 1818 lectures,[12] especially the tenth, where he picks out Dante for much the same interpretation as Browning gives him in *Sordello*. Coleridge distinguishes two things:

a combination of poetry with doctrine, and, by turning the mind inward on its own essence instead of letting it act only on its outward circumstances and communities, a combination of poetry with sentiment. And it is this inwardness or subjectivity which principally and most fundamentally distinguishes all the classic from all the modern poetry.

Although Carlyle doesn't seem explicitly to state this view in his writings before 1840, we can sense it assimilated and operative in parts of *Sartor Resartus* (1838). What is really interesting here is how Carlyle envisages a humanist, philosophical direction in literature issuing in certain stylistic qualities, qualities that are apparently strikingly like those attributed to Sordello by Naddo (2. 788–807):

Nothing but innuendoes, figurative crotchets: a typical Shadow, fitfully wavering, prophetico-satiric; no clear logical Picture. 'How paint to the sensual eye', asks he once, 'what passes in the Holy-of-Holies of Man's Soul . . .?'[13]

But if the notion of modern subjectivity is latent here it has surely been given a subtle twist. Schiller didn't quite mean that literature would become psychological when he spoke of it becoming inward. And this twist is even more evident in *Sordello*, where the hero's account of literary history, starting as a pastiche on the orthodox idealist reading, ends up as an apology for the deep and pure study of personality. By a simple but radical shift in interpretation the human soul is no longer just the conditioning factor of poetic perception, but the object of poetic study. This cognitive element explains the paradox of how a theory that owes much to the romantic can repudiate the romantic emphasis on nature. It also opens the way for the association between literature and human progress, social development, that is important in *Sordello*.

It is, by the nature of the study, impossible to be sure of anything in the history of ideas, but I feel a fair degree of certainty that this shift exhibited in *Sordello* 'explains' the change from romantic to Victorian notions about literature. Actually *Sordello* seems to be its fullest, most serious assertion at this date, but in various forms that are rather ephemeral (which is why the development has not been tracked down before) we can see this shift working among many people who were thinking and writing about literature in the eighteen-thirties.

The centre of our attention here must be William Johnson Fox, editor of the *Monthly Repository*, and the kind of opinion with which he was connected—unitarian, radical, utilitarian.

Here, in Fox's review of Tennyson's *Poems* in 1833,[14] is a pure instance of how the romantic view of a passage from naive to sentimental has given support to a new view, a propagandist view of a literature about humanity and its problems:

The first onset of poetry conquered the external world, and erected as trophies descriptions of object and action never to be surpassed: but observation has yielded the foremost place to reflection . . . the modern delineates the whole external world from its reflected imagery in the mirror of human thought and feeling . . . Poetry, in becoming philosophized, has acquired new and exhaustless worlds.

The blatancy of the sleight-of-pen with 'reflection' here (meaning both the impact of experience and philosophy—and beautifully focussing the shift in question) testifies to the depth of Fox's preconceptions. This was also the tenor of the *Pauline* review,[15] and it is not hard to imagine how phrases such as 'the great revelation which man now needs is a revelation of man to himself' and 'the mystery of our spiritual, accountable, immortal nature' might have encouraged Browning in his emphasis on 'the development of the soul'.

This sort of approach to literature sometimes takes on a significant political colouring in Fox's writings,[16] while one of his protegés, Ebeneezer Elliott, went even further in his preface to *Corn Law Rhymes*. Harriet Martineau has an interesting passage on the 'new school of poetry—the metaphysical',[17] and among unitarians across the Atlantic, such as Jones Very and W. E. Channing, the same enlisting of literature in the religio-philosophical interest goes on. The latter (from whom Fox's remarks in connection with *Pauline* quoted above were drawn) was close to the *Repository* and a friend of Martineau and Fox, and in his turgid 'The Importance of a National Literature'[18] we have, unfortunately, another major document of this development. The cliché that 'Invention and effort have been expended on matter, much more than on mind' can lead him to the new conclusion of the day that 'morals and human nature . . . form the staple of the highest literature'.

Closely bound up with the *Repository* in this matter of philosophy and literature was the *Westminster*, though the links will probably never be fully understood. Among several unitarians connected with the *Westminster* was that versatile man Sir John Bowring, editor from 1824–1836. In fact the development we are discussing might be said to date from his article on Coleridge in 1830.[19]) Here literature is not being assimilated to the requirements of nonconformity as much as to the requirements of a newly relaxed Benthamism, though the blend of the two which is the vital reagent in this whole process is as present as it is with Fox. Bowring went on to develop his idea of a 'science of man' in literature much more fully in his celebrated review of Tennyson next year,[20] a piece that is often crude and hyperbolical, but also an intelligent, daring, and comprehensive statement of this refurbishing of romantic subjectivity as a philosophical and moral instrument. Because of 'metaphysical science'

A new world is discovered for him (the poet) to conquer. The poets of antiquity rarely did more than incidentally touch this class of topics; the external world had not yet lost its freshness.

Browning is unlikely to have been unaware of the mild controversy this article caused, and even Mill, though he founded the *London* in opposition to the *Westminster*, quotes from Bowring in 'On Genius' in 1832.[21] While Mill never went as far as the older man along these lines, a pair of articles in 1834 and 1835[22] (less well known than the double essay of 1833[23]) does exhibit a more philosophical approach to literature, and at the same time he translated and published Nisard's interesting review of Hugo.[24]

In the encounter of this brand of opinion with the well-hallowed theory of poetic subjectivity we find the most fertile background to Browning's view of literature's past and future, but it is worth remarking that ideas of the same sort were occasionally voiced outside these circles. Christopher North, for example, though actually a great mocker of Bowring's article, praises Crabbe in 1834 for exhibiting something very like a 'science of man'.[25] Another influential piece in its day was Henry Taylor's preface to his successful play *Philip van Artevelde* (1834) which appeals to an empiricism of humanity in its attack on the romantics.

All this evidence shows how *Sordello* plays its part in a major shift in taste, a shift which Browning and like-minded contemporaries seem to have thought amounted to a revolution. *Sordello*, unlike the other documents we have considered, is not a fragmentary or casual discussion of these topics of poetic content and the relation of poetry to society. It is deliberated and honest, both in its striking working-out of the implications of subjectivity in the externals of the poem, and in the precision and detail with which Sordello's education, especially in politics is traced.

With Browning's strong and constant reference to the actual it would be surprising if all the poem's ideas on poetry were of the theoretical, more or less derivative variety that I have been illustrating. In fact Browning goes well beyond this point on his own account, particularly when Sordello himself is involved. Sordello's human weaknesses, his physical insignificance, his inarticulacy, are kept in the foreground. The concept of 'Genius' is most persistently deflated in the person of the hero. The most important constituent of this new, unideal figure of the poet is his reliance on his audience; poetry is not the effusion of genius, but a dynamic co-operation of audience and poet; gone is the old notion of poetry as the overheard solitary utterance, still being expressed by Mill in 1833. Closely connected with this is a fascinating notion that the poet who 'looks forth' to his audience in this way is somehow dispassionate, aloof from his work, this work being a mere chance reflection of the underlying context of the poet's whole life. This is a view that echoes so-called 'romantic irony', but Browning seems to be original in voicing it in this country.

This is part of a major theme about the degree of presentation of the author's personality in art, and Browning is of course conventional in stressing the self-effacing, anonymous character of Eglamor's, the objective poet's, writing. Shakespeare was the orthodox instance of this. When Hazlitt analyses it[26] it has become a matter of *moral* anonymity, or loss of identity, on the part of the writer, and Browning rather departs from orthodoxy in making *this* kind of anonymity a mark also of the subjective poet, of Sordello 'Beholding other creatures' attributes/And having none' (1. 718–719). We can find isolated hints of anxiety in other writers (especially Tennyson in *The Palace of Art*, but also Bowring, Nisard, and Arthur Hallam[27]) that the new subjective, psychological, humanised temper might involve a loss of moral coherence, but Browning is exceptional and far-sighted in his detailed attention to this problem. He insists on the moral relativism entailed by the poet's sympathy with mankind (3. 787–804), scorning a crude moral optimism (3. 806–825) and pointing to the reduction of moral categories to 'mood' and 'tinge' (3. 908, 5. 602–611) that results from understanding men in their individual conditions.

In fact, it is the dilemma of dramatist-analyst or synthesist, the dilemma that arises after human personality has been given its proper status in literature, that occupied Browning consistently, far more than the general demand for a psychological philosophical verse for which we have traced several precedents. Browning, in effect, made the historical concept of objective and subjective poetry, in a revised form, a live issue, not a long-solved one. In this way he was perhaps the only writer at the time who, by taking his stand firmly on the actual nature of poetic composition, was able to relate the exhilaration of a new psychological poetry to the chastening fact of a climate of moral uncertainty.

NOTES

[1] *v. New letters of Robert Browning*, ed. W. C. De Vane and K. L. Knickerbocker (1951), p. 18.

[2] It is interesting how, in the contemporary essay on Chatterton, Browning deplored 'the old principle of doing a little for every part of a subject, and more than a little for none', *Browning's Essay on Chatterton*, ed. D. Smalley (1948), p. 108.

[3] W. M. Rossetti records in 1850, among other habits of Browning's composition, that 'if an exclamation will suggest his meaning, he substitutes this for a whole sentence', *Pre-Raphaelite Diaries and Letters*, ed. W. M. Rossetti (1900), p. 263.

[4] *v.* a letter of 1837: 'give me your notion of a thorough self-devotement, self forgetting; should it be a woman who loves thus, or a man? What circumstances will best draw out, set forth this

feeling?', Mrs. Sutherland Orr, *Life and Letters of Robert Browning*, revised by F. G. Kenyon (1908), p. 97.

[5] This may clarify an obscure remark on Dante and the other early Italian poets: 'those tantalizing creatures, of fine passionate class, with such capabilities, and such a facility of being made pure mind of', *The letters of Robert Browning and Elizabeth Barrett Browning 1845-1846* (1899), Vol. I, p. 57.

[6] *v. Letters of Robert Browning collected by Thomas J. Wise*, ed. T. L. Hood (1933), p. 206.

[7] *Letters of R.B. and E.B.B.*, II, 261. This conversation was only in MS at the time (*v.* R. H. Super, *Walter Savage Landor a Biography* (1954), p. 343) though of course Browning had met Landor. Actually this new poet, author of the portraits of the imprisoned youth and Plara the bard, is not unlike Browning himself; two of the three dramatic monologues before 1840, *Porphyria* (allegedly issuing from a madhouse cell) and *Rudel and the Lady of Tripoli*, come to mind respectively, especially the latter. The youth in the Piombi prison and the associated name Zanze in fact come from an unrecognised source, Silvio Pellico's *Le Mie Prigioni* (1833).

[8] This means, however, just ignoring Browning's disclaimer about both the Germans and Coleridge (Orr, *Life and Letters*, p. 100).

[9] *v.* B. Q. Morgan, *German Literature in English Translation 1481-1927* (1938), p. 409.

[10] e.g. *Germany* (1813), vol. I, p. 307 *et seq.*

[11] *Monthly Repository*, N.S. VII, 1833, pp. 271-284.

[12] *The Literary Remains of Samuel Taylor Coleridge*, ed. H. N. Coleridge (1836), vol. I, pp. 61-241.

[13] *Sartor Resartus*, Book II, ch. 9.

[14] *Monthly Repository*, N.S. VII, 1833, pp. 30-41.

[15] Ibid., pp. 252-262.

[16] e.g. in *Monthly Repository* vols. VI (189-201), VIII (375-378), and IX (716-727).

[17] *Harriet Martineau's Autobiography* (1877), vol. III, p. 190.

[18] *Essays, Literary and Political* (1837), pp. 201-230.

[19] *Westminster Review*, XII, 1830, pp. 1-31.

[20] Ibid., XIV, 1831, pp. 210-224. This is possibly Fox's work. It is strikingly like his own Tennyson review.

[21] *Monthly Repository*, N.S. VI, 1832, pp. 649-659.

[22] *Monthly Repository*, N.S. VIII, 1834, pp. 323-331 and *Early Essays by John Stuart Mill*, selected by J. M. W. Gibbs (1897), pp. 239-267 (originally in the *London* of 1835).

[23] *Monthly Repository*, N.S. VII, 1833, pp. 60–70 and 714–724.

[24] *London Review*, II, 1835–1836, pp. 389–417.

[25] *The Works of Professor Wilson*, ed. Ferrier (1856), vol. VI, pp. 224–253.

[26] In 'On Genius and Common Sense', *Table-Talk* (1821).

[27] *v. Remains, in Verse and Prose, of Arthur Henry Hallam* (1834), pp. 137–151.

7

BROWNING'S 'MODERNITY':
THE RING AND THE BOOK, AND RELATIVISM

John Killham

Nowadays one comes across from time to time the suggestion that the reason Browning composed *The Ring and the Book* in the way he did, as an immense babble of voices endlessly discussing and pleading the rights and wrongs of a husband's killing his wife, is that he was bent on showing us that judgments of motives are hard to come at because the truth is never a simple thing. In this respect, it is said, he is at one with the leading novelists of our own time, who almost all accept in part the idea exemplified in the work of Henry James and Joseph Conrad, not to speak of Flaubert, that the reader of fiction should, in Pater's words, enjoy not 'the fruit of experience', the author's express meaning, but 'experience itself', leaving him to make his own construction of the facts and views put before him.

It is an attractive idea, if only because it makes it seem that the ambiguities of modern literature have anticipations in an eminent Victorian, and that the breach between his age and ours is not so wide as has been thought. To find that Browning may have been inclined to express the complex problems of behaviour in the modern world by elaborate poetical experiment akin to that seen in the twentieth century, does him good and comforts us. We can believe that he yielded up the search for absolute truth, and invited us to see things as they are. His modernity lay in exposing men and women as weak and gullible, acting out the brutal farce of a life for which there can be no simple formula of right and wrong. His end was to enable us to enter sympathetically into the human condition, to make us see and feel what it is like to look at things from a standpoint which the world at large is content to judge by imputation. Not only in *The Ring and the Book* but in many

153

celebrated dramatic monologues, Browning suspends moral judgment in implying that circumstances alter cases. In a word, he is a relativist.

This idea, that *The Ring and the Book* and other poems show Browning to entertain a sort of relativism, can appeal not merely because it provides reason for viewing him as 'modern': it may seem to put him in the forefront of those whose influence was to alter the intellectual climate of the nineteenth century. In 1866, when Browning was proudly telling his friends of the progress he had made in composing *The Ring and the Book*, Walter Pater, demonstrating Coleridge's by now old-fashioned struggle to apprehend the absolute, was defining the character of the time in terms of relativism.

Modern thought is distinguished from ancient by its cultivation of the 'relative' spirit in place of the 'absolute'. Ancient philosophy sought to arrest every object in an eternal outline, to fix thought in a necessary formula, and types of life in a classification by 'kinds' or *genera*. To the modern spirit nothing is, or can be rightly known except relatively under conditions. An ancient philosopher indeed started a philosophy of the relative, but only as an enigma. So the germs of almost all philosophical ideas were enfolded in the mind of antiquity, and fecundated one by one in after ages by the external influences of art, religion, culture in the natural sciences, belonging to a particular generation, which suddenly becomes preoccupied by a formula or theory, not so much new as penetrated by a new meaning and expressiveness. So the idea of 'the relative' has been fecundated in modern times by the influences of the sciences of observation. These sciences reveal types of life evanescing into each other by inexpressible refinements of change. Things pass into their opposites by accumulation of undefinable quantities. The growth of those sciences consists in a continual analysis of facts of rough and general observation into groups of facts more precise and minute. A faculty for truth is a power of distinguishing and fixing delicate and fugitive details. The moral world is ever in contact with the physical; the relative spirit has invaded moral philosophy from the ground of the inductive science. There it has started a new analysis of the relations of body and mind, good and evil, freedom and necessity.[1]

Of course, the relative spirit has been abroad at all times, as Pater implies: that 'Man is the measure of all things' is not a

difficult idea for an independent mind to arrive at. Yet Wordsworth was far more typical of western thought when he wrote
that poetry had as its object 'truth, not individual and local,
but general and operative; not standing upon external testimony, but carried alive into the heart by passion; truth which
is its own testimony, which gives competence and confidence
to the tribunal to which it appeals and receives them from the
same tribunal'. This utterance reflects in its very style the
grandeur of the humanist claim for the spiritual unity of
mankind. It is the culmination of a tradition reaching back
through the Renaissance to the foundations of our civilisation;
it is closely associated with the so-called Romantic, but truly
neo-Platonic, doctrine that the heart, or the innermost self,
is at one with Nature's central law. That this confidence in the
accessibility of absolute truth, embodied in the Christian
religion, was undermined in the Victorian period by scientific
discovery and German higher criticism is familiar to everyone.
But *laissez faire* economic theory and industrialisation were
perhaps even more immediately persuasive: the sharp diver-
gence between rich and poor led to clear signs that men could
be shaped by different and yet contiguous 'cultures' into beings
who might as well have been members of different species.
Shelley's comment that the ultimate cause of this was 'the un-
mitigated exercise of the calculating faculty' only expresses in
psychological jargon the old recognition of the schismatic
nature of man, virtuous heart pitted against cunning head. But
Shelley saw clearly that in his life-time the traditional arena in
which 'calculation' fought for its advantages, namely in politics,
was rapidly extending beyond politics to cover the whole social
life of the country as the old ties were replaced by the cash nexus
in a country undergoing rapid industrialisation. Large numbers
of people, herded in towns and cities, were to be forced to
become isolated, divorced from community. The early Victorian
intellectual thus had before his eyes as a model to which all his
speculations had to conform the image of *all* men as in fact
isolated, a conception which Arnold movingly considers in his
poems.

It is this which makes the difference between Wordsworth's
and Carlyle's estimate of the poet's rôle. Carlyle resembles

Wordsworth in seeing poets able, through their innermost
selves, to perceive the secret operations of Nature, but the
emphasis is now more upon historical change than upon
absolutes. Poets have shown their genius in their sincerity, but
this criterion is a tacit admission that their beliefs are super-
seded. Dante and Shakespeare express in their different ways
the beliefs of the middle ages, and for Carlyle these are not
true, only valuable insofar as they provide an outlet for religious
feeling necessary for human fulfilment. It seems that Nature's
operations in time (history, that is) are inconstant, that change
is the only law. Indeed, Nature will destroy those who hold on
to outmoded beliefs; but Carlyle is not always clear over what
he takes Nature to be. Sometimes he resembles Wordsworth in
thinking of it as God: but he is also tempted by the Romantic
heresy, and is capable of writing that 'The world of Nature,
for every man, is the Fantasy of himself: this world is the
multiplex image of his own Dream.'

Carlyle's case shows that a relativistic spirit was abroad in
nineteenth-century England some years before Pater wrote his
essay on Coleridge and Browning his vast poem. But it also
shows that relativism is not a simple conception. Carlyle, like
Mill, was indebted to Comte's theory of historical epochs, and
this carried with it the inescapable conclusion that history caused
institutions (and the beliefs on which they rested) to suffer
change, not regularly, but in a kind of systole and diastole of
the social organism. A similar idea underlies Matthew Arnold's
view of the post-Revolutionary period as an age of expansion,
characterised by a renewal of social arrangements in the light
of fresh thought. The relativism which grows out of this
acceptance of historical change is of a social kind, that is, it is
not primarily concerned with individual men and women in
their personal distinctiveness but rather with the beliefs and
attitudes which give society its form. Carlyle, Mill and Arnold
are all possessed of a sense of this social relativism, a recognition
that human institutions must be adapted to changing circumstances. It sees a sort of struggle on the part of human nature to
adapt itself to a changed environment while preserving its
sources of spiritual nourishment for the needs all men share.

This sort of relativism is not the same as the relativism

announced by Pater as characteristic of modern thought. It is clear from what he wrote that this has its basis in science, not history, and in all likelihood owes much to Darwin. This relativism is not concerned with changing beliefs, attitudes and the like, issuing in *social* arrangements, but relates rather to the individual's personal apprehension of the world he inhabits.[2] It is intensely materialistic at bottom, and also tends to set the individual above, or in opposition to, society, which no longer appears to have so obvious a claim to the loyalty of beings whose lives are constituted out of experiences peculiar to them. The right of society to make laws and to judge and condemn in accordance with them may seem questionable. This sort of moral relativism stands in relation to social relativism as Anarchy to Culture and it clearly looks forward to many features of our own century and its literature. (The trial of Meursault in Camus's *L'Étranger* springs to mind.)

Mention of the effect of moral relativism on an individual's attitude to social rules and laws brings us back to Browning's poem about a trial. The question we are faced with in reading *The Ring and the Book* is whether Browning, as Dowden observed, 'came more and more to throw himself into prolonged intellectual sympathy with characters towards whom his moral sense stood in ardent antagonism',[3] or whether we in fact see, to use Pater's words, that in the poem 'Hard and abstract moralities are yielding to a more exact estimate of the subtlety and complexity of our life'. Is each speaker sincere according to his lights, and thus author of his own brand of truth? And must we in consequence see Browning, not wholly consciously, perhaps, subverting the belief that men may regard themselves as entitled to judge and condemn from a sense of a law written in all men's hearts, originating from the God who governs the world?

E. D. H. Johnson has answered the last of these questions in an interesting essay on the similarity he detects between the radical empiricism of William James and *The Ring and the Book*.[4] The poem, he claims, 'most comprehensively exhibits Browning's pluralism' in that each of the speakers in the poem bears witness to the facts 'sure that he is rendering them veraciously'. The celebrated image of the gold ring symbolises the 'plasticity of factual reality' and the 'multiform nature of all truth'. Ten of the books, Johnson observes, 'present in chronological sequence the testimony of nine witnesses', who all vary from one another: yet somehow they between them reveal an ultimate unity, a universe grown out of a multiverse. That each human being *engenders* the truth upon the world is the common ground occupied by Browning and William James.

Mr. Johnson's comparison of Browning and William James is illuminating. Both do certainly accept the conditions of human life as an intelligible challenge to the individual man and woman. Moreover James's belief that on some matters we have to choose one way or the other, and that the existence of God is one such, is shared by Browning; so perhaps is the alarming corollary that if sufficient evidence to decide this and other such vital questions is lacking, then the profitability or usefulness of taking one choice rather than the other may be admitted in place of such evidence. But that *The Ring and the Book* shows Browning at one with James over pluralism is certainly less acceptable. The monologues do not show *witnesses* (in the ordinary sense), for there were none: and it is the whole point of the poem that some of the speakers have various reasons, personal or professional, for quite deliberately juggling with the 'facts' in decidedly interested fashion. To say that each speaker is sure that he is rendering them veraciously is to adapt the poem to the theory. Johnson's arguments do not really require that we believe Browning entertained pluralism and made it the structural principle of his poem. All his parallel with William James brings out is that neither poet nor philosopher saw the need to impugn or deny God for the presence of evil in the world, but rather the reverse, since the saintly heroism of such as Pompilia was thereby generated, to the edification of all good people, even a Pope. To think that life is a vale of soul-making is a moral-cum-metaphysical act of faith: its status as true or false is not in question since it cannot be verified. Browning asserts his faith in the poem, just as Carlyle did before him: their theme is the assertion of the will—heroism in fact. Both, unlike Pater, long for action, not thought. That faiths, all faiths, may not be versions of truth but only 'precious as memorials of a class of sincere and beautiful spirits' is a reflection which haunts the work of both men as they strive to recreate, in *Past and Present*, and *The Ring and the Book*, the sense of the past: but they both do their best to exorcise it, rather than permit, in the modern manner, the presence always to cast its shadow.

Mr. Robert Langbaum is most careful in his chapter on the poem in his admirable book *The Poetry of Experience* to give full recognition to the fact that Browning makes it abundantly clear, both in his own preliminary summary in the first book, and in the monologues that follow, that Pompilia is indubitably saintly and Franceschini indubitably wicked. When he speaks of the poem as 'relativist' he appears to mean something much less challenging than Mr. Johnson does when he uses the expression pluralist. 'It is relativist', he writes, 'in that the social and religious absolutes are not the means for understanding the right and wrong of the poem; they are for the most part barriers to understanding.'[5] He means by this, it seems, that the poem relates to unique people and circumstances. Ordinarily if a priest ran away with the wife of a nobleman one might think they could only be guilty. But this priest, this wife, this nobleman are to be judged for what they really are, and not simply in their life-rôles:

Browning is not saying that all discontented wives are to be rescued from their husbands, but just this particular wife from her particular husband. Why? Because of what we understand Pompilia and Guido to *be*. Hence the use of repetition and the dramatic monologue—not because the judgments are a matter of opinion but because we must judge what is being said by who is saying it. The point is that all the speakers are eloquent to a fault and make the best possible case consistent with their own prepossessions and the facts accessible to them. Our judgments depend, therefore on what we understand of them as people—of their motives, sincerity, and innate moral quality. Judgment goes on, in other words, below the level of the argument and hence the dramatic monologue, which makes it possible for us to apprehend the speaker totally, to subordinate what he says to what we know of him through sympathy.[6]

This argument overlooks that it is a quality of all fiction to deal with individual persons and events, and that in some degree we must always be guided by the author's revelations concerning his characters what to think of their actions. Some authors do admittedly leave us to work out from various sorts of clue what to think, but Browning luridly directs us at the very beginning how to judge the people in *The Ring and the Book*. Mr. Langbaum freely concedes that 'we would probably not discern the limitations of the pro-Pompilia speaker were we not specifically alerted to look for them'. So clearly it is impossible also to accept that we have to sympathise with them, that is, 'enter into their motives, sincerity and innate moral quality', before we can judge them. Yet Langbaum presses this interpretation of the poem more and more in order that it may serve as one more piece of evidence in support of his broader arguments on the subject of the poetry of experience. Thus he writes that Browning means that 'truth depends upon the nature of the theorising and ultimately upon the nature of the soul of which the theorising is a projection' and 'What we arrive at in the end is not *the* truth, but truth as the worthiest characters of the poem see it'. This view is not very far from Johnson's idea of pluralism after all.

The kind of theory I have been discussing does supply an answer to the question that is bound to occur to any reader of *The Ring and the Book*, and to treat it with scepticism imposes the obligation to supply an alternative. That question—to what end did Browning make *The Ring and the Book* an assemblage of dramatic monologues?—is intimately bound up with his remarks in the first and last books, including the metaphor of gold, alloy and ring on which so much has been written.

Browning's famous ring-metaphor has struck some critics as a curiosity of literature in that it is at variance with the facts of artistic creation. Its requiring us to replace the common phrase 'hard fact' with, as it were, 'soft fact' is curious, and it does rather suggest moral relativism, the idea that facts are malleable, and that each of us is free to impress our own meaning or sense of truth upon them. Yet at the same time Browning identifies facts with the truth, and uses the image of an alloy to suggest quite the contrary, that is, that he, at any rate, confronted with the facts of the old Yellow Book, kept exactly to them, and in no way tampered with them by adapting them to a work of art. It is tempting to see Browning's ambiguity on this question of 'truth' and 'fact' also to suggest that he somehow entertained the possibility that historical or legal evidence could not in itself supply the truth: for that one needs knowledge of character: and that he also must have meant his readers to see that the truth about human behaviour and motive is really inaccessible, a matter of personal judgment. Indeed, this view has been put forward.[7]

The whole matter is complicated by the nature of the law-case given in the Book, for, rather exceptionally, the main facts of Pompilia's death were not disputed. The difficulty of judgment turned only on motive. Theoretically, as Langbaum notices, the truth of this is *really* inaccessible; there have been miscarriages of justice in plenty. But Browning removes this possibility from the minds of his readers altogether. He knows for certain that Guido was guilty, for the truth lay in the Book for him to extract. He dug it, as it were, 'bit by bit', a 'piecemeal gain' from the Book. He knew it was the truth, an ingot of gold, not merely by assaying it (whatever that means), but from 'something else surpassing that',

> Something of mine which, mixed up with the mass,
> Made it bear hammer and be firm to file.

This makes the alloy simultaneously a touchstone of a novel kind. He knew that the Book contained truth because he could 'combine' with it, fusing his live soul with the inert stuff. It represented to him, in a manner familiar to us from accounts by Conrad and James of their sudden apprehension of a 'subject', a body of matter into which he could breathe his particular spirit. His reaction to the recognition is one of exhilaration, again a familiar enough response:

> A spirit laughs and leaps through every limb,
> And lights my eye, and lifts me by the hair,
> Letting me have my will again with these. . . .

It is not hard to see that Browning means by 'truth' what the creative artist often means—that the facts of a 'story' which have accidentally come to his attention exert an enormous appeal to his sense of life and its workings. So strong is his feeling that he can 'see' what must have happened that he has no doubt at all of the rightness of his interpretation. In this sense the original facts and the divined 'truth' are naturally one and the same. What is unusual is that Browning found his 'truth' (a goldmine of a subject, as he might have said) in such a large body of fact. As James observed in the Preface to *The Aspern Papers*, an historian cannot have too many facts, an artist too few—as a rule.

The first Book of the poem describes the long reverie in which the poet re-enacted the scenes of the crime in imagination, driven on by his sense of the perfect subject. It goes on to a highly censorious judgment of Guido and his brothers, and then, to make doubly sure that the reader makes no mistake about the motives of each of those whose speech the poet is imaginatively to create, gives a brief description of them in turn. It is quite clear, therefore, that he did not mean us to form our own judgments about the significance of a crime as in a novel of Dostoevsky. Nor are we reading an early version of *Rashomon*. The attraction of the subject consisted in the demonstration it offered of the wickedness of Guido, which is the central part of a picture made up of 'depth below depth of depravity', as Browning put it in his letter of 19 November 1868, to Julia Wedgwood.[8] 'I was struck with the enormous wickedness and weakness of the main composition of the piece' he wrote. That Guido is to be taken as the centre of interest is clear from the final book of the poem which describes 'our glaring Guido' as a soaring rocket, now declining into oblivion. (Perhaps this image reveals something of Browning's ambiguous conception of the man.) In the first book, Guido's second monologue is called 'the summit of so long ago'.

Another obvious attraction to Browning must have lain in the 'drama' of the case having been 'live fact deadened down', that is, not what really happened during the killing but what was laid before the judges as a set of documents. Browning's cry,

> Let this old woe step on the stage again!
> Act itself o'er anew for men to judge,

is quickly qualified—'Not by the very sense and sight indeed.' The interest is not in the murder reconstructed, but in the *trial*. In his letter to Miss Wedgwood, Browning states: 'The whole of his speech, as I premise, is untrue—cant and cleverness—as you see when the second speech comes . . .' In other words, Browning's interest lies in exposing wickedness through irony, an irony directed at the extreme lengths to which love of self will go, and the equal lengths to which speech will be abused to justify it. Browning makes it plain that one lesson we are to learn is that

> our human speech is naught,
> Our human testimony false, our fame
> And human estimation words and wind.

Obviously Browning could not have meant that speech is to be invariably so regarded, or he could not have been able himself to decide upon Guido's guilt and Pompilia's innocence. The suggestion is no more than that truth is very often abused because our gift of language is so capable of furthering lies and deceit that we can even persuade ourselves of our innocence. This aperçu is peculiarly Browning's own, and nowhere is it better illustrated than in his account of the ending he would have given to Tennyson's *Enoch Arden*—whereby we are to enjoy the irony of overhearing high-minded reflections upon the evil life of Enoch as his funeral-cart passes.[9]

Browning justifies his excessively liking the study of 'morbid cases of the soul' ('I thought that, since I could do it, and even liked to do it, my affair it was rather than another's') by a love of truth—God made men like this. 'Before I die, I hope to purely invent something,—here my pride was concerned to invent nothing: the minutest circumstance that denotes character is *true*: the black is so much—the white, no more.'[10] The remark that his pride was concerned to *invent nothing* brings us round to the question we started with. What it means is that to Browning wickedness justifying itself seemed particularly characteristic of human behaviour, and that this needed pointing out. Unfortunately the very nature of this truth means that the *hypocrite lecteur* would prefer to talk it away, so that the only way to authenticate it is by demonstration of the way in which excellent exculpations and evasions (such as a reader might himself use) are thought up by one indisputably guilty of crime. This is where fact comes in. What better 'argument' in support of the point could be adduced than being able to show that the fiction is also fact, attested by authentic documents?

This no doubt explains the artistic reasons Browning had for maintaining that the art-object, his poem (symbolised by a ring), was made from the gold of crude fact. But there is a psychological aspect of the matter too. Browning's creative energy found its natural outlet in irony of various kinds. In *Pippa Passes* it is an intricate irony of situation, involving various kinds of wickedness frustrated by chance. But its most remarkable form is the monologue of self-justification. (Conrad, incidentally, saw his creative power to be connected with self-justification.) This doubtless had its origin in the powerful confessional strain in Browning, illustrated in his earliest compositions, written before he had recognised that 'Art may tell a truth obliquely'. It seems reasonable, on the evidence of the number of monologues based on real people, that Browning felt most able to write when he had most assurance that he was not confessing, that is, when he was able to see himself 're-animating' rather than inventing.[11] This would mean that the long passage in the first book of the poem to the effect that only God can create and man but 'project his surplusage of soul' is really a piece of self-justification on Browning's part. He appears to be making a case for those artists (and Joyce and Shakespeare, in some degree, are others) who are not good at inventing *ex nihilo*, but need 'documents' or verifiable data to set them off and to sustain their imagination.

Browning, both in the poem and in his letter to Miss Wedgwood, makes it clear that he sees wickedness and hypocrisy to be inescapable facts of the life God has created: he is one possessed of 'a temper perhaps offensively and exaggeratedly inclined to dispute authoritative tradition, and all concessions to the mere desires of the mind'. Among the desires of the mind he counts the employment of poetic art to idealise human beings. The facts, he says, want explaining, not altering. He insists in the face of Miss Wedgwood's appeal to Sir Francis Bacon's notion of poetry, that he feels himself right in his very severe judgment upon men. So it is abundantly clear that *The Ring and the Book* was *intended* (at any rate) to impress this upon his readers. The climax of the poem, 'the summit of so long ago',

is Guido's second appearance, revealing that he was indisputably guilty, the occasion when, in prison

> death's breath rivelled up the lies,
> Left bare the metal thread, the fibre fine
> Of truth, i' the spinning: the true words shone last.
> How Guido to another purpose quite,
> Speaks and despairs, the last night of his life,
> In that New Prison by Castle Angelo
> At the bridge foot: the same man, another voice.

His companions, the Cardinal and Abate, former friends, are
awe-struck, 'So changed is Franceschini's gentle blood'.
Bearing this in mind a later passage about the poem's method
capable of misconstruction takes on a precise meaning.

Speaking of the country, or world, he is to create in the poem,
he explains that it is his deliberate intention not to write it from
a single point of view:

> A novel country: I might make it mine
> By choosing which one aspect of the year
> Suited mood best, and putting solely that
> On panel somewhere in the House of Fame,
> Landscaping what I saved, not what I saw:
> —Might fix you, whether frost in goblin-time
> Startled the moon with his abrupt bright laugh,
> Or August's hair afloat in filmy fire,
> She fell, arms wide, face foremost on the world,
> Swooned there and so singed out the strength of things.
> Thus were abolished Spring and Autumn both,
> The land dwarfed to one likeness of the land,
> Life cramped corpse-fashion. Rather learn and love
> Each facet-flash of the revolving year!—
> Red, green and blue that whirl into a white,
> The variance now, the eventual unity,
> Which make the miracle. See it for yourselves,
> This man's act, changeable because alive!
> Action now shrouds, nor shows the informing thought;
> Man, like a glass ball with a spark a-top,
> Out of the magic fire that lurks inside,
> Shows one tint at a time to take the eye:
> Which, let a finger touch the silent sleep,
> Shifted a hair's-breadth shoots you dark for bright,

Suffuses bright with dark, and baffles so
Your sentence absolute for shine or shade.
Once set such orbs,—white styled, black stigmatized,—
A-rolling, see them once on the other side
Your good men and your bad men every one
From Guido Franceschini to Guy Faux,
Oft would you rub your eyes and change your names.

The Ring and the Book, 1348–1378

We notice that the image of the glass ball's changing from bright to dark illustrates a change in men from seeming innocence to proven guilt, namely in Guido and Guy Faux: the point being made is that innocent appearances are deceptive. We can easily be taken in by the Guidos of the world; the point is made again in the last book when the Augustinian preacher (on the text of 'Let God be true and every man a liar') asserts that Pompilia was lucky to be vindicated: many like her are not.

The passage is not very happily expressed, but that it relates simply to '*this* man's act', Guido's, is clear enough from the context. E. D. H. Johnson quotes from it to explain why Browning composed the poem as a series of monologues representing 'kaleidoscopic views'. Confronted by first one, then another aspect of the story, the reader will be baffled in his inclination to settle for easy answers, to cast his 'sentence absolute for shine or shade'.[12] This suggests that the poem leaves the truth in doubt: but it demonstrates simply that many pretenders to innocence are truly guilty. Johnson's argument does not take sufficient account of Guido's speaking twice to different effect, and so showing that he was not (on the first occasion) impressing his own truth on the world, but was simply lying. The 'shine or shade' in any case relates to the image of the glass ball, not the 'views'. The 'views' are the separate dramatic monologues, and are necessary for Browning's particular gift to exercise itself—a gift not for showing that we make our own truths but for ironical exposure[13] of human failings. Browning supports his own Augustinian monk's text, 'Let God be true and every man a liar', and agrees with him that Pompilia's case showed that although human testimony was more often than not false, the truth abided with God. The glass ball is an obscure image for human beings who, by lying, put on a false appearance to the world. Browning appears to allude to the 'electric egg', an instrument used to show the effect of an electric discharge in a glass vessel partially exhausted of air. This effect was produced by passing a charge from an electric machine across a gap between metal or carbon rods enclosed in a glass chamber of ellipsoidal shape attached to an air pump. It consisted of a bright, reddish-purple glow, spreading out from the points of the rods, forming dark and light striations as the glass 'globe' is more and more exhausted. The machine could be set up with only one rod connected with the electric machine (e.g. Holtz's machine); if the other were earthed by touching it, the glow would appear in its characteristically variegated and uncertain form. This seems to be the effect Browning describes as deriving from 'the magic fire that lurks inside' (the MS has 'rolls' corrected to 'lurks'), an effect which

> baffles so
> Your sentence absolute for shine or shade,

a phrase which recurs several times in the poem. The Pope, we should notice, has no more doubt of his ability to see through the false lights and shades of Guido, than has Browning his creator. He dismisses the Comparini thus:

> Go!
> Never again elude the choice of tints!
> White shall not neutralize the black, nor good
> Compensate bad in man, absolve him so:
> Life's business being just the terrible choice.
>
> So do I see, pronounce on all and some
> Grouped for my judgment now,—profess no doubt
> While I pronounce: dark, difficult enough
> The human sphere, yet eyes grow sharp by use,
> I find the truth, dispart the shine from shade,
> As a mere man may, with no special touch
> O' the lynx-gift in each ordinary orb. . . .
>
> *The Pope*, 1234–1245

So the scientific metaphor is not a support for the relativist argument, only for Browning's explicit meaning, that appearances, helped out by lies and misconstructions, are surprisingly misleading.[14]

One point remains. Browning's rueful remarks about the British public, 'who like me not', but 'may like me yet' show, I think, that he had learned from experience that he had relied too much upon his readers' ability to see through the irony of his earlier monologues. This time he was going to spell it out—

> Perchance more careful whoso runs may read
> Than erst when all, it seemed, could read who ran.

Browning, one infers, far from intending to create ambiguity for his readers to penetrate, was bent, in *The Ring and the Book*, on eliminating it. Nothing could be further from his mind than the 'pluralism' or 'relativism' under discussion. This is not to say that he may not have encouraged it in others, only that he himself aimed at illustrating the evil that may mask itself behind specious words. His own Christianity has been shown by Hoxie N. Fairchild to be doubtful: but Browning appears to have believed that he was a Christian poet seeking to deal fairly with the world from his standpoint of special inspiration. This makes him a Victorian, not a modern.

The mistake in thinking the contrary seems to me to consist in taking the curious method of *The Ring and the Book* as tantamount to proof that Browning was a moral relativist, and then going on to see relativism as a key feature of modern literature. Even if one accepts the first part of this argument—though I have tried to show reasons why one should not—one would not I think be justified in accepting the second as a consequence of it. To do so suggests that the 'note' of modern literature is also relativist. But this, I think, is a mistaken inference from the habit modern novelists often have of putting themselves out of sight and relying upon the registration of the consciousness of participants in the action to cause the reader to assess the moral implications of what happens. This does not necessarily mean that the novelist is morally uncommitted. The true explanation is that a novelist following this method is not prepared to see morality as something that exists as an abstract set of rules

sanctioned by religious dogma but rather as something deeply
involved with actual situations and particular individuals. It is
this which underlies Henry James's really rather outrageous
tribute to Browning's poem in his centenary address on May 7,
1912. (His remark that 'Browning works the whole thing over—
the whole thing as originally given him—and we work *him*;
helpfully, artfully, boldly, which is our whole blest basis', sets
the tone of one of the most stimulating addresses that can ever
have been called forth on such an occasion.) James not only
thinks that even three characters would have been almost
excessive if he had been writing the story as a novel, but calmly
repudiates the whole method of the poem by hinting doubt
whether it ultimately succeeds, and expressing surprise that
Browning somehow gets away with endowing his Pompilia and
his Count with such gifts of expression while demanding that
we believe them to be by character or upbringing incapable of
it. His demand is for a consciousness, Caponsacchi's in fact,
reasonably and naturally capable of registering the full sense
of Pompilia's agonised life at Arezzo in the Count's hourly
presence (and on occasions that of his brother), a consciousness
also susceptible of a genuine deepening as he throws off his past
foolishness with women even as the Count tries to trap him with
Pompilia by forged correspondence ('scandalous scrawls of the
last erotic intensity'). All this is to be accompanied by an
increase of what he does find and admire in the poem, the very
feel of Italy, which Browning had soaked up during his years
there, and 'exudes and perspires' into the scenes in Rome and
Arezzo.

James is not imposing on Browning a mere preference for a
congenial method. Technique is never arbitrary. Nor is he
importing into the poem a merely 'personal' or individual
morality by having Caponsacchi estimate the significance of
events. (Moral relativism cannot, I suppose, emerge when only
one judgment is presented.) He would, if anything, deepen the
moral effect, so far as a modern reader is concerned, by making
it possible for him to see and feel the enormity of Count Guido's
conduct towards the girl who is 'hideously mismated' with him,
by following the growth of Caponsacchi's suspicions, which

spring from a profound personal incompatibility with the Count:

> We have only to begin right, only to make it, on the part of the two men, a relation of strong irritated perception and restless righteous convinced instinct in the one nature and of equally instinctive hate and envy, jealousy and latent fear, on the other, to see the indirect connection, the one with Pompilia, as I say, throw across our page as portentous a shadow as we need.[15]

In other words, by working through the eyes and mind of Caponsacchi, James would really achieve what Langbaum claims for Browning—an estimate of a man's actions and words derived from a prior knowledge, or suspicion, of his character. In reality what we have in Browning's poem is an *ex cathedra* judgment; far from believing in his own modest estimate of the poet's rôle as a mere revivifier of what only God can truly make, he illustrates in a very obvious way the old parallel between an artist and God: both are creators and lawgivers in their created worlds. Fielding makes this parallel in fun, but Browning's denial is an attempt to conceal his true estimate of his rôle: and there is something embarrassing in having the Pope in the poem shown to come right in his judgment of Guido by courtesy not of God but an intuition like that Browning himself claims.[16]

The conclusion I want to make is that Browning's strength as a poet springs from the same source as his weakness. He is by temperament, and by the forces of his time no doubt, committed to a faith in God as the prop for his moral being. His strength lies in his confidence that suffering and passion have value, and more particularly, in his feeling that he has an unassailable position from which to create through irony. In my view, *The Ring and the Book* goes back on both, and shows the weak side of his art. The method of juxtaposing his monologues within a framework of explicit moral condemnation destroys the irony which elsewhere so stimulates the reader into admiration of his art. His explicitness really does substitute 'galvanism for life' and a spark for the flame of true imagination. Fra Lippo Lippi, Browning's earlier spokesman, offered no apology for his art: nature and mankind are immensely worth the artist's labours:

But why not do as well as say,—paint these
Just as they are, careless what comes of it?
God's works—paint anyone, and count it crime
To let a truth slip. Don't object, 'His works
'Are here already; nature is complete:
'Suppose you reproduce her—(which you can't)
'There's no advantage! You must beat her then.'
For don't you mark? We're made so that we love
First when we see them painted, things we have passed
Perhaps a hundred times nor cared to see.

The Ring and the Book sees art, Browning's art in that poem at any rate, to be a matter of contriving that 'something dead may get to live again'. But truth of fact is not truth of imagination. 'Fra Lippo Lippi' lives: and it does so because Browning is not afraid to expose his doctrine (for the poem has doctrine enough) to the irony which the dramatic monologue excels in, that arising from having doctrine from a doubtful advocate. Lippi's love of the world and man as subjects for art seems not unlike the love of the world, the flesh and the devil masquerading as primal innocence:

I always see the garden and God there
A-making man's wife: and, my lesson learned,
The value and significance of flesh,
I can't unlearn ten minutes afterwards.

His worldliness persists even into heaven itself:

So, all smile—
I shuffle sideways with my blushing face
Under the cover of a hundred wings
Thrown like a spread of kirtles when you're gay
And play hot cockles, all the doors being shut,
Till, wholly unexpected, in there pops
The hothead husband!

Such frivolity permits us take or leave his claim that the artist who represents men and women realistically serves God quite as well as the conventional religious painter. It is convenient, we may think, for him to say so. In consequence, the notion remains indissolubly associated with Fra Lippo himself, part of his being like his wenching, not floating free as doctrine —even though we may recognise it as in fact part of the complex

171

of *Browning's* 'ideas' on religion and self-expression. The 'freedom' of the reader, as Sartre puts it, is uncompromised. The delicate balance of this irony is tipped ever so slightly by our externally-derived knowledge that the painter who loves women so well—

> If you get simple beauty and nought else
> You get about the best thing God invents

—is the Fra Lippo Lippi whose work has come down to us, and whose claim to be on the right course in religious painting has been validated by history. This historical testimony is a hundred times more eloquent than Browning's perfervid assertions in *The Ring and the Book*. The reader's own knowledge of the historical outcome of the events can contribute nothing to the recognition of truth in that poem, for the characters and incidents are unfamiliar. Browning has worked exceedingly hard, but his reader has nothing to do save watch a demonstration. The doctrine it conveys is commended to us not by irony but by exposure, and its culminating monologue is delivered not by a doubtful advocate but by a proclaimed liar. Moreover Browning feels himself, I suggest, so safely hedged about by his moral frame that he can admit into Guido's first monologue, and that of the Pope, 'arguments' which are more subversive of the faith supporting that moral frame than he could permit himself in any other context. Guido's monologue in particular really does point towards moral relativism if it is considered in purely intellectual terms, without respect to his known guilt. Yet the contemporary estimate of the poem is not surprising. It must have seemed to many readers who found subversive arguments attributed to the wicked Guido and moral confidence to the Pope a *counterblast* to the relativism making itself felt in that decade. It stands, in my view, as an elaborate Victorian monument to the faith that truth does not depend upon human testimony, but is absolute. Its method, that of juxtaposing dramatic monologues, serves a purpose quite contrary to that proposed by its modern apologists. Today we may find it less impressive because it has lost imaginative force as it has gained in moral explicitness,[17] an explicitness which intensifies the pessimism the poem finally displays.

NOTES

[1] 'Coleridge's Writings', in *English Critical Writings* (*Nineteenth Century*), ed. Edmund D. Jones (1916), p. 493.

[2] Edward Alexander, in his *Matthew Arnold and John Stuart Mill* (1965), p. 64, implies that Walter E. Houghton, in his pages (14–15) on relativism in *The Victorian Frame of Mind 1830–1870* (1957) did not take account of the fact that the 'idea of cultural and intellectual relativism' pervades the writing of Arnold and Mill. But Houghton is concerned with moral relativism in Pater and carefully and justly distinguishes the important respects in which it differs from Arnold's views.

[3] Edward Dowden, 'Mr. Tennyson and Mr. Browning', *Studies in Literature 1789–1877* (1892), p. 238.

[4] E. D. H. Johnson, 'Robert Browning's Pluralistic Universe: A Reading of *The Ring and the Book*', *University of Toronto Quarterly*, xxxi (Oct. 1961), pp. 20–41.

[5] Robert Langbaum, *The Poetry of Experience* (1957), p. 113.

[6] Ibid., pp. 114–115.

[7] George Levine, writing of Carlyle's growing concern, shortly after *Sartor Resartus*, with history and the primacy of fact, observes: 'At best the turn was an expression of willed faith in the notion that the world and experience are under some supernatural moral control. Although he was too scrupulously honest a man to have been able to distort his sources consciously, he never wrote a history in which the facts had not already led him to his desired conclusions.' See his '*Sartor Resartus* and the balance of fiction', *Victorian Studies* VIII, No. 2 (Dec. 1964), pp. 155–156. The final sentence, it seems to me, can apply also to Browning and *The Ring and the Book*. But Mr. Levine also connects (p. 157) Carlyle (in *Sartor*) with Browning in having it that we lean substantially upon the 'character' (i.e. the good qualities, and notably sincerity) of Teufelsdrökh when we are trying, as we read, to assess the truth (in a relativist sense, of course) of the 'clothes-philosophy'. He goes on to speak of the 'obvious connection of elements of this vision with the later work of James and Conrad—indeed with much of the modern novel'. This part of his article, arguing that Carlyle and Browning are akin in coming 'perilously close to relativism', staying clear of it largely in the same way too, seems to me ill-grounded, and particularly so in making further connection with the highly objective fiction of our present century. It seems to go back on the fact,

173

which Mr. Levine properly emphasises, that *Sartor Resartus* does not progress, that is, has no action; it employs a biographical method (the resemblances of which to fiction must, *pace* Northrop Frye, be discounted) not in the way a novelist does, but as a means of skilfully disguising what is in the last resort, doctrine. In this, surely, is the resemblance with *The Ring and the Book* and the majority of Browning's other monologues. The presence of doctrine without action is a feature which makes any connection of elements in these works with the novels of James and Conrad of minor importance at most.

[8] *Robert Browning and Julia Wedgwood*, ed. Richard Curle (1937), p. 159.

[9] Curle, op. cit., p. 75 (letter of Sept. 2, 1864).

[10] Ibid., pp. 158–159.

[11] Miss Wedgwood argued that Browning was not truly dramatic because his thoughts intruded so often. Guido was stupid and brutal, not ingenious and wily. Browning replied 'Why I almost have you at an unfair advantage, in the fact that the whole story is *true!*' ibid., p. 188.

[12] Johnson, loc. cit., p. 23.

[13] I prefer to use this phrase to describe Browning's single monologues because the alternative, used by Dowden, 'intellectual sympathy' can lead, as I venture to suggest it does in Mr. Langbaum's book *The Poetry of Experience*, to the idea that they take us into a new category of poetic art in the nineteenth century, an art depending upon a special willingness to enter into the minds of wicked and ignorant men and *ipso facto* to suspend one's normal moral attitudes. This seems to me to overlook the fact that not only all drama, but also all works employing irony—those, say, of Chaucer and Swift, to take obvious examples—have always depended upon a pretended 'sympathy'. The claim that the sympathy is, in Browning, genuine, seems to me to remove an obvious cause of our satisfaction in his poems. Langbaum's case is that we are expected to show sympathy towards his erring apologists in a manner analogous to the scientific attitude of mind. Historical or psychological considerations, he suggests, cause us to suspend our moral judgment of the duke in 'My Last Duchess'. This seems to me quite fallacious. Our moral feelings are not, admittedly, like those we would have if we were in reality the envoy *encountering* the duke, but then in art they never are. Our moral indignation is *used* by the poet, nevertheless, as an essential element in the poem's power.

[14] The electric egg was going out of use by about 1860 in favour of the 'vacuum' or Geissler tube. But Faraday demonstrated the instru-

ment at the Royal Institution in one of the lectures in his Christmas lecture-series for children (and parents) in 1859–1860. (A stenographic report of the lectures is given in *Chemical News* 1 (1860).) The lecture, delivered on Jan. 7, 1860 (pp. 126–129), contained the demonstration ('. . . we have that glorious electric light; and the moment I cut off the connexion it stops') : the report illustrates the instrument (fig. 4). The lectures were published as *A Course of six lectures on the various forces of Matter and their relations to each other*, with numerous illustrations, edited by W. Crookes in 1860; they had several editions. They were then republished by Griffin, Bohn and Co. in 1863, together with Faraday's more famous Christmas lecture on the chemical history of a candle.

[15] H. James, 'The Novel in "The Ring and the Book" ', in *Notes on Novelists*, p. 323.

[16] Those dramatic monologues depending upon imaginary reconstructions of the origins of Christianity—like 'A Death in the Desert'—are remarkably unhistorical. The 'historical' problem, whether John wrote the Fourth Gospel, is not so much shirked or overlooked in that poem, as resolved. Browning *knows*, so it appears, the true circumstances, in that John is *shown* to be the author, and speaks of the problem later doubts will create. The irony of the other poems like 'An Epistle' and 'Cleon' depends upon the 'truth' of Christianity being imposed upon the reader as an absolute. Similarly, the Pope in *The Ring and the Book*, who could quite easily have been shown to have judged wrongly, or to have decided an issue which no human being could be clear about, is in fact made both to judge the case by purely human intuition (without having *heard* any of the deponents, as we the readers have) and in fact to be right.

[17] A. K. Cook in *A Commentary upon Browning's 'The Ring and the Book'* (1920), p. 3, anticipates the conclusion of this essay in arguing against G. K. Chesterton's claim that *The Ring and the Book* could be regarded as 'the epic of free speech'. He points out that while Browning may have seen the possibility of encouraging this interpretation in Book 1, lines 1348–1378, he was fully conscious even as early as *Sordello* that the 'setter-forth' of unexampled themes had 'best chalk broadly on each vesture's hem/The wearer's quality'

8

THE RING AND THE BOOK:
THE USES OF PROLIXITY

Isobel Armstrong

I

The Ring and the Book is a long poem—too long for contemporary readers. Even an admirer of the poem has written that 'somehow, the fact emerges for us too bluntly, that the same story is being told twelve times over'.[1] Some people could take the repetition if Browning had used it in the manner of a *nouvelle vague* novelist, preserving at least the illusion of indeterminacy and openness. But he chooses to reveal from the start in blatantly melodramatic terms that Guido, 'Gilded starfashion by a glint from hell', brutally murdered his wife, Pompilia. This looks bullyingly indelicate and inartistic in the worst Browning manner. A judgment seems forced from the beginning and the Pope's assessment of the case in Book X is superfluous and only restates what the reader knows already. So, at least, Robert Langbaum has put it.[2]

The two problems of length and of predetermined judgment are related. One can begin to deal with them by assuming that Browning did not intend the poem to be read primarily for the story; the repetition is so undisguised, the facts are made so clear. It is not a work governed by what John Holloway has called the 'trajectory' of the narrative.[3] Even so, the blunt obviousness of repetition remains and it is still necessary to ask a simple formal question: is there any reason why the poem *needs* to be as long as it is? To say that the poem is really a novel because Browning is a writer of great psychological insight is to beg the question. One is still left asking what kind of novel it is. As Henry James discovered, to take the novel as an analogy only makes the problem of prolixity more difficult. He suggested a drastic restriction of points of view and would have portrayed the action mainly through the eyes of Caponsachi.[4] I think that the analogy with the novel is helpful, but rather for understanding the curiously opaque and intractable subject matter of the poem than for solving the formal problem. This nakedly metaphysical treatment of crime and punishment—a forgotten Roman murder case of 1698—set in a society where feudal and ecclesiastical authority is disintegrating under the economic pressure of a new middle class and the intellectual anarchy of what the Pope calls the 'educated man' makes a comparison with Dostoevsky more useful than a comparison with James. Dostoevsky's interests are eschatological, Browning's epistemological and psychological, but both are fascinated with the nature of belief and unbelief and with what it does to people.

Another way of approaching the prolixity of the poem is to accept it as a relativist poem displaying a multiple interpretation of a single event. John Killham has discussed the difficulties of this position and certainly relativism provides the reverse of an organising principle, implying that the poem could have been even longer than it is: there are as many views of the situation as there are participants in it and there is no reason why Browning should not have gone on writing monologues almost indefinitely. He could have included, as he does not, monologues by Pietro and Violante, Caponsachi's friend, Guido's brother, all of whom, on the face of it, have a greater claim for inclusion than the lawyers or Tertium Quid. Yet this premise, it is clear, makes the existing termination of the poem purely arbitrary and ignores Browning's firm assertion that the poem is completed, formally and morally, by Guido's last monologue. The poem, in fact, is not to be seen as a modernist poem, as an amorphous gathering of points of view and of endless moral possibilities. The relativist view, besides being unable to provide an adequate solution to the form of the poem, makes the problem of Browning's tactless didacticism even more embarrassing because the end of the poem is so clearly stated at its beginning, a procedure which violates the aims of a relativist art.

The great difficulty in the way of accepting that *The Ring and the Book* may be controlled by a shaping principle which justifies, at the same time as necessitating, its length is that modern or post-symbolist criticism of poetry has evolved what is really an aesthetic of the short poem. Valéry, concluding that the economic length for a poem could never be more than a hundred lines, may seem absurdly dogmatic now: Pound, on the other hand, does not. His description of the image 'which presents an intellectual and emotional complex in an instant of time' seems perfectly right if one assumes a poetry which will always mime the instantaneousness and suddenness of experiences like Joyce's epiphany.[5] Our familiar critical vocabulary of concentration, intensity, complexity and multiple ambiguity is appropriate to this sort of poetry and describes the rhetoric of brevity. This vocabulary does not do justice to the seeming messiness and certain ramifications of poems like *The Ring and the Book* where to talk about the 'texture' of the verse—a metaphor designed to emphasise intricate verbal relationships— often means to talk about a verse which is loose-textured and suggests the unpleasing notion of something full of holes. We need to evolve ways of thinking about long poems. A short poem is like an object, a thing which one can, as it were, roll about in the palm of one's hand, easily perceiving it as an entity, easily accepting the experience we have as an instantaneous 'whole'. The experience of reading a long poem is different. It silts itself up in the mind. Reading a long poem is more like the slow process of growth or of gradual discovery.

In *The Ring and the Book* the reader is moved through a process of growth or of discovery and this is done by means of a spiral of repetition. The poem continually doubles back on itself in order to go forward. 'I suspect that much of growth starts out by our turning around on our own traces', J. S. Bruner has said, talking about the psychology of learning. We say, 'I see what I'm doing now', or 'So that's what the thing is'.[6] I find this helpful for thinking about the repetition in *The Ring and the Book*. The facts of the case are given unequivocally in the first book; but to know that Pompilia was innocent and Guido guilty is only to have a bare abstract hold on the story. Even the complete outline reveals very little of the actual content, the moral nature, of the case. Browning's insistence that 'dead truth', the paraphrase of historical fact, is to be changed into 'live truth' (I, 696–697) by a creative act of the imagination and in the process *transformed* indicates how the poem is to be read. The reader is to feel his way to a discovery of the nature of the situation, just as Browning redeemed through his imagination the inert facts of history—'The life in me abolished the death of things . . . I saw with my own eyes . . .' (I, 520, 523). Browning is attempting to make here the kind of distinction which Newman made when he talked of the difference between 'notional' and 'real' assent, an abstract or mechanical and a felt understanding of something.[7] Of course, Newman only repeats a distinction generally understood in earlier Romantic poetry. Wordsworth recognised that the truth 'carried alive into the heart by passion' is radically different from one which is simply known. 'Nothing ever becomes real till it is experienced', Keats said.[8] The uniqueness of *The Ring and the Book* lies in its deliberate attempt to move the reader through a 'notional' to a 'real' understanding of a situation and in the form which Browning evolved to make possible this process of discovery. By repeating different versions of the same story from monologue to monologue, recoding and transposing the facts into different moral and emotional keys, he evolved a poem which continually amplifies and at the same time continually modifies itself. Each monologue becomes a control upon the others. A reading of the poem is a dynamic activity because the reader has to corroborate the initial judgment by inhabiting a series of monologues imaginatively and because the poem demands a continuous process of adjustment, discrimination and reformulation in the light of what is already known, from what has been read up to that point. A choric trilogy, representing legal and ecclesiastical judgment in the persons of Hyacinthus, Bottinius and the Pope, follows the central monologues of Guido, Caponsachi and Pompilia. It directly echoes, sometimes through parody, the positions adopted in the first choric trilogy by Half-Rome, The Other Half-Rome and Tertium Quid. This return of the poem upon itself, reincarnating yet again, but with further shifts and conflations, some of the notions which have already been displaced by the central monologues, enables the reader to multiply distinctions, to achieve a fuller imaginative grasp of the nature of the moral questions Browning explores so that we end by knowing in a richer way what we already know. It is a way of bringing about the discovery 'So that's what the thing is'. 'The moral sense grows but by exercise', the Pope says (X, 1415). Here the poem itself is the exercise.

Some people might feel that the Pope's assessment of the case deprives them of this experience by seeming to explain the meaning of the poem too clearly. The Pope, in contrast to the intellectual dilettantism of Tertium Quid, exercises the rational and moral faculty in a profoundly serious way. His judgment, though more anxious and less gothic than Browning's, is identical with the one given in the first book. Browning, for instance, in order that the reader shall be in no doubt about the villainy of the villains, falls into a luridly grotesque descriptive style—there is something self-consciously cloak-and-dagger about it. The Pope, speaking of Guido's brother, Paul, uses some of the same epithets ('fox-faced', for example) as Browning uses in the first book and regards him with the same kind of moral disgust, but he spends far longer in analysing the nature of Paul's offence, pushing the analysis towards as complete an understanding as possible. He takes the two brothers singly. Browning discusses them together.

> . . . a dark brotherhood, and specially
> Two obscure goblin creatures, fox-faced this,
> Cat-clawed the other, called his next of kin
> By Guido the main monster,—cloaked and caped,
> Making as they were priests, to mock God more,—
> Abate Paul, Canon Girolamo.
> These who had rolled the starlike pest to Rome
> And stationed it to suck up and absorb
> The sweetness of Pompilia . . .
>
> (I, 548–556)

Compare the Pope's account of Paul:

> Twice Guido, all craft but no violence,
> This copier of the mien and gait and garb
> Of Peter and Paul, that he may go disguised,
> Rob halt and lame, sick folk i' the temple-porch!
> Armed with religion, fortified by law,
> A man of peace, who trims the midnight lamp
> And turns the classic page—and all for craft,
> All to work harm with, yet incur no scratch!

While Guido brings the struggle to a close,
Paul steps back the due distance, clear o' the trap...
(X, 884–893)

The Pope's is the most authoritative statement of the para-
phraseable moral content of the case. Yet it is important to
realise that this *is* moral explication. The truth which he has
found 'Evolvible from the whole' (X, 231) is explained as
clearly as the limits of paraphrase, the diagram of moral judgment, will allow. The conclusion is the same, but of a different
order, from the one evolved by the reader from the lived
experience of the monologues, and I think that the Pope's
soliloquy is there to underline this, just as the repetition of
judgment emphasises that, after the experience of the poem an
assent even to a moral diagram will be different from the mere
grasp of the essentials achieved in the first book. The Pope's
'whole' is the documents of the case. Our whole is the experience of the poem up to this point. And the Pope's judgment is
less than the experience of the poem which is not complete
until the spiral ends with the final monologue of Guido.

The Ring and the Book is arranged in convolutions of repetition
so that the reader can 'learn' or discover the poem; it is like
this so that something can be discovered as well about the
processes of judgment itself, and the nature of judgment is one
of the things the poem is about. 'Everyone who reasons, is his
own centre', Newman said.[9] The reader of these monologues is
forced to rely on his own centre, on the authority of a delicate
sense of moral 'feel' in order to evaluate them. This is also the
authority claimed by every speaker in the poem and so one is
in a circular relationship with these monologues. Caponsachi,
for instance, asserts the authority of the self in the intuitive act
of moral judgment when he makes an analogy between an
aesthetic and a moral judgment. He believed involuntarily in
Pompilia's innocence just as his knowledge of the genuineness
of a Raphael would be based on an intuitive leap. Nevertheless,
he is amazed by Pompilia's 'self-authorised and self-explained'
certitude (VI, 920). Pompilia, the most assertive speaker in the
poem, sees her conscience as the 'clear voice' of God (VII, 1615)
and makes the irreducible non-rational impulse a sanction for

action. And yet her monologue implies the potential solipsism and anarchy of the self-authorised judgment when she recalls the fearful delusions of a maniac she saw in her childhood who ran through the square crying 'I am the Pope, am Sextus, now the Sixth . . . The angels, met in conclave, crowned me!' (1173, 1176). The grounds on which Pope Innocent XII condemns Guido to death are no other than these—'Therefore I stand on my integrity' (X, 276); 'I know just so, nor otherwise. As I know,/I speak' (X, 1290–1291). The great Romantic doctrine of self-derived intuitive insight celebrated in *Paracelsus* (1835) thirty years before—'Truth is within ourselves . . . There is an inmost centre in us all/Where truth abides in fulness . . .' is exhaustively questioned in this poem.

Tennysons's ultimately unqualified 'I have felt' (*In Memoriam*, CXXIV), the glorification of the 'Spontaneous Me' by Whitman (whom Santayana called Browning's half-brother), the subtle equanimity with which Newman accepted the circularity of judgment—'there is no ultimate test of truth besides the testimony borne to truth by the mind itself'—Browning could not accept these positions in the same way.[10] They raise epistemological difficulties, difficulties which are restlessly exposed and reiterated from monologue to monologue in *The Ring and the Book*. Browning accepts that the ultimate basis of judgment may well be 'I have felt', but the status of an evaluation—even if it is the right one—based on the moral 'feel' of a situation, and the infinite regression involved in the evaluation of *that* evaluation, is the central problem of the poem. *The Ring and the Book* is a poem about itself because it examines its own assumptions. It attempts to break out of the problem by demonstrating that the things which rest on an appeal to a non-rational authority differ not in kind but in value: they are debased or refined species of one another—revelation, vision, moral intuition and their analogues in the working of the imagination (no wonder that the poem is so obsessively concerned with the status of fictions), instinct, impulse, the hunch. These notions are continually redefined and evaluated through juxtaposition with one another. I can show this best by discussing the multiplicity of redefinitions evolved in the slow silting up of the language of the poem. On a large scale it happens because each monologue exemplifies various kinds of judgment involving the non-rational, imaginative process of inference and selection. The *process* is the same in all the monologues but the product is different. The Pope, for instance, considers that the capacity for insight endowed by God is the means to revelation, to truth. His judgment, diagram though it is, is construed through a full engagement of the moral imagination and emerges only after saturation in the facts of the case. The lawyers claim to construe the case with analogous, almost seer-like, powers of imagination but here imagination moves into the aesthetic realm of possibilities and probabilities and the art objects which are produced are as different from the Pope's soliloquy as they are from the products of fantasy to be found in the monologues of Half-Rome and The Other Half-Rome. The notions of insight which these speeches both embody and exemplify all differ again from Pompilia's belief in her rightness which comes almost inspirationally, *sui generis*. Pompilia's speech exposes those of the lawyers but in important ways the Pope's speech qualifies hers. The poem is a self-qualifying structure, re-examining its presuppositions and values as it proceeds. Whether its elements are rearranged in slightly differentiated paraphrase or in wild parody enough analogies and cross-references are built up for the poem to arrive at a controlled statement about the nature of a 'self-authorised' intuitive act of judgment.

Perhaps it seems incongruous that these strenuously nineteenth-century concerns should appear in the context of brooding, chaotic violence, as if Browning used Shakespearian or Jacobean tragedy as a model. But the pastiche has its uses, partly because it sanctions a bold handling of sex, class and religion, but more particularly because it creates a mood in which good and evil have a moral and metaphysical reality. The question of conscience invites here a sharpness of response which could not have been paralleled if the poem had been set in a nineteenth-century context and blurred with all the tender susceptibilities and reservations of the intellectual in that culture. The late seventeenth-century setting is also treated for the purposes of the poem as a historical watershed. The institutions created at the high peak of Christian achievement are in

decay and a moral authority located in the individual is super-
ceding them. The picture of a society in transition enables
Browning to expose one of the main worries of the poem. This
is not so much that a reliance on the 'Spontaneous Me' will
encourage relativist assumptions which undermine morality
but that our response to morality will become aestheticised.

II

I have said that the structure of *The Ring and the Book* becomes
meaningful if it is seen as a poem about itself. It is also a poem
about its own language and an understanding of the form of
the poem depends upon a grasp of Browning's attitude to
language. In a very real sense the theme of the poem is its
style or one could say that it is a poem about style. Instinct,
impulse, nature—the vocabulary is the same but these are
protean concepts and their significance depends upon their
formulation, the structure of a sentence, the cadence, the tone.
The total context of each monologue gives the words a meaning
which then undergoes successive shifts and gradations of value
as the poem proceeds, shifts which are all the more surprising
because the formulations are so ostensibly alike. In the event
the repetition is never exact because the meaning of the words
is transformed. Language is the only precise index of value if
we are forced back upon sensing the moral feel of each monologue and so the poem is intensely concerned with the corruption of language, values which debase language and language
which debases values. The involuntary total impression may
seem to pre-judge analysis, but words are the signs from which
the impression is extrapolated and the initial impression can be
checked from the nuances and details of the language.

'For how else know we save by worth of word?' Browning
says in the first book (I, 837) to vindicate his method. Many
people have assumed a distrust of language in *The Ring and the
Book* on the evidence of such statements as 'Language that
goes, goes easy as a glove,/O'er good and evil, smoothens both
to one' (I, 1180–1181) or 'Art may tell a truth/Obliquely, do
the thing shall breed the thought, . . . missing the mediate word'
(XII, 859–861). Yet these comments do not invalidate the first

185

statement. Browning breeds thought by allowing the language of the monologues to expose one another and this presupposes the closest attention to language. As if to make this clear a deceptive parody of his method is built into the poem in the monologue of Hyacinthus, the lawyer pleading for Guido, who is one of the failed poets in the poem. His monologue is a violent joke against the misuse of reiteration. He is a manipulator of language, endlessly duplicating rhetorical alternatives— 'Here repeat charge with proper varied phrase' (VIII, 191), 'So many varied sorts of language here' (VIII, 1517)—and carrying synonym to a grotesque extreme in the proliferation of diminutives for his son, Giacinto—Cinone, Cinozzo, Cinoncello, Cinuolo, Cinincello. For this debased poet ('Unluckily, law quite absorbs a man,/Or else I think I too had poetized' (VIII, 150–151)) language is rhetoric and rhetoric a series of formulae. The continuous alternation of Latin formulas for the same English words plays mechanically above the gourmet's avid anticipation of his celebratory dinner party and makes his speech take off into a kind of verbal fantasy. Mechanical repetition of this kind never gets to grips with reality. There is not much to choose between Hyacinthus and Bottinius, the second lawyer, who has more grandiose notions of the shaping power of the imagination. He intends to recreate Pompilia's story in terms of the archetypes in myth and legend to which it aspires (IX, 86–107; 119–139; 182–212). In both cases a corrupt art all too easily patterns and transmutes experience and language creates empty structures, fictions which are parasitic on actuality in the same way that the lawyers exploit the murder case economically.

These are demonstrations of the misuse of language but the poem also celebrates its power. I am not thinking here primarily of local effects of poetic intensity. Although the poem can achieve these when it is necessary, Wordsworth's primitive distinction between metre and prose is probably the only description of poetry which would allow the poem to have the status of a poem rather than of prose. The language is stiffened by metre. It is also integrated by the continuous transitions of alliteration and assonance every four or five lines from one very limited group of vowels and consonants to another very different and equally limited group. There is a compelling energy and economy about this which certainly differentiates the poem from prose in a more than nominal way but these are essentially devices for keeping the poem going. The power of language is exhibited on a much larger scale when the monologues are set against one another for then *The Ring and the Book* becomes a poem in the more important sense that every word matters. Parallels even of the most casual phrases betray the quality of the speakers' feeling—often the closer to duplication the more sharp the betrayal. When Pompilia is described in her desperate visit to the Archbishop as 'shrieking all her wrongs' (Half-Rome, II, 881) or as having 'sobbed out her prayer' (The Other Half-Rome, III, 1004), the phrases are easily passed over in the context of each monologue, but there is a significant difference between 'shrieking' and 'sobbed', 'wrongs' and 'prayer' which goes far beyond synonym. The first is hostile and suggests the violent exaggerations of a hysterical woman while the second is imbued with romantic sentimentality and religiosity, a portrayal of helpless femininity.

In the same way, the language in which the image of the Fall of man is expressed (an image repeated by all the speakers in the first choric trilogy) takes on the colour of different fears and fantasies. The same image is transmuted by varying kinds of verbal squint and Pompilia's story is mythologised in a thoroughly private way. Women are a threat to the speaker in Half-Rome so he sees marriage in authoritarian terms, as an institution where male dominance must be preserved, just as he wishes to preserve the feudal aristocratic privileges of a society which he sees being displaced by aspiring merchant people like Pietro and Violante. Therefore Violante is the Eve of the situation, manipulating both her husband and Guido, the down-at-heel aristocrat who is her victim. Pietro is the duped Adam who 'Crawled all-fours with his baby pick-a-back', doting in his 'cabbage-plot' of a 'fools'-paradise', falsely believing that Pompilia is his legitimate child (II, 253–262). The Other Half-Rome sees Pompilia as an innocent Eve victimised by a satanic Guido. His is a conventional romantic view presented with indulgent charity which half disguises his sexual curiosity. Pompilia, the child of a prostitute ('This fragile egg, some careless wild bird dropped ...' (III, 215)), lived in a pre-lapsarian 'garden-plot' of virtue when once rescued from vice by Violante's motherly instinct. She was 'a chance sliver, branchlet slipt from bole/Of some tongue-leaved eye-figured Eden tree,/Filched by two exiles and borne far away' (III, 234–236), and so became a bloom—sentimentality and sexual euphemism unite here—'To be toyed with by butterfly or bee' (III, 245). For the speaker in *Tertium Quid* the situation is entirely simple. Pompilia is a modern Eve, the unsatisfied wife of an ageing husband, overprotected by him but sexually rapacious—'Adam so starved me I was fain accept/The apple any servant pushed my way' (IV, 858–859). This is why 'Fancy-and-flesh' fell for 'Brisk-and-bold' and eloped with Caponsachi, the attractive priest. The language moves through precise structures of feeling so that these formulations define one another. The disgust and violence of the first is exposed by the soothing, easy romanticism of the second and these together define the thinly sophisticated cynicism of the third.

Now that I have suggested how the 'varied sorts of language' in the poem work by revealing shifts of meaning and emphasis it is possible to show how Browning uses the vocabulary of feeling and impulse to explore the implications of the intuition and insight claimed as a moral sanction by all the speakers in the poem. The three participants in the action, Pompilia, Caponsachi and Guido represent, to adapt William James, varieties of intuitional experience and the circularity of 'the testimony borne to truth by the mind itself' is immediately evident from these monologues. Pompilia expresses the naked, Romantic innocence accepted in *Paracelsus*—'truth is within ourselves'. She insists with absolute authority 'I am clear it was on impulse to serve God' (VII, 1600). Guido uses the same vocabulary in his first false testimony. The murder resulted from what was in essence a sudden conversion, almost a visionary experience. He was 'rapt away by the impulse' to kill when he saw Violante (V, 1662) because he had experienced a 'voice beyond the law' (V, 1548), an 'inner call' (V, 1596) making him aware

Of the first conscience, the anterior right,
The God's-gift to mankind, impulse to quench
The antagonistic spark of hell.

(V, 1574–1576)

Caponsachi also moves into an area of experience not governed by rational intelligence to recognise the 'live passion' of moral feeling rather than the dead forms of the Church (VI, 1001). '"Thought?" Nay, Sirs, what shall follow was not thought' (VI, 937). But his conversion is slow, muddled and full of ambivalent feeling. The first sight of Pompilia makes him rededicate himself so that he swears 'Never to write a canzonet any more' (VI, 467), a feeling all mixed up with regrets that he is 'priest and celibate' (VI, 493). Ultimately he acts without consciously choosing to act. He goes to meet Pompilia for the rather inglorious reason that she might think he is afraid and his crisis is resolved without a decision.

Though it is primarily through the 'instinctive theorising' of the choric monologues that the moral centre of these speeches and their significance is exposed, the closed circuit created by the language of impulse can be evaluated here. Caponsachi's slow honest doubt suggests something thin about Guido's rhetoric of conversion and his acknowledgment of live passion is different from Guido's abstract battle between good and evil. When Pompilia talks of impulse she means involuntary feeling created by an impassioned need to affirm life when she discovered about her child. Her refusal, until she is advised by the Archbishop, to undergo sexual degradation by consummating her marriage with Guido is part of the same feeling. The sense of the word is far shallower in Guido's 'rapt away by the impulse', where it means not involuntary feeling but feeling beyond control, a sudden unpremeditated overwhelming of the faculties by violence for which he takes no responsibility.

One of the strengths of the choric comment, from the aesthetic constructs of the lawyers to the hunches of the citizens, is the sense it gives of the appropriation of the murder by a public, the 'general mind', as Browning calls it (I, 844). One is reminded of Arnold's concern with what, borrowing from Renan, he called the 'general intelligence' in *Culture and Anarchy* and I think the same kind of concern lies behind these parts of *The*

Ring and the Book, manifesting itself as a critical worry about the integrity of language. The mobs who stampede the dead bodies and break down the balustrades, the crowds who gather round Pompilia's death-bed, epitomise anarchic and irrational feeling which gets into the speech even of the self-appointed artists, Hyacinthus and Bottinius. As these speeches are the point at which the whole poem doubles back on itself, reforming or refracting the notion of impulse and intuition, I shall use them to show how the concepts are debased by the values which leak into the words. These gross burlesques are part of a huge semantic cats-cradle suggesting that an ultimate reference in the sanction of inner feeling can be self-defeating

All the speakers except the Pope posit some kind of innate 'natural' morality to explain the case. In the monologues of the lawyers this is carried to a grotesque extreme by being expressed in comically absurd deterministic terms. For Hyacinthus 'blind instinct' (VIII, 533) is aggression; for Bottinius it is sex. Both blandly assume the fallacy that what is natural is excusable because it is spontaneous. Hyacinthus claims with ridiculous pomposity that if 'beasts, quadrupedal, mammiferous,/Do credit to their beasthood' (VIII, 510–511) in instinctual aggression then man, 'creation's master-stroke' and 'intellectual glory' (VIII, 534) vindicates himself by revenge. The argument that 'Revelation old and new admits/The natural man may effervesce in ire' (VIII, 686–687) is ludicrous but it is only the more modest and plausible position of Half-Rome enlarged and simplified in the process. Half-Rome has an atavistic yearning for a primitive morality of 'natural justice'—'*Honoris Causa*, that's the proper term' (II, 29). He sees a simple moral dignity in the dictates of 'natural law' (II, 1477) which impel men to take upon themselves the vindication of their honour—'No—take the old way trod when men were men!' (II, 1524). The Romantic notion of the 'Spontaneous Me' exemplified first in the ethic of 'natural law', reduplicated in Guido's melodramatic 'impulse' and enlarged into 'blind instinct' becomes suspect through these formulations. Pompilia's amazing spontaneous rightness seems as much lucky as good.

Spontaneity is the theme of the monologue of Bottinius and true to his belief in the synthesising power of the imagination he presents the case in thoroughly literary terms as a pastoral of sexuality—'He is Myrtillus, Amaryllis she' (IX, 541). Sexuality is harmless because it is natural and whatever Pompilia's actions she is innocent in the more radical sense that she acted instinctually. Her guilt is a mere 'foible' (IX, 1470)—'Even the blessed Magdalen mistook/Far less forgiveably . . .' (IX, 938–939). He undermines the possibility that Pompilia is really innocent by suggesting that the easy, innocent sexuality of youth which 'nature gave' (IX, 227)—'vernal pranks', 'easily-imagined Hebe-slips/O'er sward which May makes over-smooth for foot' (IX, 235–236)—must flower again after the cruel repression of her marriage and 'spring forth,—sprout here, spread there' (IX, 292). Tiring of Guido, Pompilia beguiled the men of the town, Caponsachi among them, with feminine arts—'armoury thus allowed for natural' (IX, 431). And Caponsachi, seducing her while she slept on the journey to Rome, only gave way to nature.

> For, curiosity—how natural!
> Importunateness—what a privilege
> In the ardent sex!
>
> (IX, 750–752)

This trivialisation acts as a control upon the much less obviously meretricious sentimentality of The Other Half-Rome. 'Men are men' (III, 880), this speaker says, echoing the phrase of Half-Rome, but his doctrine of nature is different. He means that men easily give way to the finer feelings of pity and compassion, 'natural weakness' (III, 836) though this might be. Thus he romanticises Caponsachi's feeling for Pompilia and 'impulse' is put in the context of action taken at the dictate of arbitrary feeling.

> And heart assured to heart in loyalty,
> All at an impulse! All extemporized
> As in romance-books! Is that credible?
> Well, yes.
>
> (III, 920–923)

When declined by Bottinius as 'natural' importunate sexual curiosity the immediate impulse of feeling described by The

Other Half-Rome seems dubious. This is another demonstration of the unstable language of impulse. Tertium Quid says of Caponsachi's action, 'the truth was felt by instinct here,/ —Process which saves a world of trouble and time . . . what do you say to it,/Trying its truth by your own instinct too?' (IV, 1006–1009). Here the same word shifts from meaning sexual to moral instinct. By the ninth monologue it has taken 'a world of trouble and time' to make the most exact discrimination between the values implied in the same words—as they are used, say by Guido and The Other Half-Rome or again by The Other Half-Rome and Pompilia. By this stage in the poem so many variations of meaning have accumulated that every monologue stands in relation to every other monologue.

III

I shall move from the language of the poem to its form in this final section to consider the relevance of the last monologues in the poem, those of the Pope and Guido. After the distortions comes the Pope's recapitulation which establishes a moral norm by using the protean language of impulse in a firmly controlled way. Of Guido he says, 'Not one permissible impulse moves the man' (X, 537). Yet this, just like the poem itself, is a self-qualifying monologue because it is an overt debate on the premises of the poem, and exposes the dilemmas inherent in it. The Pope trusts in 'The Word' (X, 377) though he is aware of the betrayals of language (X, 349–354). Though he gives an unqualified 'self-authorised' moral judgment he acknowledges the historical evidence for the fallibility of papal verdicts (X, 24–162) and constantly recognises the limits of knowledge and perception (X, 1239–1252; 1321–1332). Furthermore he is prepared to understand the cultural and moral consequences of locating judgment in the self and not in institutions or fixed codes. The collapse of institutional morality is inevitable and necessary because the disintegration of these dead forms might bring with it a rebirth of moral energy (X, 1614–1630). Yet once the inner authority of the 'Spontaneous Me' is recognised there is no real need to make the transcendental leap to the ultimate sanction of God. The Pope contemplates the obvious possibility that Caponsachi's miraculous aid to Pompilia could, and with perfect respectability, be described as the prompting of 'an instinct of the natural man' (X, 1583). A noble morality can exist without the sanction of Christian values, but the Pope considers the culture emerging in his own time without equanimity, because it is Comtian and humanistic—the most glaring anachronism of the poem! Worse than the anarchy of individualism, worse than the easy, relativistic morality of 'Ask your hearts' (X, 1924), the tribunals of this culture will be those of 'the educated man's' (X, 1977), the intellectual. The possibility is of a morality impoverished because it is expressed in thin and rational terms or assimilated to the vocabularly of aesthetics. This aestheticised morality speaks in 'the spirit of culture' and 'Civilization' (X, 2017, 2018) which the Pope imagines pleading for the release of Guido—'mercy is safe and *graceful*' (X, 2059). The morality of the heart carries its own weakness within itself because it so easily becomes stale and arid. The new anti-Christ is the debasement of feeling.

Once again the formulation counts here, the exact language used, for the Pope dramatises the implications of the self-authorised judgment effectively by expressing it as 'the spirit of culture' would express it. Yet ultimately the sanction of inner feeling is the only one. The monologue ends with the Pope acknowledging the circularity of judgment and confirming the validity of his own insights exteriorised as a voice—'A voice other than yours/Quickens my spirit . . .' (X, 2099–2100). Yet in spite of this there is a Gerontion-like tone about his soliloquy, the weary dismay of an old man analysing a culture on the ebb.

> I have worn through this sombre wintry day,
> With winter in my soul beyond the world's.
>
> (X, 212–213)

Guido's monologue modifies that of the Pope although it is not easy to see how this happens. It seems at first to have been created simply to corroborate the Pope's (and Browning's) judgment. Guido sees his murder as a consummate work of art ruined only by Caponsachi's unaccountable integrity and the honesty of a petty official (XI, 1560–1563). Claiming total intellectual autonomy and freedom, dismissing belief as at best consolatory—he will not make a formal repentance and die 'the edifying way' (XI, 433) simply to console the church—and at worst propagating an enslaving prudential morality which rests solely upon a meaningless denial of life's 'absolute use' (XI, 1487), he seems to confirm all that the Pope expects of the new authority of the educated man. God is dead, or at least, Jove and the ancient deities resuscitated, foisting upon man the evils for which he is expected to take moral responsibility— 'Irrational bunglers!' (XI, 1975). Guido refuses to take moral responsibility for being 'a mistake' (XI, 939) or for instinctively following the bent of his own nature. Like the other speakers, he makes his instincts the sanction of his actions—'Heart upon dungy earth that's warm and soft' (XI, 758).

But this monologue is more than a ferocious coda displaying an extraordinarily destructive energy and intelligence. Browning says that the Pope's judgment is 'the ultimate/Judgment save yours [the reader's]' (I, 1220–1221) and judgment is finally shaped by Guido's soliloquy. At the same time as it modifies the Pope's verdict it brings to rest the problem teased out in the earlier parts of the poem, the notion of the inner voice of feeling and its implications. Both these things are achieved through Guido's account of his relations with Pompilia —as so often in this poem sexual feeling is an index of moral nature.

The Pope's account of Guido's motive as greed, revenge and self-interest is not entirely complete. The motive is revenge but revenge on her for failing to fulfil his sexual fantasies. Tired and disappointed at fifty, he had hoped to renew himself through her but was enraged by her involuntary disgust—'The thirteen-years' old child, with milk for blood' (XI, 965); 'She eyes me . . . As heifer—the old simile comes pat—/Eyes tremblingly the altar and the priest' (XI, 979). He resented Violante's hint that Pompilia would endure him only because 'nature helps the woman in such strait,/Makes passiveness her pleasure' (XI, 1065–1066). Her patience gives her power over him because he is goaded into fury by it and throughout the monologue he is obsessed by her appalling endurance and the possibility of her unwanted forgiveness.

Occupy your patch
Of private snow that's somewhere in what world
May now be growing icy round your head.

(XI, 2078–2080)

He thinks of Pompilia as having consumed him, 'sucked me dry
of juice' (XI, 211). Both wife and child are a threat to his
identity and he refers ironically to his heir as a 'Treasure' (XI,
220). In Book I Browning says that Guido 'Speaks and des-
pairs' (1283). It is the self-eroding despair of the person who is
governed by a fear of deprivation so strong that he seems to be
without any notion of his own being. Guido feels that death,
paradoxically, may open the possibility of self-discovery. It may
reveal

something changeless at the heart of me
To know me by, some nucleus that's myself.

(XI, 2394–2395)

Meanwhile hate, at least is self-affirming 'Nor is it in me to
unhate my hates,—/I use up my last strength to strike once
more/Old Pietro . . .' (XI, 2400–2402).

Guido's recognition that he lacks the sense of a 'nucleus' of
the self completes the spiral of the poem for it suggests that
whatever weaknesses the sanction of 'self-authorised' action
carries within itself it at least posits some feeling of identity, a
centre, a stable ego, by which the world can be given shape and
meaning. Disintegration and despair follow upon the loss of
belief in 'Something changeless at the heart' of being. The
emotions, which for Pompilia are validated and directed by her
belief in herself, have, as it were turned bad on Guido; they
have taken on a destructive life of their own. And so the poem
returns to its starting point, reasserting the value of self-
authorised insight, the truth 'within ourselves', which has been
so heavily qualified in the convolutions of the monologues. So
heavily qualified, indeed, that there is something of a desperate
last-ditch stand in this poem. Browning shows that Pompilia's
tough, healthful primitivism is an anomaly—she has escaped
some difficulties through a lucky incompleteness. It is no accident that she is illiterate. She is an antidote to Guido, perhaps,
but she is no antidote in a society which must exist through its

intelligence and sophistication. Unlike Pippa, an early Browning innocent, she is a victim. The real opposites of both Guido and Pompilia are Caponsachi and the Pope who are over-burdened with the responsibility of trusting in the 'testimony borne to truth by the mind itself'.

The Ring and the Book sustains itself by virtue of repetition rather than in spite of it. The ring of the title which Browning is at pains to describe in Book I is the autonomy of the created life of the poem smelted from history. It is also the unbroken unity of idea emerging from successive reformulations, binding the monologues together and imaginatively realised through them. Yet in suggesting the shaping principle of the poem I do not mean to imply an extreme formalism and to make every element of the poem 'fit in' to a rigid pattern. A great deal does fit in but a poem of this kind must live by the largeness of the world it creates. In Book I Browning talks of the poem swelling into life, a world reached by the shooting 'beanstalk' of his imagination (I, 1347). One of the primitive advantages of length is that it allows for the sport of creative power and the play of aesthetic exuberance. Keats recognised this when he defended the long poem as 'a little Region to wander in',[11] a description sometimes unreasonably assumed to be an indication of his immaturity. The long poem is a place where sheer imaginative energy can be set in play, as in Browning's description of a Bernini fountain in Book I. It plays a functional part, perhaps, in establishing the locale of the poem, but this is a trivial justification, as grudging as it would be to dismiss this liberated dance of the imagination as an example of 'waste fertility'.

> Where the old Triton, at his fountain-sport,
> Bernini's creature plated to the paps,
> Puffs up steel sleet which breaks to diamond dust,
> A spray of sparkles snorted from his conch,
> High over the caritellas . . .

(I, 898–902)

NOTES

[1] Hugh Sykes Davies, *Browning and the Modern Novel* (Hull, 1962), p. 17.

[2] Robert Langbaum, *The Poetry of Experience* (1957), pp. 112–135.

[3] John Holloway, *The Charted Mirror* (1960), p. 99.

[4] Henry James, *Notes on Novelists* (1914), p. 322.

[5] Paul Valéry, *The Art of Poetry* (1958), vol. VII, p. 315; Ezra Pound, *Literary Essays* (1960), p. 4.

[6] J. S. Bruner, *Towards a Theory of Instruction* (Cambridge Mass., 1966), p. 21.

[7] J. H. Newman, *An Essay in Aid of a Grammar of Assent* (1870).

[8] Wordsworth, *Lyrical Ballads* (1802 Preface), ed. R. L. Brett, A. R. Jones (1963, revised ed., 1965), p. 257: Keats, *Letters of John Keats*, ed. H. E. Rollins (Cambridge, 1958), vol. II, p. 81.

[9] Newman, op. cit., p. 338.

[10] George Santayana, *Interpretations of Poetry and Religion*, Torchbook Series (New York, 1957), p. 199. Newman, op. cit., p. 343.

[11] Keats, op. cit., vol. I, p. 170.

References to Browning's poetry are from *The Works of Robert Browning*, ed. Frederic George Kenyon, 10 vols., (1912).

MATTHEW ARNOLD AND THE PASSAGE OF TIME:
A STUDY OF *THE SCHOLAR-GIPSY* AND *THYRSIS*

Philip Drew

The everlasting substance of the hills
Hath frayed and slidden down, and we no more
Touch the same surface which our fathers trod.

But she with prodigality brings forth
On every bank the virgin saxifrage,
Waving her myriads of white fairy blooms,
This morn, as ever . . .
　　Fragment written on a blank leaf of Herder's
　　Ideen zur Philosophie der Geschichte der Menschheit
　　　　　　　　　　　　　　(Allott p. 584)

A wanderer is man from his birth.
He was born in a ship
On the breast of the river of Time.
　　　　'The Future' (ll. 1–3)

The *movement* he [the poet] must tell of life,
Its pain and pleasure, rest and strife;
His eye must travel down, at full,
The long, unpausing spectacle;
With faithful unrelaxing force
Attend it from its primal source,
From change to change and year to year
Attend it of its mid career,
Attend it to the last repose
And solemn silence of its close.
　　　　'Epilogue to Lessing's Laocoön'
　　　　　　　(ll. 143–152)

Motion is more easily lost than got and is
continually upon the decrease.—Newton

I

One of the infuriating things about Dr. Leavis is that even his asides are remembered and respected as much as his more considered assessments. The passage on the Victorian poets at the beginning of *New Bearings* and the casual dismissal of Arnold in the essay 'Mr. Eliot and Milton' are often quoted not only as being true in themselves but also as indicating by the very cursoriness of their treatment the sort of concern which the poets in question merit. The bright student soon learns how thoroughly to read the authors the professor makes little jokes about.[1]

It is, however, one thing to resent Leavis's offhand scorn for detailed argument and another to imagine how the detailed defence of specific poems should be conducted. *Empedocles*, for example, seems to shrink when confronted with Arnold's own pitilesss critique from the 1853 Preface: 'The suffering finds no vent in action . . . there is everything to be endured, nothing to be done.' The same is true of all his long narratives, such as *Balder*, *Sohrab* and *Tristram*, in which the individual is forced to learn and acknowledge his own powerlessness. He must either act blindly, like Hoder or Rustum, and suffer the consequences, or accept patiently, like Hermod or Iseult, and endure his fate. 'In such situations there is inevitably something morbid, in the description of them something monotonous.'

Many of the shorter pieces are equally hard to defend but, for a different reason. Quiller-Couch said that Arnold seemed to regard himself as Wordsworth's widow: the jibe is unfair enough to be funny and true enough to be damaging. Time and again, even in well-spoken-of poems such as 'Resignation', 'Heine's Grave', or 'Obermann', there is the sense that Arnold is forcing a dutiful emotion of despair or bleak resolution and attaching it to an appropriately misty or austere landscape. What is so difficult to accept when he does this is the conscientious dullness of the language.

The reader may be forgiven for suspecting that Arnold often writes on the forbidding principle laid down in 'Morality' that '. . . tasks in hours of insight willed/Can be through hours of gloom fulfilled'. The result is that in poem after poem Arnold's profoundest insights into the human condition are subdued to the authentic Lake District flatness, often indeed to the point of fatigue and frigidity. If therefore a critic insists that what we ask of poetry is a combination of memorable utterance and a sense that what is being said is worth saying it is no real answer to complain that his terms are unacceptably naïve. We must prepare to meet the blunt question, 'You say that Arnold writes superbly in some poems, and that in others he offers us an argument of great subtlety and importance, but does he ever do both at once?'

To establish a keep on which to base a defence, the friend of Arnold must discover a body of poems in which all the poet's characteristic strengths, such as his powers of natural description, his clear view of his own times, and his flexibility in argument, are simultaneously displayed, not loosely and in isolation, not as a number of separate 'moments', like the end of *Sohrab*, but centrally and in combination. The poems I propose to consider for this Palladium are 'Dover Beach', 'The Forsaken Merman', perhaps 'Isolation', and in particular 'The Scholar-Gipsy' and 'Thyrsis'.

II

'Dover Beach' and 'The Forsaken Merman' are those rare objects, Victorian poems without a single weak line.[2] Even Professor Jump, whose book on Arnold is in general so damning that the reader trembles to think what Jump would say about an author he really disliked, has a good word for 'Dover Beach', as indeed have most critics. At the lowest estimate the poem provides an invaluable concise conspectus of Arnold's major preoccupations and his favourite ways of expressing them. Here I am not thinking so much of his sea-imagery, which many critics have remarked, or of his acute sense of 'the eternal note of sadness', as of the implications of the last section of the poem. Arnold has already used the striking phrase 'the turbid ebb and flow/Of human misery', and in the poem's concluding lines he defines in a pregnant simile his apprehension of the human condition as one of pointless random collision:

201

And we are here as on a darkling plain
Swept with confused alarms of struggle and flight,
Where ignorant armies clash by night.

In this world from which Faith has retreated there is only one
resource suggested—'Ah, love, let us be true/To one another!'
Humphry House has well observed that the desire of the
Victorians to establish abiding human relationships often
reflected their need for warmth, certainty and consolation in
face of the isolation engendered by the uncomfortable discoveries of the scientists.[3]

It is not hard to see how the geologist and the biologist destroyed the idea of special creation, or the way in which theories
of evolution called in question the validity of ethical systems.
But nothing seems to have offered such obvious ground for
pessimism as the laws of thermodynamics, which have become
so notorious in another context. For the obvious implication of
the first law is that in every mechanical process, and indeed in
every form of activity a certain amount of the energy involved
will be converted into heat, which is the least defined form of
energy. The second law, if generally true, describes a Universe
in which energy once dissipated in the form of heat cannot be
recovered except at the cost of an even greater quantity of
energy of some higher kind. It seems to follow that the whole
process of the Universe is one of gradual degeneration from an
earlier state when all matter was charged with potentially useful
energy to an ultimate state in which all energy has been converted to heat, everything is the same temperature, and no life or
identifiable motion exists. Whether we call this a condition of
maximum entropy, or the heat-death of the Universe, or a state
of total randomness is not of any importance. The point is that
if we have this view of the world we must see it as a clock that is
running down; indeed we may think of the gradual increase in
entropy as itself a kind of measurement of time.[4]

Anyone who understood the laws of thermodynamics in this
sense, and such interpretations were not uncommon in the
nineteenth century, would have strong grounds for a pessimistic
view of all human activity. For the picture that represents the
span of the Universe is of two forces at work. First, through

living matter, which implies organisation, and is most clearly exemplified by purposeful communities of creatures, determining and controlling their own environment, there appears to be a steady progress in redeeming Earth from the primal Chaos. At the same time a slower, but surer, tendency of the kind I have described draws everything irresistibly to a state of total disorganisation. The history of the Universe is thus a chronicle of inevitable decay, terminating at the point when nothing is available except general information in a statistical form.

It is but a short step to the use of this picture of the physical world as a metaphor for any kind of human behaviour which, while it may in fact impose some kind of organisation on matter, is short-sighted, careless, heedless, or reckless of its consequences for society. We use 'disorderly' quite correctly for any conduct which offends against our sense of organisation or fitness for purpose. Hence we have a complex of ideas in which randomness or lack of particularised information, purposeless human activity, and the passing of time are intimately linked, and stand as symbols for one another. Thus emotions such as regret for lost youth or vexation at the sort of unintelligent human behaviour that resulted in the great urban slums of Victorian Britain are but different faces of the same coin. Either emotion can be transposed into grief that in time the entire fabric of the Universe will be without energy or movement or meaning: either emotion thus offers an immediate route to a pessimism of the most thorough-going kind, especially difficult to combat because it is justified by an apparently irrefragable chain of scientific reasoning.

A precisely similar complex of ideas finds linked expression in many of Arnold's poems.[5] 'The Future' is one of many obvious examples: Arnold says that as the world grows older

> Our minds
> Are confused as the cries which we hear,
> Changing and shot as the sights which we see.
> And we say that repose has fled
> For ever the course of the river of Time.
> That cities will crowd to its edge
> In a blacker, incessanter line;
> That the din will be more on its banks,

Denser the trade on its stream,
Flatter the plain where it flows,
Fiercer the sun overhead.

(ll. 55–65)

The use of a model of this kind serves also to place Arnold's
ideas of artistic creation as one of the few modes of human
activity which, with only a minimal dissipation of energy as heat,
really do impose an organisation on the world and thus apparently arrest the resistless flux of time. 'These fragments I have
shored against my ruins.' This is why Arnold's most poignant
moments of desolation occur when he feels that human beings
cannot, by their nature, communicate even through art, but
are eternally separated by the 'unplumbed, salt, estranging
sea'.

It is this quality, the 'pity and mournful awe' which Arnold
speaks of in 'Grande Chartreuse', that seems to me to be the
most powerful informing force in Arnold's best poems. In
'Resignation' and 'Isolation' the terms of the poem so qualify
any tentative expressions of hope that it is hard to be certain of
more than the quality of Arnold's initial despair, while in
'Dover Beach' the frailty of personal defences against the
impersonal forces of darkness is so strongly emphasised that the
final impression is one almost of desperation. 'The Forsaken
Merman' is, I think, a genuinely pathetic piece, and is not
fairly accused of sentimentality, but its short lines, its insistent
rhythms and refrains, the reminiscences of Hans Andersen, and
the carefully paternal tone combine to place it in the category
of a nursery poem, and thus to diminish its value as a mature
comment on life. All that remains of my chosen few of Arnold's
poems is 'The Scholar-Gipsy' and its sequel and counterpart,
'Thyrsis'.

III

The closeness of the two poems is easily established. They have
the same metre, the same stanza-form, the same *locale*, the same
deliberate reminiscences of the diction of earlier poets, the
same characters, and the same mythology—the public pastoral
mythology and the private Scholar-Gipsy mythology. Arnold

said of 'Thyrsis' in his note of 1867, 'Throughout this poem there is reference to another piece, "The Scholar Gipsy" ', and in lines 28–30 of 'Thyrsis' he refers directly to the Gipsy-Scholar himself. In the remainder of this essay I shall examine the consequences of regarding 'Thyrsis' and 'The Scholar-Gipsy' not as separate poems but as two parts of the same poem. I shall try to show that these parts represent successive stages in the development of an argument by poetic means, that the poem as a whole is an achievement of great complexity which it is impossible not to admire, and that it offers a view of the world and of man's place in the world which is of importance.

At first sight the poem seems to be a collection of familiar Arnoldian tricks. Anyone acquainted with his poetry must have noticed his extraordinary capacity for extracting a melancholy reflection from the landscape. So uniform is this habit that it is almost impossible to find in Arnold's poems a tract of countryside which is not in one way or another charged with emotion, the emotion being invariably grief or regret.[6] Arnold has many routes to the same destination. First, Nature, being what man is not, implies the incompleteness of man, at which Arnold grieves. 'Rome-Sickness', 'Self-Dependence', 'Youth of Nature' and 'Youth of Man' are examples of this technique. Specifically Nature is unchanging, but man grows old, at which Arnold grieves. This is illustrated in 'Growing Old' and many other poems, notably the first stanza of 'The River'. (The point becomes so firmly established that in 'Thyrsis' Arnold can contrive an additional pathos from the fact that man has changed part of the countryside—'How changed is here each spot man makes or fills'.) Thirdly Nature is unified, especially the sea, but man is isolated, at which Arnold grieves. For this use of natural imagery see the last two stanzas of 'The Terrace at Berne', 'To Marguerite' ('Yes, in the sea of life'), and 'Obermann Once More' (lines 209 ff.). Finally Nature was everything that noisy, pushful, urban Victorian Britain was not. This appears in poems such as 'Lines Written in Kensington Gardens' and 'On the Rhine': Arnold knew enough of the world to realise that Britain was certain to grow steadily more urban. The countryside thus represents the past, the 'old haunt', and is a symbol of the inexorable forces of time and a constant reminder of human powerlessness. Hence a further sort of grief.

All these ways of charging a landscape with emotion are employed in 'The Scholar-Gipsy' and 'Thyrsis', the third much less noticeably than the others. Such devices are normally local, not structural, except in very short pieces. If they occur in isolation they gratify the rhetorical not the poetical sense of the reader, to adopt the terminology of the 1853 Preface. But in the diptych Arnold shifts from one stance to another with amazing fluidity, using the simple features of the Berkshire countryside to establish again and again the incompleteness of human existence. The change of focus becomes almost an end in itself, corresponding to the great waves of irrational yearning that sweep over Arnold.

To a countryside charged with emotion in this way Arnold introduces a small cast of characters, notably himself and Clough and the figure of the Scholar. In 'The Scholar-Gipsy' Arnold uses the anecdote from Glanvil as a myth expressing the need to avoid contagion by 'the world's slow stain'. The question it poses in its simple form is whether it is possible for a young man to avoid the challenge of the modern world. In 'Thyrsis' the question is put in another way: if a middle-aged man is immersed in 'the world and wave of men' does this mean that the ideal world he dreamed of when he was young and indeed for a time enjoyed, is in fact thereby destroyed? The two questions are shown to be related when the Scholar-Gipsy is formally identified with a particular tree in the familiar landscape ('Thyrsis', ll. 26–30). The importance of the landscape is confirmed in lines 101–104, where Arnold lays down the equivalence between time and place on which so much of his poem turns:

> Well! wind-dispersed and vain the words will be,
>> Yet, Thyrsis, let me give my grief its hour
>>> In the old haunt, and find our tree-topped hill!
> Who, if not I, for questing here hath power?

'The old haunt' is a richly charged phrase, which is defined more closely as the poem proceeds. Just as the Scholar-Gipsy hoped to draw down poetic inspiration by retiring from the world (line 50), so Arnold's desire to rediscover 'the old haunt' is intimately connected with his and Clough's vocation as poets.[7] 'The old haunt' is not simply the country as opposed to 'the rank life of towns'. It is the life of the countryside, innocent, restorative, and making for easy natural poetry, while the 'city-noise' and 'the great town's harsh heart-wearying roar' represent all the forces that overtask and ultimately silence a poet's voice. Again 'the old haunt' stands for Arnold's own youth, when poetry flowed comparatively easily, whereas now 'the mount is mute, the channel dry'. Finally it is the world's young time, when it was natural to write poetry. 'We had not lost our balance then', whereas now the poet is confronted at every turn by the 'bleakness, barrenness, unpoetryness' of 'the damned times'. The two poems, which at first appear to be simply a collection of skilful rural vignettes, or a box of colour slides of Best-Loved English Scenes, are thus Arnold's instrument for expressing some of his deepest intuititions about his world, about poetry, about human relationships and about the human condition.

In particular Arnold embodies in the fabric of his poem the one ultimately irresistible force of destruction, Time.[8] This is apparent when the Scholar-Gipsy is the main focus of attention but it is even more sharply conveyed in 'Thyrsis', which reaches back through layers of past time. They may be schematised as follows.

1. The present moment, or time of writing the poem.
2. The 'winter-eve' on which the poem is set.
2.1–2.9 Constant references to points between 2 and 3. For example, Clough's death, Arnold's departure from Oxford, Clough and Arnold both find it progressively more difficult to write poetry, Clough leaves Oxford, Arnold experiences the emotions embodied in 'The Scholar-Gipsy', and so on. These occur and recur like episodes in a 'long unhappy dream'.
3. The 'jocund, youthful time' when Arnold and Clough were together at Oxford. This is, of course, another way of regarding 'the haunt beloved'. In this context it is first the time of physical vigour, 'thine height of strength, thy golden prime,' what Arnold described in a letter to his brother Tom (15 May 1857) as 'that life at Oxford, the *freest* and most delightful part, perhaps, of my

life, when with you and Clough and Walrond I . . . enjoyed the spring of life and that unforgotten Oxfordshire and Berkshire country'. Secondly it was the age when truth seemed attainable, and finally the age when it was possible for Arnold and Clough to 'sing' naturally.

4. The time when the Scholar-Gipsy was alive, a doubly happy time, since 'the strange disease of modern life' with its 'divided aims' had not yet begun, and poetry came naturally, because it was 'the bent of the time'. Eliot, like Arnold, placed the crucial dissociation of sensibility in the seventeenth century.

5. The age of pastoral, in which we must locate the world of *Lycidas*, of Spenser, and of Greek and Latin pastoral poetry.

6. Even behind this there are (*a*) the time when men really were shepherds and (*b*) the mythical age of Orpheus and Daphnis. Arnold does not distinguish between these two in point of remoteness. 3, 4, 5 and 6 are used, singly or in combination, to express the happy past, which stands in constant contrast to 1, 2 and 2.1–2.9. It is clear that 4, 5 and 6 are vanished beyond recall, and it is Time which has vanquished them—'Time, not Corydon, hath conquered thee': but what of 3? Has this also been destroyed? If so, then Time has indeed conquered all things.

In this way Arnold generates his characteristic sensation of helpless despair at the inevitable ebbing away of Time, an emotion very close indeed to that with which many of his contemporaries regarded their own subjection to unalterable physical laws. Thus Arnold's lightest rural image carries an extraordinarily potent charge of feeling, for the countryside becomes a vast clock—that which measures the swallowing up of human hopes, the hardening of human sensibilities, the drying up of poetic inspiration, and the encroachments of the towns.[9]

IV

The movement of the double poem is simple and massive and not difficult to trace. Having established the scene and the multiple equivalences to be attached to the countryside, Arnold reinforces his imagery by an invocation of the Scholar-Gipsy, the *genius loci* of Cumnor. Arnold does not at once explain whether the Scholar owes his immunity from 'disease' to the happier times in which he was born or to his prescience in leaving the world early, or to both. All Arnold tells us is that the Scholar has not felt 'the lapse of hours': he is 'exempt from age' because he has avoided the life of the modern world. At this point (141 ff.) Arnold moves from the vivid description of an actual landscape into the language of abstraction—'change to change', 'repeated shocks . . . numb the elastic powers', 'bliss and teen', 'a thousand schemes'. In contrast to the firm physical imagery which characterises the Scholar and his world, modern man is marked by vague, widely-applicable *classes* of experience. The effect is of an almost Oriental passivity, as if men were only vehicles for happenings. This is enhanced by the Omar-like cadence of lines 147–150:

> Till having used our nerves with bliss and teen,
> And tired upon a thousand schemes our wit,
> To the just-pausing Genius we remit
> Our worn-out life, and are—what we have been.

Here and in the following stanza[10] Arnold is deliberately speaking in terms which await their explanation—'we are— what we have been', 'Thou hadst—what we, alas! have not'.

In particular we have to learn what gave the Scholar his immunity: the explanations follow. First he fled while he was young 'with powers/Fresh, undiverted to the world without'.[11] Those who have to go on living find that age itself brings dis- satisfaction. The unsatisfactoriness is rendered in Arnold's intangible, slippery vocabulary—'sick fatigue', 'languid doubt', 'much to have tried, in much been baffled', 'nor knows for what he strives', 'casual creeds', 'vague resolves', 'new begin- nings, disappointments new'. The faults and griefs of modern man are touched in the widest possible terms in phrases such as 'Who hesitate and falter life away,/And lose tomorrow the ground won today'. These idle fluctuations 'without term or scope' contrast painfully, by their generality and randomness, with the Gipsy's '*one* aim, *one* business, *one* desire'.[12]

The mysterious stanzas about Tennyson[13] serve partly to emphasise that the diptych, like *Adonais* and *Lycidas*, is a poem about poetry, partly to demonstrate how impossible it is to write with nobility, sanity and precision, when all that the world has now to offer us is a 'store of sad experience'. We, and this includes Clough, can only pine, wish for the end, and endure. The hope that we can no longer nourish remains with the Scholar-Gipsy because he is still a 'truant boy' and still has the resilience of youth.

Arnold has by now come close to the second reason for the Scholar's immunity, his good luck in being 'born in days when wits were fresh and clear'. This was doubly fortunate, since earlier ages were not simply easier to live in, because they were calmer, but easier to write poetry in. The idea which occupies the rest of 'The Scholar-Gipsy' is the importance for the Scholar of avoiding 'feverish contact' with the modern world. A series of imperatives, reinforced by images of disease, exhort the Scholar to keep clear of 'the infection of our mental strife'. 'Fly hence, our contact fear!' Exactly what the Scholar has to preserve and precisely how the modern world would corrupt him need not be specified: it is enough for him to be warned that 'thy cheer would die,/Thy hopes grow timorous, and unfixed thy powers,/And thy clear aims be cross and shifting made'. It is also plain that if he is to preserve his 'free onward impulse' his refuge must be 'far on the forest-skirts, where none pursue', and in the liquid beauties of lines 211–220 the country-side receives its final idealisation in the poem as the only place of health.

This stanza and the next epitomise, in their firm confrontation of different kinds of language, the method of 'The Scholar-Gipsy'. The first in characteristic Arnoldian lover-language about nature (he takes a voluptuary's pleasure in the recesses of the countryside) indicates that the Scholar can preserve his 'unconquerable hope' and his 'inviolable shade' only by plunging ever deeper in 'the bowering wood'. He must avoid 'us' for we are plague-ridden. There follows a catalogue of symptoms, characteristically abstract, which would impair the Scholar's hopes, powers, aims, and, as a climax, his youth. His salvation can lie only in flight. This suggests an explanation of the concluding simile of 'The Scholar-Gipsy', a notorious point of difference among critics.

Setting aside its obvious *punctuating* rôle in the poem[14] and the way it provides a bridge to the Greek myths which lie behind 'Thyrsis', we may say that it sums up in itself all that Arnold has said so far. The Tyrian trader with his gravity of demeanour and settled habits resents the coming of a different way of life, symbolised by the youthful Greeks with their cheerfulness, their novel methods of commerce, and their exotic consumer-goods (doubtless with trading stamps). The Tyrian, however, cannot stop the advance of time, any more than Arnold could. His only resource is to change location, to travel Westward back through space and time to a more primitive people. This device, though not, as Saintsbury points out, immediately applicable to the Scholar, is precisely that adopted by Arnold himself when he returns to 'the old haunt', that is to say a place which is further back in time than metropolitan life.

The opening of 'Thyrsis' picks up 'The Scholar-Gipsy' as exactly as one movement of a symphony picks up another. The landscape is the same. Arnold presents his credentials for using it—'Once passed I blindfold here, at any hour'. He hints at a pastoral frame by the use of the name 'Thyrsis', but otherwise the emphasis is on reality: all that suggests a poetic convention is the insistent inversion, and even this sounds a little weary and middle-aged. He begins by exclaiming that 'each spot *man* makes or fills' has been altered, and asks 'Are ye too changed, ye hills?' The poem, that is, is to be about the alterations wrought by Time, and the question to be asked is whether Nature is as mutable as human institutions. Finally Arnold distances the earlier poem, making it part of a younger, happier time; this difference is signified by a change in the figure in each half of the diptych.

In 'The Scholar-Gipsy' the correlative is a mythical figure of a young man, about to be a poet, who has somehow managed to avoid the contagion of the world and moves freely through a countryside of which he has become a part. In 'Thyrsis' the correlative is an uphill journey on foot at the end of a winter's day by a middle-aged man finding his way by memory through an altered countryside in search of a tree whose position he has forgotten and which may no longer be where it was. He is not to write very much more poetry. The countryside which he once knew so well but which is now so altered is of course the first half of 'The Scholar-Gipsy'.

That single elm-tree bright
Against the west—I miss it! is it gone?
We prized it dearly; while it stood, we said,
Our friend, the Gipsy-Scholar, was not dead;
While the tree lived, he in these fields lived on.

('Thyrsis', ll. 26–30)

As I have suggested, the journey which Arnold has to make in
'Thyrsis' is not simply by the Great Western. He is travelling
back through time.

That Arnold was completely in control of these complex
temporal manipulations can be seen from lines 31–40, where the
pastoral convention is not used as a way of avoiding direct
speech about the world as it is, but as a symbol (not just the
words that refer to a symbol, but as an actual thing present in
the poem, a sort of concrete poetry) of Arnold's youth and of his
earlier poetry.

Ah me! this many a year
My pipe is lost, my shepherd's holiday!

(ll. 36–37)

The plural 'them' in line 38 shows that these are not in loose
apposition, but are two distinct deprivations. This change in
Arnold between the time of 'The Scholar-Gipsy' and the time
of 'Thyrsis' is of course crucial in the operation of the double
poem. It is a simplification, but a venial one, to say that
'Thyrsis' is 'about' a re-reading by the poet of 'The Scholar-
Gipsy' fifteen years after he had written it. The recurrent
question can be briefly put in the form

Now times are altered; if I care
To buy a thing, I can;
The pence are here and here's the fair,
But where's the lost young man?[15]

The themes of this stanza are taken up at the conclusion of the
poem.

As I have said, the progression of the poem is easy enough to
follow. No commentary is needed, except to draw attention to
the way in which the clichés of pastoral convention are restored
to life and interest by their placing in a progressively more

complicated time-scheme. In line 80 a further term is introduced, the originating age of pastoral poetry. In the past poets
had 'easy access to the hearer's grace' and Proserpine would
listen to a 'Dorian pipe'

> But ah, of our poor Thames she never heard!
> Her foot the Cumner cowslips never stirred;
> And we should tease her with our plaint in vain!

> Well! wind-dispersed and vain the words will be . . .

The time when you could 'descend into yourself and produce
the best of your thought and feeling naturally' is past: to do so
now requires 'an overwhelming and in some degree morbid
effort'.[16]

Each apparently artless and purely decorative natural image
is thus infinitely extended in time and space, so that, for
example, the 'warm green-muffled Cumner hills' and 'the
sweet spring-days' with their 'whitening hedges and uncrump-
ling fern' stand for whole tracts of Arnold's life and happiness,
and the phrase 'our happy ground' represents everything that
Time devours. To demonstrate how intricately yet effortlessly
this is brought about would require a detailed analysis of the
double poem, but an account of a short passage (lines 111–150)
will illustrate many of the things I have been saying.

> 'I know these slopes; who knows them if not I?'

Arnold once again gives his credentials: to know Cumnor is a
kind of talisman. But even the country, which was a visible
token of his youth, has changed. Many woods have been
ploughed up and 'since our day put by/The coronals of that
forgotten time'. The primroses, which were the pledges of
spring, have been forced into more retired spots. Using here
with entire appropriateness the old *Ubi sunt?* formula, Arnold
laments also the passing of the tutelary figures of the countryside, such as the mowers and the lock-keeper's daughter. 'They
all are gone and thou art gone as well!'

At this turning-point in the poem the emphasis falls heavily
on the loss of youth, and in particular on Arnold's feeling that
old age is upon him. He grieves not so much for the physical

symptoms (though he details these with candour) as for the loss of vitality, sensibility and hope (ll. 138–140). Even more painfully he has lost the sense which he had in youth that it was possible to reach some sort of certainty: now 'unbreachable the fort/Of the long-battered world uplifts its wall'. It is impossible to bring clarity out of 'the earthly turmoil' and thus everything a man does appears 'strange and vain', until he longs for death. The transition from regret at the changes in an actual landscape to grief for the universal condition of man is flawlessly exhibited. Just as the night is the 'winter-eve' of the poem and the grave, so the revenant is looking for an actual tree and for Truth. What he learns when he comes back is that the landscape which he has invested with his golden memories is itself a mutable thing. The pastoral images no longer console, since they are seen to be themselves figures for a harsher truth, 'For Time, not Corydon, hath conquered thee'. By line 150, then, Arnold has taken the despair and disgust of 'The Scholar-Gipsy' and re-established them on a much more convincing basis, using as his instrument the passage of time between the two poems, which has taken his youth from him and brought the world closer to its ultimate end in featureless disorder.

V

If I am confronted at this point with the objection that Arnold himself in the 1853 Preface raised to situations of this kind— 'when they occur in actual life, they are painful, not tragic; and the representation of them in poetry is painful also'—it is clear that I shall contend that Arnold does offer us a legitimate pleasure even though he represents the plight of modern man as one of helpless suffering and an inevitable progression away from the sources of light and energy. 'The mind naturally loves truth', Johnson says, and Arnold gives pleasure because he tells the truth, to put the matter in deliberately naive terms; because, moreover, he sets his own grief for Clough, for his lost youth and for his ill-luck in falling on an uncongenial age in the context of a universal lament for the fate of modern man he avoids making a personal appeal for our pity, which distinguishes him from, say, Housman. He is equally far from the luxuriant melancholy of Swinburne or FitzGerald, and from the bleak pride of Hardy.

If Arnold had ended his poem at line 150, one might indeed apply to it his own verdict on Lucretius,—'overstrained, gloom-weighted, morbid'—but there is a final turn to come. Arnold welcomes the advancing night in terms which make it quite plain that 'night' is 'death', the total eclipse of 'life's morning-sun'. Then, just as it seems that he must abandon the quest and return to the present, unable to find any evidence that the past time he has sought to discover even existed, there is a Wordsworthian 'moment':

> See,
> Backed by the sunset, which doth glorify
> The orange and pale violet evening-sky,
> Bare on its lonely ridge, the Tree! the Tree!
>
> I take the omen! Eve lets down her veil,
> The white fog creeps from bush to bush about,
> The west unflushes, the high stars grow bright,
> And in the scattered farms the lights come out.
> I cannot reach the signal-tree tonight,
> Yet, happy omen, hail!
>
> (ll. 157–166)

It is an error to suppose that this is offered as a triumphant climax. Arnold does not reach the tree. In fact he recognises that he cannot reach it *'tonight'* (i.e. before he dies); what the epiphany does grant him is the assurance that the tree was not imaginary, that the vigour, certainty and happiness of youth are realities, even though he can no longer recover them.

Clough, now dead and buried in Florence, has, like the Scholar, found a way of escaping decay and corruption, by flight to his 'boon southern country'. He has escaped, that is, back into time and is now listening to 'the immortal chants of old' in the mythical age which lay even before Classical pastoral poetry. He is among 'the flowery oleanders pale' leaving Arnold among the 'brambles pale with mist engar-landed'.[17]

> There thou art gone, and me thou leavest here
> Sole in these fields! yet will I not despair.

Despair I will not, while I yet descry
'Neath the mild canopy of English air
That lonely tree against the western sky.
Still, still these slopes, 'tis clear,
Our Gipsy-Scholar haunts, outliving thee!

(ll. 191–197)

Arnold now moves close to identifying himself with the Scholar. 'A fugitive and gracious light he seeks,/Shy to illumine; and I seek it too.' This quest is prophylactic against *tempus edax rerum*:

the smooth-slipping weeks
Drop by, and leave its seeker still untired;
Out of the heed of mortals he is gone,
He wends unfollowed, he must house alone;
Yet on he fares, by his own heart inspired.

(ll. 206–210)

This is because the whole idea of a quest implies a fixed object in life, which in turn implies that all activity is not random, since some principle of order is to be discerned.

In the last two stanzas the country imagery is used in what is by comparison a slightly less brilliantly original way. From the time of Wordsworth the fourth use of Nature-as-a-source-of-woe had been a commonplace, and a poetic resource exploited by all the great British poets of the century except Browning. Arnold freshens it a little, but perhaps not enough for some tastes, by stating the contrast in terms of poetic art, recalling the earlier lines 'Ah me! this many a year/My pipe is lost, my shepherd's holiday'. At the beginning of 'The Scholar-Gipsy' Clough was addressed in terms designed to recall *Lycidas*. As a shepherd he has a duty to his flock, the work of the world must be done, and the 'bawling fellows' must be kept quiet: but when this is done he will return to the poet, who is set among, but insulated from, the sights, sounds and scents of the countryside. 'Here till sundown, shepherd, will I be.' The shepherd's life thus established as one of hard work, the pastoral convention lapses and the idealised countryside merges with the actual fields and woods of Cumnor.

At the end of 'Thyrsis' Clough is again addressed in the

language of pastoral, but with a significant change. The shepherd's life is now seen not as one of labour but as a desirable, though unavailable, refuge from the still harsher life of the city. This contrast is economically conveyed in the image of Clough's 'rustic flute', now silent for ever. It is a flute because it symbolises a kind of simple spontaneous melodic poetry. It is rustic in tribute to the pastoral convention, which in turn stands for a 'jocund, youthful time'. It is rustic too in opposition to 'the great town's harsh, heart-wearying roar',[18] and Arnold, bearing all these meanings in mind, and weighing his situation in life, comments without self-pity:

> Too rare, too rare, grow now my visits here!
>   'Mid city-noise, not, as with thee of yore,
>   Thyrsis! in reach of sheep-bells is my home.

(ll. 231–233)

'Growing Old' and 'The Progress of Poetry' echo in these lines.[19] What keeps them from being simply a bid for the reader's pity is their placing in a universal context. 'The night/In ever-nearing circle weaves her shade' about us all. Arnold's comfort is but a 'whisper': *'Why faintest thou? I wandered till I died./Roam on! The light we sought is shining still.'* It is a scanty, unheroic message.[20] The point about it however is not its content: the wonder is that it can be transmitted at all. Normally in Arnold we meet with the assumption or conclusion that 'we mortal millions live alone' and that no communication is possible between beings separated by 'the unplumbed, salt, estranging sea'. Yet the whole movement of his great double-poem turns on his avowal in the last few stanzas that Clough, whether alive or dead, can in some sense 'speak' to his friend and fellow-poet.

It is important to note the qualified and provisional nature of the hope which Arnold embraces (and by implication, extends).[21] It is equally important to notice the passive rôle played by the poet: he is literally passive of course in the sense of being a sufferer, but he is passive also in the sense that his part in the poem is confined to waiting for the spark from heaven to fall, urging the still active Scholar to fly from contact with him, and turning back with his quest still unfulfilled. The result is that we have in this poem a fine example of something rare

217

in verse—a limited, measured effect deliberately chosen to represent a constricted situation. 'Constricted' is I think the right word to express the quality of the poet's unease. It is not, as we have seen, an inflexible despair, such as Arnold detected and reprobated in Lucretius, or in his own *Empedocles*, but can best be described in the words Arnold himself applies to a greater poet than Lucretius:

> Over the whole Aeneid there rests an ineffable melancholy: not a rigid, a moody gloom, like the melancholy of Lucretius; no, a sweet, a touching sadness, but still a sadness; a melancholy which is at once a source of charm in the poem, and a testimony to its incompleteness.
>
> ('On the Modern Element in Literature')

The last few words of that quotation point to a line of criticism which is frequently taken against Arnold. What I have been trying to show is that the melancholy in the double-poem is not a symptom of the failure of poetic control or of the lack of moral fibre; it is what the poem is all about—the feelings of man at the passage of time, the fear that life is no more than an inevitable process of decay and disintegration, an inert world created by reference to inert poetic traditions, the personal and the cultural dismays interpenetrating, and the limited scope of the dramatic action reflecting the limited choices available to modern man. It is the territory of *The Waste Land*. What distinguishes Arnold from Eliot is the finesse and assurance with which he handles this complex of ideas while remaining strictly within the confines of traditional form.

Eliot's problem in 1922 had been Arnold's nearly sixty years earlier, that what he had to say about his life and the world he lived in was to be expressed only in an image of constricted man. This makes it very hard for Arnold to obey his own desires to write pragmatic poetry.[22] He seems to be quite conscious of his own dilemma. About ten years earlier in 'The Grande Chartreuse' he had written:

> My melancholy, sciolists say,
> Is a past mode, an outworn theme . . .
> Ah, if it *be* passed, take away,
> At least, the restlessness, the pain;

Be man henceforth no more a prey
To these out-dated stings again!

(ll. 99–106)

He meets his critics by challenging them to show that his dejection is not amply warranted by the miseries of existence:

> The kings of modern thought are dumb;
> Silent they are, though not content,
> And wait to see the future come.
> They have the grief men had of yore,
> But they contend and cry no more.

(ll. 116–120)

Byron, Shelley and Senancour cried aloud, but what good did they do? 'Have restless hearts one throb the less?' On the whole the 'sons of the world' ignored the poets and went on their self-confident way. To them Arnold remarks in the same tone of unemphatic irony:

> We admire with awe
> The exulting thunder of your race;
> You give the universe your law,
> You triumph over time and space!
> Your pride of life, your tireless powers,
> We laud them, but they are not ours.

(ll. 163–168)

Unlike the 'sons of the world' Arnold recognises his own inability to conquer time and space, and his twin poem is devoted to demonstrating his own thraldom to Time. But since he maintains that the constriction which he expresses is at least as important an element in Victorian life as its superficial buoyancy and expansiveness, he is able to claim in 1869 that his poetry, if not obviously pragmatic, nevertheless embodied one of the main currents of Victorian thought:

My poems represent, on the whole, the main movement of mind of the last quarter of a century, and thus they will probably have their day as people become conscious to themselves of what the movement of mind is, and interested in the literary productions which reflect it. It might be fairly argued that I have less poetical sentiment than Tennyson, and less intellectual vigour and abundance than Browning: yet, because I have perhaps more of a fusion of the two than either of them, and have more regularly applied that fusion to the main line of modern development, I am likely enough to have my turn, as they have had theirs.

I have no intention of awarding gold, silver, and bronze medals; it is enough to consider the justice of Arnold's account of his own qualities. His claim to fuse 'poetical sentiment' with 'intellectual vigour' can, I think, be granted with respect to 'The-Scholar-Gipsy-and-Thyrsis' and some other poems, which I have quoted and which come, so to speak, under its aegis. The following stanza, for example, has seldom been denied 'poetical sentiment'. If, as we read it, we bear in mind the whole context in which it is set, I think that we can grant it also intellectual abundance and vigour, just as we recognise these qualities in the Odes of Keats:

> So, some tempestuous morn in early June,
>   When the year's primal burst of bloom is o'er,
>   Before the roses and the longest day—
> When garden-walks and all the grassy floor
>   With blossoms red and white of fallen May
>   And chestnut-flowers are strewn—
> So have I heard the cuckoo's parting cry,
>   From the wet fields, through the vexed garden-trees,
>   Come with the volleying rain and tossing breeze:
>   *The bloom is gone, and with the bloom go I!*

My argument is thus that we should value Arnold's twin-poem for its 'truth and seriousness' as 'a criticism of life', to use his own familiar phrases. The crucial step, which I have tried to take in this paper, is to show that we find in the poem an understanding of man in the modern world as precise and comprehensive as that which we willingly acknowledge and admire in his prose works.

VI

In conclusion let us look once more at the most influential of modern critics of Arnold. Of 'The Scholar-Gipsy' Dr. Leavis writes:

'Thou hadst—what we, alas, have not.' And that is *clearly* all that

Arnold knows about it. He exhibits the Scholar as drifting about the Oxford countryside in an eternal week-end. 'For early didst thou leave the world'—and what the poem *actually* offers is a charm of relaxation, a holiday from serious aims and exacting business.

And what the Scholar-Gipsy *really* symbolizes is Victorian poetry, vehicle (so often) of explicit intellectual and moral intentions, but unable to be *in essence* anything but relaxed, relaxing and anodyne.

(*The Common Pursuit*; my italics)[23]

The worth of such a passage as a piece of connected argument is not hard to judge. What is most interesting about it is Leavis's total disregard of all the features of 'The Scholar-Gipsy' and 'Thyrsis' which I have tried to draw attention to. Possibly they simply do not exist in the poem, in which case Leavis is possibly right. But if they are there, then Leavis is wrong about Arnold, and may therefore be wrong in the argument or chain of assertions which he bases on his reading of Arnold.

In short, when our century undertakes the serious rereading of Victorian poetry to which this book is a contribution, I think we shall find that the 'ideas' of the Victorians are not as 'inferior in vigour and force' as it is at present fashionable to maintain. Nor are they without relevance to our own concerns. A final quotation from Leavis, this time from *Two Cultures?*, makes the point:

Really distinguished minds are themselves, of course, *of* their age; they are responsive at the deepest level to its peculiar strains and challenges: that is why they are able to be truly illuminating and prophetic and to influence the world positively and creatively.

NOTES

[1] Especially if he makes the same joke twice, cf. *Revaluation* (1936), p. 191. A comparison of the two passages is not without interest. We notice, for example, that in the earlier essay Dr. Leavis observes that it is an error to try to examine Wordsworth's thought. 'His triumph is to command the kind of attention he requires and to permit no other' (p. 156). 'In the key passages . . . the convincing success of the poetry covers the argument' (p. 159). In the later essay Arnold is held up to scorn for precisely the same attribute:

'The nobility and sonority go with a subtly "musical" use of language—the "emphasis" is sufficiently "on the sound" to save the "idea" from close scrutiny' (*The Common Pursuit*, 'Mr Eliot and Milton'). If the two essays are taken together they provide an example of an exceedingly scarce type of argument. From *The Common Pursuit* we find that one of the most telling arguments against Milton is that he exercised a pernicious effect on Arnold. Those who ask how we can be sure that Arnold was a bad poet may be referred to *Revaluation*, where they will learn that his poetry belongs in ethos with the 'Georgian week-enders'. 'Such pastoralists as the late John Freeman, in fact . . . show obvious marks of his influence.'

[2] Kenneth Allott thinks that 'Dover Beach', 23, is 'dubiously "poetical" ', but A. Dwight Culler (*Imaginative Reason*, p. 40) seems to me to make a good case for it.

[3] *All in Due Time* (1955), p. 133.

[4] Arnold indeed makes Nature say at one point, speaking of her own earlier days, 'I knew not yet the gauge of time,/Nor wore the manacles of space' ('Morality', 31–32).

[5] I am not, of course, arguing that Arnold was familiar with the work of Carnot or Clausius or Kelvin when he wrote *Empedocles on Etna*, any more than Pope was when he wrote Book IV of *The Dunciad*, or that Tennyson had read Darwin and Wallace when he wrote *In Memoriam*; simply that a construct of this kind, with the additional attraction of the coincidence of dates, makes Arnold's ideas about time and human behaviour easier to follow.

[6] Of course, in many places Arnold explicitly *recommends* a more positive attitude to the natural world, but what I am concerned with here is the way in which he actually *uses* the countryside in his own poetry.

[7] Note how this is corroborated by the language of the poem, which deliberately recalls Keats, who died young, and Gray, who was never able to speak out. The most interesting example of this is to be found in 'The Scholar-Gipsy', ll. 136–140, where Arnold tells himself that the Scholar must by now be dead and have become part of 'some country-nook': he has been reabsorbed into the countryside and is neatly laid to rest in quotations from Gray's 'Elegy'.

[8] Richard Giannone if anything understates the point when he says '*Thyrsis* is a poem in which the sense of time is crucial, as central, I would say, as in *Tintern Abbey*' ('The Quest Motif in *Thyrsis*', *Victorian Poetry*, III (1965), 71–80). It is not too strong to

say that 'The Scholar-Gipsy' and 'Thyrsis' represent the most serious scrutiny of the meaning of Time since the Mutability cantos.

⁹ See the motto from his own '*Lucretius*, an unpublished Tragedy which Arnold set before the poem in 1867:

> Thus yesterday, to-day, to-morrow come,
> They hustle one another and they pass;
> But all our hustling morrows only make
> The smooth to-day of God.

Kenneth Allott comments, 'The lines are without a particular application to *Thyrsis*'.

¹⁰ Note the extraordinary number of archaic 2nd person singulars in 151–160. The dramatic appropriateness of this convention here does not need stressing.

¹¹ Here Kenneth Allott well draws attention to *Adonais* 356:

> From the contagion of the world's slow stain
> He is secure, and now can never mourn
> A heart grown cold, a head grown grey in vain.

¹² Cf. also Arnold's frequent use of the word 'eddying' to express aimless, pointless motion.

¹³ These lines seem to me to refer to Tennyson beyond any doubt, although Leopardi, Goethe and Carlyle have all been suggested as candidates.

¹⁴ As at the end of *Sohrab and Rustum*, and many poems of Tennyson's.

¹⁵ A. E. Housman, 'When first my way to fair I took'.

¹⁶ Letter to his sister, 1857.

¹⁷ For a similar antithesis see 'lily' (95) and 'cowslip' (99).

¹⁸ Note that the flutes and bells of the country, with their sharp, separate notes have given way to the indistinct, random and meaningless 'city-noise'. Cf. 'Birds here make song, each bird has his,/Across the girdling city's *hum*', 'the huge world, which *roars* hard by', 'men's impious *uproar*', 'the city's *jar*' ('Lines Written in Kensington Gardens').

¹⁹ Cf. also 'Palladium' 12, 'We visit it by moments, ah, too rare!'

²⁰ It is perhaps helpful to notice in passing the not dissimilar structure of 'Rugby Chapel', also published in 1867, in which the poet is at first plunged in gloom by Nature, but by the end of the poem recognises his father's great power to help others. An even closer parallel is provided by the two 'Obermann' poems (published 1852, 1867). What is important at the end of 'Obermann Once More'

is not the rather commonplace sentiment which the voice of the dead Senancour utters, but the fact that he is able to communicate with Arnold at all.

[21] Cf. Lionel Trilling, *Matthew Arnold* (1939), Chapter X; in which he represents Arnold as entertaining at this period of his life fairly sanguine hopes for mankind in general.

[22] For Arnold's use of this word to describe poetry with a serious purpose see his Preface to *Poems* (1853), line 200 in Allott's edition.

[23] See also the essay 'Gerard Manley Hopkins', e.g. 'What he [Arnold] offers poetically as thought is dismissed as negligible by the standards of his prose', and 'The Victorian-romantic addicts of beauty and transience cherish the pang as a kind of religiose-poetic sanction for defeatism in the face of an alien actual world—a defeatism offering itself as a spiritual superiority'.

THE IMPORTANCE OF ARNOLD'S *MEROPE*

Gabriel Pearson

Leave we the unlettered plain its herd and crop;
    Seek we sepulture
On a tall mountain, citied to the top,
    Crowded with culture!
              Browning: *A Grammarian's Funeral*

Any appreciation of Arnold's *Merope* has to run the gauntlet of a daunting unanimity of hostile or bored report. Lionel Trilling simply finds it 'uninteresting',[1] while J. D. Jump, more decisively, rejects it as 'almost unreadable'.[2] These are but current forms of the coolness of its original reviewers, of Froude, of Clough, of Arnold's sister. Arnold's own claims for it sound edgy and evasive.[3] *Merope* fell still-born upon an unreceptive world and few have found much life in it since. The present essay does not set up to reclaim or even defend it. More modestly, I would rather indicate ways in which *Merope* has, in fact, interested me, ways in which it has become readable. Admittedly, the interest is an oblique one, but I shall argue that it is in the nature of the case that it should be so. Again, to read *Merope* as other than an exercise in charity or antiquarianism is to read it, or perhaps one should say 'scan' it, in a rather special sense, but one which has some general implications both for Arnold himself and for other poets of his period. To show this, I will have to approach *Merope* cork-screw-wise, dislodging meanings from it by a process of controlled obliquity. I trust to the intention—to present Arnold's poetic career as less random and anticlimactic than it appears when *Merope* is viewed as its not wholly unheroic culmination—to excuse so much indirection.

    Arnold's critical writings continue to command wide respect

—respect, rather than authority. Surprisingly, though, scant attention has been paid to *Merope* as the one whole-hearted attempt by Arnold to confirm in practice his critical and cultural programme. One senses some embarrassment here. Why has *Merope* not been found to serve as a means of transition between Arnold as poet and Arnold as critic? The reason must be that we have never supposed the criticism to be operational or credited Arnold with believing it to be. We just do not grant it that kind of validity. Responsiveness to Arnold does not depend on our believing his judgments or evaluations to have much practical bearing on how we should judge or what we should read. Yet he is felt as important, even exemplary, and this, I would suggest, is because he transmits so distinctly, by virtue of the misguided clarity and luminousness of his mind, the contours of a predicament which we still share. We interpret his elaborated reactions—which embrace both his poetic and critical practice—as a measure of the intractability of that predicament which is, to put it at its most bland, the predicament of humanist values and imaginative sensitivity seeking to make sense, in and of, mass industrial society.

Arnold recommends solutions; indeed, his whole activity as a critic is itself a solution. Yet these solutions come over as fabrications—even though they are in the main decent ones. They are wise and humane and civilised—and not true. Not true, because they do not match the predicament, because we can see space all round them in which they are suspended, because they are not grounded in any existential or psychological grasp of the actual human and historical situation.

This I suspect is more widely felt than admitted. One can continue to admire the aesthetics of Arnold's stance, the cool mobility of his polemical strategies. Pleas for disinterestedness, for a free play of intelligence, for what, in alien traditions, has substance and permanence, all these seem admirable and must have had their own edge of refreshment in the overheated interiors of Victorian controversy. Yet there remains a singular failure of impingement or engagement. Arnold fails consciously to reveal the substance of his predicament by failing to be caught struggling in it, in the way that flawed, passionate energetic writers like Carlyle or Ruskin or Morris are. In these, the struggles, the defeats, the powerfully motivated miscalculations come over as revelatory. They are half dissolved in the stew of the situation but this tells us what the stew was and displays a heartening demonstration of a necessary courage. Essentially, they are in history in a way that Arnold never was and did not believe in being.

Arnold was off, up in the high cool air of the mountains, getting an all-round look at the terrain, but suffering the attendant disadvantages of his aerial inspection. When he descended to the plain—to employ one of his favourite topo-graphical tropes—he carried his aerial perspective with him. The result was that he could make nothing out, but only register the intolerable close-upness of everything. It is remark-able, for instance, how all the letters which discuss his work as an inspector seem curiously lack-lustre in observation, while conveying a genuine sense of oppression.

Arnold was outside history, looking down into it. But he was not really outside and his inability to let himself down inside was his constitutional expression of the predicament. Poems like 'The Buried Life' and 'Dover Beach' prove how much he wanted to descend, how much the failure to do so was felt as a kind of negative imprisonment, a matter of being shut-out. How did Arnold know that

> . . . we are here as on a darkling plain
> Swept with confused alarms of struggle and flight,
> Where ignorant armies clash by night

except by aerial inspection of 'the world/Which lies before us like a land . . .'? He does his best to be simultaneously up on the heights and down in the arena, but the best he can manage is a fine, military trope and a metrical stutter in the last line— on, nicely enough, the word 'ignorant', which implicates Arnold the observer as much as the struggling citizens of the plain. There is a give-away phrase in *Culture and Anarchy* that comes to mind here, 'from the point of view of culture', which shows how much culture is a matter of extra-historical vantage-point. Culture—'the best that has been thought and said', with all equivalents of the same kind—rises clear from the embarrass-ments of historical inherence. It appoints a permanent and objective order against which all merely local experience is to be measured and into which a kind of sublimed essence of experience is lodged.

This order is a series of categories all of which can be translated into each other to form the perpetual, extra-historical vantage-point: touch-stones, disinterestedness, the state, culture, Sophocles, the academy, Thomas Arnold, the grand style, the Hebraic, the Hellenic, Rugby school, France, Germany. And, one should add, whatever faculty conceives the social triad, Barbarian, Philistine, Populace, which allows a measure of social fact to be assumed, as a suitably sublimed essence, without any mere grubby factuality clinging to it. Given this order of categories, argument becomes redundant. Basically, the categories are deployed by a series of inter-translations. And their final term, into which they all fold, is Arnold himself, Arnold in an attitude of one who gazes from his height and is to be seen by those below as so gazing. Such an attitude is a disposition to watch yourself being watched as one who watches while pretending unawareness of being watched. It is peculiarly maddening and was, at the deepest level, intended to madden. It was his form of engagement, a revenge against society, and, for all its urbanity and obliqueness, both desperate and aggressive.

The 'Wragg is in custody' passage[4]—so often cited as evidence of Arnold's social involvement—confirms how unengaged he really is. Arnold is not really interested in Wragg ('poor thing') as anything but a counter in his game of playful but wary prodding at antagonists carefully pre-selected for their suitability as victims. The passage takes its force from its aggressiveness: Roebuck and Adderley were safely conspicuous targets, so much so that collision was unlikely to damage Arnold himself. The fact that Arnold consciously announced a policy of deliberate non-collision in his polemical writing itself requires explanation. The aggression is nonetheless real and comes into view when Arnold enacts for us the way in which he habitually wields such a missile as Wragg against the enemy: 'Mr. Roebuck will have a poor opinion of an adversary who replies to his defiant songs of triumph only by murmuring under his breath, *Wragg is in custody* . . .' The richness of implication, even of this half sentence, is astonishing. Arnold, in effect,

228

asserts that he and Roebuck are totally antagonistic within a common polity of which Arnold is silently subversive. Yet this subversion ('murmuring under his breath') is now being uttered aloud, suggesting that Arnold's kind of critical activity is in turn, vis à vis society in general, nothing but a subversive whisper, meant only for a few judicious ears and that this in turn—its silence, its ineffectuality—is itself an indictment of that society. As an attitude, this is superb, but its panache should not disguise how intricately self-cancelling it is. Arnold's mobility turns out to be, on inspection, an extraordinarily flexible immobility.

For Arnold, the Wragg case is less a social atrocity than bad aesthetics. The trouble with names like Wragg and 'Higgin-bottom, Stiggins, Bugg!' is that they are hideously un-Attic, secretions of an endemic social ugliness. This is a local instance of the degree to which Arnold's social criticism is derived from aesthetic, though from an aesthetic charged with the energy and authority of religion and morality. What we have is a curious series of displacements: morality and religion are enacted as aesthetic and aesthetic becomes the attitude towards society. The aesthetic is the middle term between morality and society. I use the ungainly term 'aesthetic' to suggest something different from imaginative apprehension (the term 'imagina-tion' is largely absent from Arnold's critical vocabulary; one presumes that it was too debased for him by its association with romantic subjectivity). Aesthetic is the detached cultural repository of achieved (almost wholly verbal) artifacts, which, by their persistence, have acquired hierophantic significance. Literature, we know, was to replace religion, but it was also to replace literature as imaginative activity. Such activity requires constant renovation of experience; but the aesthetic exists precisely to order, not enter experience.

There is a paradox at the very heart of the term, criticism, as Arnold uses it. Arnold gives an absolute authority to an activity designed to dissolve and qualify absolute assumptions. Attempts to absolutise the relative are central to early nine-teenth-century metaphysics and most nineteenth-century thinkers until Nietzsche, knowingly or not, are deliberating the aftermath of Hegel. Arnold was no metaphysician and recoiled constitutionally and out of persistent moral habit from paradox. He himself had sacrificed his own life to an inner call to duty and, despite the implicit relativism of his critical position, he did want it to operate as though it were authoritative. Yet he ostentatiously disclaims authority replacing it by a social tone, a display of fierce superior manners, that implies authority too delicately organised and too diffused to be directly unveiled to the vulgar. It becomes a matter of manners, even of manner. Arnold plays at amused reasonableness, leavened with real earnestness, so as to invite a discernment of an authoritative centre between the lines.

A somewhat later account of this state of affairs would call it a mask and prescribe artifice and the dramaturgical as a sufficient way to reality. But Arnold, for any number of reasons, could not have admitted to his own performance. He needed the mask to have the mobility and naturalness of his own features. The result is that he lost touch with his own motives for adopting the mask and these motives become an inner self, buried but still troublesomely alive. This catastrophe is what the poetry is really about. It is explicit in 'The Buried Life' and 'Growing Old', though the very explicitness of those poems is itself a form of numbness, part of the loss. Our pity derives from the pathos exuded by the externality of their tropes, themselves manifestations of the failure they seek to recover. The effectiveness of these poems derives from their paralysis of lyrical mobility, from their badness. All the poems are in this sense partly bad, have bad patches, tend to the explicit and the assertive. 'Rugby Chapel' is an extreme instance, where a genuine, baffled bereavement is let out for fifteen lines, only to be contained by the deployment of a willed topographical trope in the next one hundred and ninety.

'Rugby Chapel' is a late poem and Dr. Arnold a dangerous subject. But one can look at the matter in another way. Arnold seems to distrust his own poetry when it proceeds unimpeded directly from his own sensibility. He does not trust it to reveal truth or he distrusts the truth that it reveals. 'Poetry'—creative, sensuous imagination, as opposed to versified statement or assertion—plays a highly problematic rôle in any Arnold poem. It comes across as a form of indulgence to be reproved, interrogated or abolished by the will. One can construe this distrust of his own spontaneous, poetic nature auto-biographically (as I would), but whatever its personal genesis, it focuses a larger, post-romantic problem about what status to allow the imagination. Is the imagination socialisable, or is its essential nature anarchic and disruptive? Does it preserve archaically the lineaments of lost humanity or is it simply a self-indulgence (with all necessary sexual overtones) in private reverie made shamelessly public?

The romantic imagination had at its inception been implicitly justified, because social life seemed one way or another analogous to artistic creation, growing like an organism or reforming itself out of its own depths. But in a post-revolutionary or non-revolutionary period—above all in England after 1848—the social substance, though enormously dynamic, is so dense and massive as to feel like a man-created yet uncontrolled force of nature. It enforces a choice between some sort of acceptance or compromise on the one hand, or exile (either inner or outer) or positive opposition or eccentricity or madness, on the other. Sometimes, it can produce all of these at different levels, even within one mind. Hence some of the disjunctions to be found in Victorian art between depth and surface, instinct and repression.

The tradition remained romantic; even where this was not a conscious choice, it was impossible to escape the endemic, implicitly romantic historicism of the age. And romanticism involved—to throw off the definition that seems relevant here—a conception of poetry as deep or profound rather than elevated or sublime. One model might be Gray's 'The Bard', where the poet, an elevated figure at the beginning of the poem, confirms his alien identity by plunging to the depths at the end, earning Johnson's sneer that 'suicide is always to be had without expence of thought'.[5] The poet, as well as being wilfully suicidal, is improvident at every level. With poetic activity conceived in this way, how was the Victorian poet to sustain his identity as a poet against a society whose confident and anti-imaginative ethos—whatever lip-service was paid—was enforced through that most penetrative of organs, the bourgeois family? Browning and Tennyson, significantly enough, emerge from unconventional families, earlyish in the century. Hopkins's family, however amiable, was nearer the norm; the wrench was that much more violent and takes the form of embracing a sanctioning authority more rigorous than theirs, which had to be silently rebelled against in its turn and whose rigours killed him. But all these poets wear some disguise, are variously evasive, hypocritical, self-protective. They project their deepest life into legend, costume, decoration, abnormal states of mind, 'characters' who can be forgiven as foreign or belonging to disreputable epochs.

But one must not over-dramatise. One has also to register the enormous confidence that Tennyson or Browning repose in their lyric imagination. They credit it as a source of reality in a way that Arnold never does. True, imaginative vision never quite disengages itself from these guises and mazes; it remains as oblique and partially disowned (as displaced in dramatic monologue) or issues as an uncomprehending cry or becomes the atmospheric or pictorial suffusion of larger structures (as in much Tennyson). It protects itself from premature exposure by all kinds of pseudo-ratiocinations and narrative elaborations. The poems become artful ducts through which the idle (and indigent) tears arise, unsanctioned by a meaning and bright with import.

This confidence of, say, Browning emerges clearly as against Arnold's deep diffidence if we compare 'Saul' (which could have influenced it) with Arnold's *Empedocles on Etna*. There is a parallel in situation: a young lyric poet is sent to soothe and perhaps cure an older man's soul-sickness. Browning's David succeeds and generates the poem which describes his success; he is both actor and narrator. The larger poem acts for its audience much as David's song works on Saul. It relaxes the embattled will (just as the fresh lilies relax the taut wires of David's harp). Saul, who at the beginning 'relaxed not a muscle, but hung there as, caught in his pangs/And waiting his change, the king-serpent' is offered, at the poem's culmination, the birth of Christ and a regenerated Paradise; the imagery is religious, but its action psychological:

Anon at the dawn, all that trouble has withered from earth—
Not so much, but I saw it die out in the day's tender birth . . .
In the startled wild beasts that bore off, each with eye sidling still

Though averted with wonder and dread; in the birds stiff and chill
That rose heavily, as I approached them, made stupid with awe:
E'en the serpent that slid away silent,—he felt the new law.

The healing power of poetry is vindicated, Adam is renewed
and renames his creation, while the banished serpent of Eden
becomes one with the serpent of the *caduceus* and, as a Shelleyan
emblem of time's bondage, he knows his change. The lyric
impulse is here orphic and redemptive. The case of David's and
Saul's counterparts, Callicles and Empedocles, is painfully
different. There is no healing here. The split remains between
the baffled will and lyric emotion. 'He fables yet speaks true'
is Empedocles's response to Callicles's rendering of the myth of
Typho. 'Fable' and 'truth' are the poles of the antinomy
between which Empedocles, and the very textures of the poetry,
are torn apart. They can only be collapsed by suicide, by
splitting beneath the tension, rather than by relaxing it. True,
the drama appears to resolve in Callicles's high, cool lyric
celebrating the Apollonian vision: but this is a conclusion, not
a release: 'Not here, O Apollo!/Are haunts meet for thee'.
But if they are not 'here' in the hot arena of the breaking mind,
are they usably anywhere? Besides, Apollonian mastery has
been shown as exacting too great a price in lost humanity and
naturalness in the earlier account of Apollo and the defeated,
flayed Marsyas. Browning and Tennyson could still claim a
societal use for poetry as therapeutics, something Arnold toyed
with too, though with no great conviction. In any case, there is
desperation in finding a use for art in its non-utility, in its
irresponsible play.

Callicles celebrates the lyric and mythic, which the doctor
(Pausanius) prescribes for Empedocles's condition, and they do
not work. They fail internally and dramatically (Empedocles
is not cured) and externally, as part of the texture of the whole
poem: they are qualified, discounted, allegorically violated by
Empedocles's harsh, didactic ode and by the torsions and
splittings of his free verse. The composition itself enacts
modally as well as dramatically Arnold's predicament. The
last lyric fails to resolve: it simply gets away—from the volcano
—from the menace of an opposing poetics. This escape from
pain is in fact dealt with by Callicles in the myth of Cadmus

233

and Harmonia which directly follows Empedocles's ode. Cadmus and Harmonia are transported to Illyria and transformed into snakes. The outcome is however quite different from that at the end of 'Saul':

> . . . and there
> Placed safely in changed forms, the pair
> Wholly forget their first sad life, and home,
> And all that Theban woe, and stray
> Forever through the glens, placid and dumb.

This, in essence, is what happens to the whole poem. It opts for safety and oblivion and freedom from pain; Arnold's suppression of it, whatever he may claim as the reason, is an act which buries the pain yet deeper. Callicles's potentially redemptive knowledge is locked inside his myths as images which resist its release. The knowledge is there, but unusable, because Arnold dare not trust imagination as a source of knowledge. Faced with such knowledge, Arnold prefers to be 'placid and dumb'. Much of his subsequent poetry and all his critical prose is, in a crucial sense, a form of dumbness.

The poem knows more than Arnold himself. It discovers, imagistically, that he was committed to a model of depth rather than of elevation. The volcano is marvellously iconic and graphic: a high place whose summit points the shortest way to the profoundest depth—a hollow elevation up which the inner self might erupt. The energies are pent and writhing at the root, while the repressive will assumes the mask of mandarin superiority worn by the Olympian gods, whom Callicles depicts as horribly lifeless and lovely, arrested and relaxed:

> As he lets his lax right hand,
> Which the lightnings doth embrace,
> Sink upon his mighty knees . . .
> While o'er his sovran eye
> The curtains of the blue films slowly meet.
> And the white Olympus-peaks
> Rosily brighten, and the soothed Gods smile
> At one another from their golden chairs,
> And no one round the charmed circle speaks.
> Only the loved Hebe bears
> The cup about, whose draughts beguile

Pain and care, with a dark store
Of fresh-pulled violets wreathed and nodding o'er;
And her flushed feet glow on the marble floor.

This is classic poise with a vengeance. Yet there is something
enervated about the syntax, indicated by the inert 'ands'.
This is rigour with a deadly softness at the core. The rich colours
(blue, gold, violet) seem strangely stilled against the whiteness
of the marble which seems to have stolen its colour from the
spilt energies of Typho, much as the marble floor encloses and
mirrors and chills the warm feet of Hebe. Again, the freshness
of the violets is painfully detached ('pulled') and deadened into
décor.

This remarkable passage points to two paths, neither of
which Arnold could pursue. One leads to Parnassian preciosity
and artifice, the other to a plunge into depths from which he
feared he might not return. The first possibility is only indicated
(by this passage in particular). The second is presented in
greater detail, as a cycle of eternal recurrence. Empedocles
plunges into elemental chaos from which he is resurrected as
Callicles, the spontaneous principle of growth. The poem
views Callicles and Empedocles as two segments of a revolving
circle. As Empedocles falls downwards, on the inside, he pushes
Callicles up on the outside towards the crater. Such a cycle
seems hopelessly interminable, without the consolation of
tragedy, which defines life in terms of a destiny. This at least
makes some sense of Arnold's rejection of *Empedocles on Etna* as
untragic.

Arnold's suppression of *Empedocles on Etna* indicates a recoil
from these alternatives between depth and artifice. In their
place, he proposes neo-classical principles and practices that
issue in those epic torsoes, *Sohrab and Rustum* and *Balder Dead*.
By general agreement, these poems exhibit a psychological and
imagistic inwardness that contradicts their overt intent. They
were to have manifested grand style, high seriousness, archi-
tectonics. Practically, the reader elucidates meaning from
behind or in spite of their presented facades. So, the epic
similes of *Sohrab and Rustum* come over as more than stylistic
declarations of intent; they instance a seepage of contemporary

reality into what should be monuments of a timeless order, to
the point where the narratives can no longer be taken on trust
in their own terms but demand a psychological or even an
autobiographical reading. To take a notorious instance:

> As some rich woman, on a winter's morn,
> Eyes through her silken curtain the poor drudge
> Who with numb blackened fingers makes her fire—
> At cock-crow, on a starlit winter's morn,
> When the frost flowers the whitened window-panes—
> And wonders how she lives, and what the thoughts
> Of that poor drudge may be; so Rustum eyed
> The unknown adventurous youth . . .

By general consent, this is a Victorian cameo (indeed, the
similes are, as it were, inset into the poem): the middle-class
housewife, warm from bed, peeps out at the skivvy, not so much
with compassion, as with baffled curiosity (the drudge is a
better placed Wragg, say!). Her silken curtains suggest the
cluttered exoticism of mid-Victorian interiors—a taste which,
indeed, the whole composition can be seen as existing to cater
for. (Poetry not now as therapy but as mental interior decoration.) The simile frames an intimate awareness of social distances which reverberates into and from the narrative. The
whole composition is about gaps and distances: between cultures, generations, classes, sexes; between, indeed, medieval
Persia (or any spacial or temporal remoteness) and the contemporary world whose onrush consumes the past as exotica.
These splits and gaps fracture both his sensibility and his social
being. They are registered as a violation, a tearing apart of
delicately organised structures. The 'frost-flowers' (nostalgic
evocations of childhood) dissolve in the hot presence of the
adult and social world, just as the flower-like Sohrab will be
torn on his father's spear. The inner meaning of *Sohrab and
Rustum* is about such violations, such fracturing. The Oxus
passage that concludes the poem completes the process of dis-
solution, separating out the elements into the motionless fluid
of the Aral sea and the cold fixity of the stars.

Sohrab and Rustum was to be a demonstration of classic art in
which 'the tone of the parts was perpetually to be kept down, in
order not to impair the grandiose effect of the whole'.[6] The

expression 'kept down' is symptomatic of the degree to which Arnold instinctively felt his neo-classic discipline as a matter of repression; and nothing better illustrates the Freudian law of the return of the repressed. At its deepest levels, Arnold's imagination encountered dislocation which the conscious Arnold tried to overcome by a deliberate act of will. The result is an artifice that betrays its inner dislocation. The architecture is built on quick-sand and the cracks and crumblings declare the nature of the foundations. The poetry takes continual revenge upon the poem. The attempt to decree unity by fiat ended by revealing to Arnold himself that his 'poems are frag-ments'.[7] It is the result of Victorian character-building (his neo-classicism looks like a retarded, specialised form of this) that Arnold ascribes this fragmentation to his 'weakness' and has to promise, in the same letter to his sister to 'do better some day'. This 'better' it may well be, is *Merope*, which, as I shall argue, is, in an interesting way, a worse. Meanwhile, I cite this letter to show how even when Arnold knew what was wrong he failed, in a characteristic way, to understand it.

'The Scholar-Gipsy', composed approximately between *Empedocles on Etna* and *Sohrab and Rustum*, more than most of his poems, exposes the problematic nature of the lyrical impulse and reveals the alternatives which Arnold substituted for it. As in *Empedocles on Etna*, the lyric impulse is mythopoeic and idyllic and issues from the intergrated sensibility of earlier epochs and phases of the individual life. Here, as he hints at the Gipsy's mesmeric powers—ineffectual though they seem to be— he recalls the Romantic claim that connects imagination with magic. He himself does not make the claim: rather, he defers it, viewing it hopelessly, as an irrecoverable possibility, much as Tennyson defers the coming of Arthur and the defeated whole-ness he represents. But the magic is only dream-magic to be indulged in and then despairingly dismissed. The Gipsy is at best momentary consolation. It is a vacation-Arnold who for a moment identifies with him in the dream land-scape of the Berkshire countryside where the present world of mental toil and fatigue can be, for the duration of a few stanzas, annulled. One can see the point of Arnold's campaign against romantic subjectivity. The Berkshire stanzas are an extended allusion to

just such romantic subjectivity with its longed-for and prepos-
terous claims. Keats—and the slightly iced Keatsian fulness of
texture alludes to Keats—could talk of 'vision' or at least 'a
waking dream', but Arnold had been awakened too often by
the inner thwack of Dr. Arnold's moral imperatives not to be
able to distinguish between them. The dream of the Gipsy was
buried or had been killed:

> And thou from earth art gone
> Long since, and in some quiet churchyard laid—
> Some country-nook, where o'er thy unknown grave
> Tall grasses and white flowering nettles wave,
> Under a dark, red-fruited yew-tree's shade.

It is worth remarking how much unknowledge or ignorance is
a theme of Arnold's poetry. We have 'the unknown, adven-
turous youth' of *Sohrab and Rustum*, the blind, unknowing Hoder
of *Balder Dead*, the 'ignorant armies' of 'Dover Beach', while one
of the choruses of *Merope* celebrates a positive orgy of ignorance:

> Knowing he did it, unknowing pays for it.
> Unknowing, unknowing,
> Thinking atoned-for
> Deeds unatonable . . .

The burial of the gipsy buries the lyric sensuousness of the poem
itself. The stanzas that follow are the equivalent of Empedocles's
bald, didactic ode. True, there are bald patches in the Keats
Odes, as in 'the weariness, the fever and the fret' stanza of
'To A Nightingale'. But Keats works through his passage back
to an affirmation of the imagination as not merely escapist
fantasy but implying a human solidarity in the face of its final
incapacity to console: 'the sad heart of Ruth'. Arnold's anti-
lyrical stanzas much more damagingly take up the burden of
Berkshire idyll and destroy it. Thus, the sensuous imagery of
the yew's red fruit (themselves a death-fruit) die into trope:

> and we . . .
> Who never deeply felt or clearly willed,
> Whose insight never has borne fruit in deeds . . .

The defeated relapse into argument manifests, verbally, the
separation of feeling and will, depth and clarity as antithetical

terms, while 'fruit in deeds', so unfruitfully dead, crumble, before our eyes, on the page, like dead-sea fruit.

Yet Arnold does push beyond this antithesis. He inserts a third kind of poetry. He urges the Gipsy to 'fly our paths' and, as he puts distance between dream and reality, he tries desperately to plug the widening gap with verse that is rigidly, almost aggressively solid—a series of sculptured attitudes, salient and arrested forms, at once pugnacious, defensive and stoically inert. Thus the Gipsy is transformed into Dido; she assumes, and so arrests, his flight, and turns it into repudiation:

> Still fly, plunge deeper in the bowering wood!
>> Averse, as Dido did with gesture stern
>> From her false friend's approach in Hades turn,
> Wave us away, and keep thy solitude!

The passage names its own attributes—'gesture', 'stern', 'averse'—and so these really become its subject, what it is about. Dido and the Tyrian trader are both Punic and the gipsies are reputed to have a similar origin and so quite naturally continue the sequence of lost, exotic peoples that have gone under in the imperial march of progress.[8] Of course, this gipsy is not really a gipsy, only one of their 'crew'. He was to be a mediator between magical and rational knowledge, but with the defeat of such a possibility, the only possible attitude is one of stoic withdrawal. The substitution of Hades for burial removes the issue to the realm of permanent literary culture; the classicism of the *Aeneid* serving for Arnold much as the sacrifice of Dido for Virgil or of Cleopatra for Horace served as a reminder of how much of value the triumph of their times had permanently abolished.

'The Scholar-Gipsy' is a critically much-traversed territory and so it is with reluctance that I resurrect the perennial topic of its concluding simile. Critics have remained puzzled as to how it connects to the body of the poem. In view of the Dido passage, its function, indeed its meaning, is an asserted disconnection. The simile works, paradoxically, by asserting its dis-similitude. Again, it names its own attitude, 'grave', identifies its enemy, 'merry', 'light-hearted', and enunciates its own posture and the aggressive will that compels it, 'indignantly'. The fruit recur, this time transformed into luxuries:

Freighted with amber grapes, and Chian wine,
Green, bursting figs, and tunnies steeped in brine . . .

'Amber' suggests unnatural preservation and, more sinister, the figs as well as being unduly laxative (we remember that catharsis is a form of poetic therapy and that, when Wordsworth's medicine is administered, we become children again: 'Smiles broke from us and we had ease') are both premature and over-ripe; 'steeped in brine' again implies sterile excess. At this point, both the buried world of imagination and its anithesis, the world of labour and fatigue, are being decisively repudiated. The whole cluster combines the world of idyll and the world of activity—here, of commerce. But the Tyrian is also a trader, though his goods are never exposed to view. One supposes them to be cultural wares, conveyed to the 'ignorant armies' that clash, as at another world's end, in 'Dover Beach'. ('Culture' has, in some sense, to be sold and Arnold's famous banter is not so very far from the merchant's patter. The answer to the child in the Beerbohm cartoon, who asks Arnold why he can never be wholly serious is, none the less, 'because I wholly am'.)

As with the named attributes, so the syntax becomes the import of the last stanza:

> . . . and unbent sails
> There, where down cloudy cliffs, through sheets of foam,
> Shy traffikers, the dark Iberians come;
> And on the beach undid his corded bales.

The unbending attitude unbends with something of a creak. The syntax picks its way, intricately, through a considerable complication of punctuation, to achieve the last, over-resonant resolving line. The line emerges in detached salience to become a microcosm of the detachment of the whole simile. It thrusts, with a sudden lunge, from the complicated machinery of the sentence: its past tense (thunderously final), chimes somewhat disturbingly against the present tense of 'come'. And, as a statement, its verbal sequence contradicts its meaning: the bales, which were undone, remain, to the end, still 'corded', as though their contents were a mystery to be protected from the acquisitiveness of wordly sensationalism.

The simile demonstrates the construction of the architectonic as a response to the mutually incompatible pressures of dream and reality. The virtue of 'The Scholar-Gipsy' is that it describes the process and reveals its motives. It reveals the genesis of an essentially synthetic poetry which enacts an extra-historical order from which the aerial perspective can operate. Indeed, the end-of-the-world transactions of the Tyrian trader are, quite suddenly, viewed from an unlocatable height, in which he and the dark Iberians, are reduced to minute figures within a vast temporal and spacial sweep. The gipsy has been viewed at ground- (or beneath ground-) level, much as the Grecian coaster is 'descried' at sea-level by the Tyrian. The Tyrian's flight transforms his view-point until it bisects the poet's own from his lofty elevation above history; the Tyrian too becomes an object of elevated but sympathetic scrutiny. The Tyrian's final act is a negative act, frozen before it can be fulfilled: 'And on the beach undid his corded bales'. Process is arrested, fixed beyond the reach of time, as irrecoverably past.

The architectonic seems impenetrable in its catatonic arrest. Yet, as has been observed, it is also aggressive and defensive. It reproaches the disorder of the world as worthless and flies from it as if under threat. Its import as gesture nullifies its overt content; yet it does have content of a special kind—negative content. The meaning of Arnold's architectonic poetry is all that it is not: subjective lyricism (his own and that of his tradition), the sick hurry of the world of mechanical toil and fatigue, the special predicament of the poet which compels a choice between suicide and immolation by the world, between depth and surface. It follows from my account of *Empedocles on Etna* and *Sohrab and Rustum* that what is repressed returns and that the act of denial is a complete negative expression of what is denied. The retreat to the height conceals and thereby reveals the depth.

Merope deserves applause as an act of intrepid, grandiose bloody-mindedness. Here Victorian men and women stagger about under the massy breast-plates of their polysyllabic Greek names. It hibernates, at the wintry end of Arnold's poetic career, like a Galapagos tortoise, with its huge, horny carapace and its soft underbelly. Ferocious in appearance, with its chilly reptilian externals, it is really a lettuce-eating animal, a blown-up version of the domestic garden curiosity. It is quick to retract beneath its shell at the least cold breath of criticism. And, to abandon the analogy, since *Merope* is Arnold's most complete assertion of the architectonic in all its elaborated rigour, it might be expected to be, negatively, the most expressive of his works.

Curiously enough, critics have tended to accept it, at its face value, as an unsuccessful exercise in Sophoclean *gravitas*. It is this, of course, and they are right to construe it as somewhat inept, soft-centred, Victorian academic pastiche, so long as they persist in allowing Arnold any of his terms. If these terms are granted, then of course it can be faulted all along the line. Thus, its problematic quality makes it Euripidean rather than Sophoclean. Merope's moments of sympathy with the murderous usurper, Polyphontes, are a little too close to Gertrude and Claudius for comfort. The action is very weak: Merope, after her one nearly disastrous excursion into action, spends the last third of the play as a passive spectator of deeds of which she disapproves. The choruses carry Sophoclean sententiousness to the point of caricature. Where these do come to life, it is in the idiom of Arnold's own 'Buried Life'. Finally, the verse is stilted and monotonous, the speeches wordily over-protracted.

Yet these objections imply some kind of imaginable success. But success is really unimaginable; there surely has been no imaginatively satisfying or unproblematic neo-classicism since Racine in France or Ben Jonson in England. Arnold quite rightly locates himself, in his *Preface to Merope*, in a tradition which includes *Samson Agonistes*, Goethe's *Iphigeneia*, the tragedies of Maffei, Voltaire and Alfieri, and all of these would, I imagine, be considered problematic works. This suggests that success of an unproblematic kind is not to be had. Such projects are to be seen as wilful artifices, an attempt to compensate, in terms of the work, for a cultural order either under threat or already destroyed. The neo-classical work is inevitably demonstrative and programmatic. Its unsatisfactoriness as imaginative experience interrogates the quality of such available experience.

Still, Milton and Goethe do have positive content. *Samson Agonistes*, however Attic in form, remains distinctly calvinist-independent in theology and politics. Arnold follows Lewes in blaming Goethe for not achieving a fully Sophoclean effect: '. . . he produces it, not in the manner of Sophocles, but . . . in a manner of his own; he produces it by inculcating it; by avoiding agitating matter; by keeping himself in the domain of the soul and conscience, not in that of the passions'.[9] In other words, *Iphigeneia* has genuinely contemporary content. Goethe explores the transition of individuals from a lower to a higher level of ethical consciousness. Such extra-classical concerns make for the obvious interest of *Samson Agonistes* and *Iphigeneia*. Yet, at first glance, little such interest attaches to *Merope*, which is unremittingly the classical artifice, defiantly and uncompromisingly willed and asserted.

We have to switch our attention to another focus. The notion of negative meaning, both in respect to the act that produces the poem and to its ostensible content, is the way, or at least must be our way in terms of our own historical consciousness, to its meaning. *Merope* must be regarded as a monumental tomb with the word Culture inscribed upon it. The poem explores the significance of its own commemorative function. Rightly then the drama centres about an actual tomb. It opens with a young man and his uncle for whom the tomb is 'the goal/Of our night-journey'. There follows a mourning procession in black and next Merope herself, described in terms that belong to the kind of effect the whole composition aims to produce:

> And look, to meet them, that one, grief-plunged Form,
> Severer, paler, statelier than they all . . .

The description of *Merope* as a 'Form' (with that capital letter) shows how essentially marginal the action of the play is to its real meaning as an instance of 'Form', severity, austerity. The play wants, really, to be a ritual of arrested grief which recovers the quality of classic art as a static, total image. And yet, there is an obstinate sense in which the action of the play accumulates its own, explanatory significance. The characters all occupy some potential or actual familial rôle in relationship with each other, and Merope is crucially at the nodal point of these relationships. For twenty years she has mourned her slain husband and her two—out of the original three—dead children. She is mother to Aepytus, the third child, who escaped the slaughter and returns now for revenge. To Polyphontes she is emotionally related through her endured hatred of him for killing her husband, Cresphontes, but of recent years, a curious half-respect has attenuated her hatred. The play opens at another critical point. Polyphontes has come to offer marriage. (It is interesting that Arnold was twenty when his father died and the play begins twenty years after Cresphontes's death. Aepytus, we are to understand, is aged about twenty.)

The relationship between Merope and Aepytus or Merope and the dead Cresphontes or even Merope and the Chorus has very little reality. Curiously, the only relationship that has the complex savour of one is that between Merope and Polyphontes. Here, Merope herself assumes inwardness and so becomes real to us by apparently responding to a genuine complexity in Polyphontes. Polyphontes is himself able to distinguish between his 'character' as a defensive solidifying of his nature and some more total rejected self-hood:

> The long repressive attitude of rule
> Leaves me austerer, sterner, than I would.

It is as though the brazen-footed clip and chilly diction of the verse has become an object of knowledge within the play to one of the characters. Polyphontes tells us, in effect, that he knows he looks absurd, lumbered with such a name, such a rôle, such a language; he would much rather discard them, he hardly knows how he has come by them, but since he has, he must make the best of it. That 'I would' sounds a note of pathos to which, we feel, Merope genuinely responds. Continually, as the play progresses, we sense her as reaching out beyond her own and Polyphontes's rôles to an inner reality denied them by the convention in which they have been trapped. This gives their relationship the substance of a kind of marriage, the pathos of a shared, institutionalised and half-acknowledged inauthenticity. More, Merope, as the central consciousness of the drama, registers Polyphontes as mysterious and opaque. True, the chorus generalises this:

... more than all unplumbed,
Unscaled, untrodden, is the heart of man.
More than all secrets hid, the way it keeps.
Nor any of our organs so obtuse,
Inaccurate, and frail,
As those wherewith we try to test
Feelings and motives there.

And it is presented as one of the extra-classical interests of the neo-classical play analogous, say, to the politics of *Samson Agonistes* or the ethics of *Iphigeneia*. But its real interest is that opacity and mystery are qualities responded to by Merope herself. At the conclusion of the play any interest in Aepytus's triumph is deflected by Merope's interrogation of the dead Polyphontes:

What meantest thou, O Polyphontes, what
Desired'st thou, what truly spurred thee on?

This response almost of affection for Polyphontes, lends their ding-dong stychomithia and heavy-breathed tirades a spurious air of routine rôle-playing. Arnold here is dutifully gesturing towards 'the domain ... of the passions' which remain well beyond the range of his capacity to feel.

Merope's expressions of maternal passion also look routine. In her first important speech to the Chorus she first denies that as a woman she can interest herself in revenge. But this is a tricky line to have her take since it calls into question one main ethical premise of the play. (Arnold seems continually about to raise this question, only to sheer off in confusion.) But, she continues, she will encourage revenge, so long as it returns her son to her:

Can [vengeance] bring home my child? Ah, if it can,
I pray ...
                                   ... the all-seeing sun:
'Sun, who careerest through the height of Heaven ...' etc.

This elaborate rhetorical distancing seems designed to suppress the novelistic quality of the relationship of Polyphontes and Merope. It redirects it to the officially sanctioned passional relationship—the ostensible core of the drama—between

Merope and her son. Arnold has to try hard to make this relationship work. We are to gasp with horror when Merope nearly murders her son in error. This is supposed to provide the authentic archaic *frisson*. But there is another response possible: Merope is actually represented as nearly killing her son and this must connect with her suppressed relationship with Polyphontes, an inadmissible possibility which Arnold uses every rhetorical means to put out of mind.

Merope herself is split all ways. She cannot carry through her obligation to revenge her husband because she doubts the ethics of revenge. Her relationship with Polyphontes mingles official repugnance and uneasy affection. Her relationship with her son is even more ambiguous. She longs for his return, blames him for rashly embracing personal, unaided revenge—though she rationalises this on prudential grounds—and, finally, unheeded, has to witness, as a passive spectator, a butchery which she repudiates. When she does at last brace herself to action, she nearly kills her son with the axe meant for Polyphontes. Whatever significance this has for the plot it is hard not to read here a hidden wish—a wish on Merope's part, on Aepytus's part, on Arnold's part. Such a wish, successfully acted, would of course have destroyed the whole artifice and, as in Empedocles, left Arnold face to face with his sphinx.

Aepytus is even more split, not in terms of the plot, but in terms of the way he is represented. He adopts the device used by Orestes—a report of his own death—to lull Polyphontes's vigilance. Arnold, interestingly enough, gets this wrong: it is Orestes's tutor who reports it, not Orestes. Obviously, to report one's own death raises interesting possibilities. It implies a vision of suicide—or of alternate destinies. Aepytus's account of his own death is so richly circumstantial that it comes over as imagistically true. Arnold discovered, as he tells us in his Preface, a passage in Pausanius about 'an Arcadian hunter drowned in the lake Stymphalus, down one of those singular Katabothra, or chasms in the lime stone rock' and believing that invented features of his own work should have some basis in tradition, applied this event to Aepytus. But why that event, we may wonder, and can we believe that that incident in Pausanius did not haunt his imagination before he found a use for it? We seem to be left with two Aepytuses: one who returns, as a dutful son, to revenge his father, and the other, a night Aepytus who returns, via Arcadia, to the depths. That this is a kind of suicide gains support from the ready credence given to the idea that Aepytus is his own murderer. Merope, while about to cleave him with the axe, remarks upon his similarity to her son:

> How often have I dreamed of thee like this,
> With thy soiled hunting-coat, and sandals torn,
> Asleep in the Arcadian glens at noon,
> Thy head drooped softly, and the golden curls
> Clustering o'er thy white fore-head, like a girl's; . . .

How telling that just here, of all places, we should find the one rhyme almost in the whole play! Sohrab too was compared to a girl, and described by his father, Rustum, as effeminate.

I have no wish here to invoke factors in Arnold's own psychology. Whatever its personal source, this sexual confusion focusses a general and profound predicament—one that begins as a crisis located within the middle-class family, to become, at another level, the predicament of the artist in a society that denies him a genuine function. Thus it seems incorrect to associate artistic personality with neurosis though neurosis may well, in a sense, protect the dissipation of natural, childhood artistic impulse by an adult world that despises or can find no use for it. It is only from the eighteenth century and increasingly thereafter that artists—and in particular poets—are thought of as effeminate, girl-like or namby-pamby. Milton may have been known as the Lady of Christ's, but this did not, apparently, cause him to be thought unmanly. The continuing strength of this tradition makes poetry difficult to teach to boys even now.

The whole question seems connected with familial rôles and their implications for sexual differentiation. In the nineteenth-century bourgeois family, the mother was made to play a particularly ambiguous rôle. On the one hand, she is the angel of the house, promoting, within the household circle, the compassionate sensitivity disallowed in the outer world. On the other, she channels the wordly ethos into the household. She mediates between fathers and children, particularly sons: she is the source of tenderness and simultaneously the teacher of paternal values. And this last, in a paternalist society, brings about a contradiction between her socialising rôle and her biological and carnal being. She has both to cherish the son as an object of maternal love and yet to destroy those aspects of his affective nature which her love has created. The son, in the extreme instance, will feel that the very source of his life is the means of its destruction.

That this can lead to a virtual deadlock between ethos and emotion is witnessed by Swinburne's *Atalanta in Calydon* composed six or seven years after *Merope*. Here Althaea, in accordance with the legend, holds the life of her son, Meleager, in her hands and, compelled by her own sense of what the familial ethics demands, burns the brand on which his life depends. Meleager, attempting to make sense of his fate in the hour of death, can produce only a statement of total verbal and logical *impasse*:

> Mother, I dying with unforgetful tongue
> Hail thee as holy and worship thee as just
> Who art unjust and unholy . . .

while earlier Althaea voices an equal cry of hopeless contradiction:

> I am severed from myself, my name is gone,
> My name that was a healing, it is changed,
> My name is a consuming . . .

If this predicament is what lay at the source of Swinburne's catastrophic career, it is no wonder that it led him, religiously, to conceive a universe tortured by malign divinity, psychologically, all relationships as sado-masochist and, poetically, a language in which these contradictions had been magically eliminated in favour of a self-generating, non-referential, autotelic verbal universe. Nineteenth-century poetry, despite or because of its indirection, sounds deeper levels of psychological reality than the novel often does, because as an activity it is suspect and hence secretly subversive. So, often, was the novel, but it could always get by by pretending to certain quasi-positivistic aims which sometimes seep into and modify its content. These levels are nonetheless sounded frequently by Dickens and the Brontës. But to show Swinburnian insights operating in George Eliot may seem a more hopeless task. Still, there is this extraordinary passage in *Felix Holt* published a year after *Atalanta in Calydon*. Mrs. Transome is talking to her maid about her son (Chap. 39):

'Denner,' she said, in a low tone, 'if I could choose at this moment, I would choose that Harold should have never been born.'

This as it were is Mrs. Transome as Althaea. The context at least makes this something more than regret for youthful indiscretion. A page earlier, George Eliot makes the fundamental point about the contradictory nature of the woman's position: it is about the woman as wife rather than mother, but the point holds:

'Not true that she will ever master him. No woman ever will. He will make her fond of him, and afraid of him . . . A woman's love is always freezing into fear. She wants everything, she is secure of nothing . . . What is the use of a woman's will?—if she tries, she doesn't get it, and she ceases to be loved. God was cruel when he made women.'

However, *Merope* manifests an implicit political as well as psychological content, though the two concerns are really one. Merope is an Arcadian princess and Arcadia is a pre-political realm with a naturally legitimated order:

> . . . but what cause to our Arcadia gives
> Its privileged immunity from blood,
> But that, since first the black and fruitful Earth
> In the primeval mountain-forests bore
> Pelasgus, our forefather and mankind's,
> Legitimately sire to son, with us,
> Bequeathes the allegiance of the shepherd-tribes,
> More loyal, as our line continues more?

Cresphontes, one of the Hericlidae, had, with the help of his Dorian allies, conquered Messenia and built his new capital, Stenyclaros, the scene of the action of the play. Cresphontes appears to have been rather like Culture in *Culture and Anarchy*,

249

above classes. His aim was the creation of a unified polity out of a fusion of Dorian overlords (Barbarians?) with conquered Messenians (Philistines?). Polyphontes claims that Cresphontes was deliberately undermining the power of the Dorian aristocracy until its existence was endangered and that this was why he had to be killed.

Here, surely, autobiographical factors come into play. Dr. Arnold had himself urged the same sort of fusion of all Christians—and so of all classes—into a national church. Arnold, as Trilling makes clear, assumes much of the import of his father's mission, though in altered form. It is hard not to construe Aepytus's mission of restitution as Arnold's assumption of his father's burden. The notion of unity haunts Arnold's poetical and critical work. Dr. Arnold's unity is not, however, exactly what his son was after. And in assuming his father's mantle, Arnold jettisoned a part of himself. There is something oddly shorn and featureless about the triumphant Aepytus. Merope herself feels it in her incapacity to rejoice in the successful completion of his mission. Dr. Arnold's conception of unity was a fabrication; it failed to attach to the social roots. And Arnold's own search for unity, at the political as at the personal level, required more than his cultural criticism, a modified version of his father's national church, permitted. He seems, even in *Merope*, to half apprehend a deeper kind of unity including the Arcadian innocence of social childhood, which the other Aepytus carried down with him to the depths. Merope represents Arcadian innocence trapped in a social, class-ridden world. Subjected to contradictory pressures, her will is paralysed, so that she becomes what she complains of being: 'a pale, unmeaning ghost', and nothing in the action of the play does anything to alter this.

Merope is Arnold's last fling. It is the act by which he apparently assumed the paternal, authoritative rôle, stationed himself on his elevation and, like Polyphontes, took on 'the stern, repressive attitude of rule'. The façade is finally complete, the *rigor mortis* confirmed. Yet Arnold continued to believe, not exactly in being a poet, but in poetry as a cultural activity or, if sufficiently authoritative, as a cultural order. *Merope* is Arnold's attempt to give this order a palpable existence. The diverging ethical and imaginative sides of his own nature are rammed together into a monumental massing of hard, cold form. Arnold tries to disappear into his own monument, to wear it like armour for protection and wield it like a weapon for defense. But its very massiveness slows him down, makes him vulnerable. The criticism is a much lighter form of armour; it permits more mobility. The discarded *Merope* stands where Arnold dropped it, slightly inscrutable as to purpose, but still, for all its elaboration of stiffly articulated joint and massive plate, visibly his.

At the same time, the content of the poem re-enacts the process by which the total composition became the cold, blank thing it is. It presents the riven—and, in combination, touchingly real—figures of Merope, Polyphontes and Aepytus. There is the final disconnection of the man of duty from the Arcadian youth dragged, like Phlebas another Phoenician, into the fertilising depth of water. And with the failure of *Merope*, Arnold emerges fully, but half-dead (we have his own continuous word for this), into the public world of action, there to work his father's will. Yet this world continues to remain unlived and unliveable in, except as the brazen prison, in which he has chosen to thrust himself. Another Arnold retreats further, to the heights, whence he articulates laws for the world which he has never quite inhabited, and beneath which are depths which he has disowned. Of course, however much a life's basic, existential issues may be fudged, life, of a sort, goes on, and Arnold's, productively enough, did. Indeed, it manifests the utmost success that such a life can dispose of: sane, serviceable, characterful, courageous. Its consistency of self-abnegation exemplifies how much social existence in the nineteenth century, even at its most distinguished, could fail to unify or include. Arnold, one feels, had counted the cost, and knew the score. His last poem, *Kaiser Dead* (shades of *Balder Dead*) celebrates a departed dachshund. Arnold, in its last stanza, seems to tell us that he had lived something of a dog's life too:

> Well, fetch his graven collar fine,
> And rub the steel, and make it shine,
> And leave it round thy neck to twine,

Kai, in thy grave.
There of thy master keep that sign.
And this plain stave.

Another late poem is about a dead dog called Geist, but at this point the self-inflicted ironies should be allowed to pass beyond the necessity for comment.

NOTES

[1] Lionel Trilling, *Matthew Arnold* (1939; 3rd impression 1955), p. 157.

[2] J. D. Jump, 'Matthew Arnold' in *From Dickens to Hardy* (*The Penguin Guide to English Literature* vol. VI), ed. Boris Ford (1958), p. 309.

[3] Arnold's comments are quoted by Kenneth Allott in his ed. of *The Poems of Matthew Arnold* (1965), pp. 398–399.

[4] 'The Function of Criticism at the Present Time', *Lectures and Essays in Criticism*, ed. R. H. Super (Ann Arbor, 1962), pp. 273–274.

[5] Samuel Johnson, *Lives of the English Poets*, ed. G. B. Hill (Oxford, 1895), vol. III, p. 440.

[6] 'Preface to *Poems*', 1853, *On the Classical Tradition*, ed. R. H. Super (Ann Arbor, 1960), p. 6.

[7] *Unpublished Letters of Matthew Arnold*, ed. Arnold Whitridge (New Haven, 1923), p. 18.

[8] See G. Wilson Knight, '*The Scholar Gipsy:* An Interpretation', *R.E.S.* ns. VI (1955), pp. 53–62.

[9] 'Preface to *Merope*', *On the Classic Tradition*, ed. R. H. Super (Ann Arbor, 1960), p. 59.

CLOUGH'S SELF-CONSCIOUSNESS

Barbara Hardy

To speak of Clough's modernity is understandable but misleading. Perhaps no other Victorian writer is so visibly imprisoned in his Victorianism, breathing with difficulty under its
glass dome. The breathing, the difficulty, the restraints and the
visibility, are all found in his poetry. His idealism, his doubts
about his idealism, his troubled sexuality, his ethical brooding,
his views of work and political action, all would of course have
taken different forms had he truly been a modern, but the play
of his passion and his intelligence brings him close to us.

Richard Gollin's remarks on Clough always command respect, and in a review of two recent books in *Victorian Studies*
(Vol. X. No. 3, March 1967) he takes Paul Veyriras to task for
occasionally mistaking Clough's moral concern for his personal
compulsion'. I have to begin by admitting that I find myself
unable to feel as confident as Mr. Gollin about distinguishing
Clough's detached and controlled criticism from his 'self-
directed utterances'. While acknowledging Clough's variousness and toughness, I see his analytic mode as inextricably
bound up with his personal compulsions, and indeed welcome
his attachment to the personal as a source of warmth and acceptance even in satire. In this essay I want to emphasise in turn
three aspects of the poetry: its lyric structure; its use of narrative;
and its intellectual argument and analysis. Since I see Clough's
strength in his combination of lyric with argument, narrative
with lyric, and irony with passion, there will be some overlap
and repetition.

I

Clough's lyrical utterance is given its intensity by being
connected with a full sense of life in a way that usually works

against the lyric grain. Lyric poetry, like George Eliot's Lydgate, often raves on the heights, cut off from the habitual self that waits below. Clough's strength of feeling is not bought at the expense of his habitual self. His characteristic breadth and awareness is plain in the well-known letter to Blanche Smith, which he wrote in 1852, two years before they married:

> Fortified by bread and cheese I return and rise to the sublime . . . here in this dim deceitful misty moon-shiny night-time of existence we grope about and run up against each other, and peer blindly but enquiringly into strange faces, and sooner or later (for comfort's sake for the night is cold you see and dreary) clasp hands and make vows and choose to keep together and withdraw again sometimes and wrench away hands and seize others and do we know not what. . . .

It is true: he does rise to the sublime, here and in his poetry, and his sublime is a matter of concept and feeling, and seems to achieve the heroic by refusing the heights. The qualities of the human being are the qualities of the poet. There is his candour, warmer than most candour; his toughness, gentler than most toughness; and his affectionateness, more scrupulous than most affectionateness. There is the ability to analyse and still appreciate, criticise and still celebrate. He dissects feeling while feeling, and the pains of exposure and probe become part of what is felt. His materials are transformed by the act of inspection, as in all genuine science and genuine poetry.

The vivisective impulse is what Joyce saw as essentially part of the modern spirit. In Clough it is never a matter of the mind operating on the heart. One of Gerard Manley Hopkins's best sonnets, 'My own heart let me more have pity on', is an excellent model for critics of Clough as well as for critics of Hopkins:

> My own heart let me more have pity on; let
> Me live to my sad self hereafter kind,
> Charitable; not live this tormented mind
> With this tormented mind tormenting yet.

In this poem the poet struggles visibly against the temptation to diagnose conflict in the facile terms of a heart/mind antithesis. He begins by dividing 'my own heart' from 'me', then speaks of the object of the pity as 'my sad self', and then sets against this expansion the notion of the 'tormented mind' tormenting not a heart, nor a self, but 'this tormented mind' itself. Clough is like Hopkins in his refusal to condense the difficulties of being human into a conflict between intellect and feeling. He sets out the difficulty of analysis and diagnosis, and the difficulty becomes part of the pain and effort. His is a typically modern inability to identify the problem, and it is an inability which often creates poetic forms which shuttle to and fro, or which are tortured in convolution rather than progressive and developmental. The only one of his three fine long poems to have a progressive form is *The Bothie of Tober-Na-Vuolich*, and its progression towards an affirmative conclusion depends on an outline, a fable, rather than on a full exploration of an action or a complex picture of living. *The Bothie* has its beginning, middle, and end, but its form is a foreshortened, erratic, and collapsed form. The other two long poems, *Amours de Voyage*, and *Dipsychus*, are convoluted and even circular in form, and their conclusions, if that is the right word, do not seem to complete a development. Clough's forms of poetry come out of the honest experiments of his strong passions and intelligence; they present more than usual feeling in frank disorder. He writes from the centre of his doubts and anguish and this often means that the poems seem to lack a centre. It is no wonder that we compulsively call him modern.

Disorder in Clough comes both from an inability to work through to a final answer, and from a related inability to isolate the experiences of belief, desire, ideal, and dream. What struck some of his friends—Matthew Arnold, for instance, when he had begun to 'settle down' and of course, Mrs. Clough—as an excessive fastidiousness and fussiness in analysis and scruple, may strike us as fine refusal to compromise, to lie, or to live partially. Clough's tenderness of conscience is visible in his arguments about idealism and in his approach to the practical commerce of living. My formulation immediately hardens into falsity under the glare of Clough's *lumen siccum*: he so seldom felt able to say what was ideal and what was practical. The apparent 'ideal' might be fantasy luring us away from work and action, while 'practical demands' might borrow the peremptory voice of duty in order to disguise the solicitations of passion and worldliness. In a pre-Freudian world, Clough is painfully alert to the masks which desires can wear, and most of his poetry is an analytic attempt to strip down the masks, for he knows that human beings can wear them in layers, may be made up of them. The analysis is not performed by the clear exercise of reasoning and logic: he admits the pain, fatigue, hope, hopelessness, frustration, longing, doubt, and fear of the analytic process. The feelings are seen and discovered as analysts and as analysands.

The double self, as he calls it in *Dipsychus* (whose title and form at once conflict* to show up the crudeness of concepts of mere duality) is most simply present in the love-letter I have quoted. He sets down the bread and cheese then rises to the sublime. Having set down in duality and tension what he is doing, he then does it. He composes an image which is *also* divided: In 'the dim deceitful misty moonshiny night-time' there is the cold, the obscurity, the need and isolation, but there is also allure and beauty. Moreover, moonshine has perhaps helped to make the image, which looks cynical at first glance but turns out to have a Platonic tinge of hopefulness in its implied possibility of daylight. The shiftingness of this image, and the self-consciousness of its setting-down are found everywhere in Clough's poetry. He warned Blanche that her heart was not 'a priceless treasure' and told her not to dream of 'everlasting unions and ties that no change can modify'. Change and modification are conspicuous in his poems. His analysis proceeds by setting up a pattern and then qualifying it.

Sometimes the sense of modification is compressed into a single complex image like the ambivalent moonshine, as in the cutting second line of this almost (but only almost) innocuous hymnlike list of human qualities:

> A mind for thoughts to pass into,
> A heart for loves to travel through,
> Five senses to detect things near,
> Is this the whole that we are here?
>
> ('What we, when face to face')

* I take the poem to be an argument and struggle *between* the divided *Dipsychus* and the ambiguous Spirit.

Sometimes it is set up in a polarity, as in the 'double' dreams of Cain in 'The Song of Lamech', where we move from one extreme to another, or in the movement from a narrow winding street to the top of the campanile, in *Dipsychus*, or in Claude's labyrinth, in *Amours de Voyage*, where he feels lost but keeps the 'clue' in his 'bosom unbroken', or in the sinking fall through a fissure where he still feels 'the strength of invisible arms up above me'. It would be easy to pile up instances. But it is not only in imagery that we find the duality, tension and contradiction. It is there in his elaborate structures of feeling, in the ordering and patterns of his 'sense of musical delight', in the refrains which can give a specious sense of stability and a profound sense of mutability, in his habit of quotation and self-quotation, in his fluency and variations, his metrical power and self-consciousness about prosody: 'Hexameters, by all that's odious', as the Spirit says. Clough uses lyric analytically.

He can pose form against form, in a truly lyric argument, not only when he makes Shakespeare answer Dipsychus's revolted

> But to be swilled with animal delight
> And yield five minutes' pleasure to the male—

with

> It was a lover and his lass

but when he puts the gravity of the rhyming hexameter

> Yes, it is beautiful ever, let foolish men rail at it never.
> Yes, it is beautiful truly, my brothers, I grant it you duly.

against the Spirit's

> How light we move, how softly! Ah,
> Tra la la la, the gondala!

One of the most moving and powerful examples of integral lyric argument is from *Ambarvalia*:

> Why should I say I see the things I see not,
> Why be and be not?
> Show love for that I love not, and fear for what I fear not?
> And dance about to music that I hear not?
> Who standeth still i' the street
> Shall be hustled and justled about;

257

And he that stops i' the dance shall be spurned by the dancers'
   feet,—
Shall be shoved and be twisted by all he shall meet,
And shall raise up an outcry and rout;
And the partner, too,—
What's the partner to do?

Clough argues in image and motion: the sick distaste for
pretence and conformity shows itself in the monotonous and
insistent rhymes and repetitions of the first four lines, and then
arrests the flow abruptly and discordantly; but the argument
moves, we leave the deflating image of the compulsive crowd
and its threats and obstacles for the possibility of harmony.
Clough moves through the marvellous fragmentary 'And the
partner, too,—/What's the partner to do?' into an image of
real hearing and responsive movement in 'the living dance'.
He reaches the odd conclusion that the thing to do is to keep
moving in imitative fashion 'amid the throng', waiting for the
music to become audible—except that Clough's perception
always races ahead of his readers, and just as we catch up with
the point about the temporary conformity, turning and bounding not to nothing but to a music to be made by the expectant
soul, his suggestion is eroded by doubt, and replaced by the
melancholy beating question,

> Alas! alas! alas! and what if all along
> The music is not sounding?

In the second part of the poem Clough revises image and
music, and poses the existence of two musics, one loud and
coarse, the other 'soft and low,/Stealing whence we do not
know'. Clough constantly trips our expectation, whether it is the
expectation of heart or the reason, and the distinction here is
characteristically cross-hatched. The first music is not the
public music of conformity and social harmony, it is bred from
fancy and only sounds in the head; the second music is 'easily
forgot', and we must keep the ear alert, painfully, and not
listen to any other sound,

> But listen, listen, listen,—if haply be heard it may;
> Listen, listen, listen,—is it not sounding now?

In the last stanza the image of sight joins that of sound, to present something like Arnold's 'bolt shot back' on the buried self,

> Yea, and as thought of some beloved friend
> By death or distance parted will descend,
> Severing, in crowded rooms ablaze with light,
> As by a magic screen, the seer from the sight
> (Palsying the nerves that intervene
> The eye and central sense between);
>   So may the ear,
>   Hearing, not hear,
> Though drums do roll, and pipes and cymbals ring;
> So the bare conscience of the better thing
> Unfelt, unseen, unimaged, all unknown,
> May fix the entranced soul 'mid multitudes alone.

The poem dissolves and rejects its own imagery, and Clough's word 'conscience', into which is gathered the senses of moral and aesthetic consciousness, has to stand 'bare', its object 'unfelt, unseen' like Keats's unheard music. The poem works by its own momentum, like all good poetry, and its address to the ear and eye, like its tone and pattern, moves a considerable distance in these three stanzas. Clough's ability to shift feeling over such distances within an individual form which is sufficiently an enclosure to define and imprint, makes his lyrics remarkable and disconcerting. This poem sets up a music, sharp and intricate, and transforms it into something slower, heavier, more confused and groping, while using the same set of instruments—question and answer, the pivoting 'yets', the anticipations and echoes. Eventually, with no flourishes or triumphant climax, we move out of the high-pitched lamentations and exhausted sighs, and the solicitous and affectionate advisings and hopes, into a recognition and an answer. It is not a metaphysical answer, either to questions of faith in the human or the more than human, because Clough's imagery has allowed him to be expansive and vague, to accommodate all or any of these questions in the structure and symbolism of music and the 'entranced soul'. The formal continuity and argument is made out of the ordering of feelings.

Not only do image and music set up such complex movement

within individual poems, but can be seen across the poems, in larger correspondences and conversations. Clough quotes 'Easter Day' and *Amours de Voyage* in *Dipsychus*, and often revises, continues, and answers earlier poems. This cohesiveness is perhaps more unusual than we might expect, considering the nature of his poetry, and it seems to be a direct result of writing right from the human centre: all Clough's poems are equally grave and personal and—I believe—always deal with the same problems. There is no sense of dramatic striving for variety, or of conspicuous creation of separate beautiful pieces. Each poem performs an analysis of the passions and the intelligence by the passions and the intelligence and the process goes on and on. The poems send out sensitive antennae to each other, and come to create a body of work which has the integrity and wholeness of a man's diary or his correspondence: every piece is a whole and urgent message straight from the centre of suffering heart and mind. In the winding melancholy and sternness of 'Easter Day, Naples, 1849'[1] and the briefer, more static and emotionally unvaried reply, by 'another voice' in 'Easter Day 11', in the echo of 'Jacob's Wives' at the very end of *The Bothie*, and in 'Bethesda's' answer to the first poem in *Ambarvalia*, the relations are those of resonant echo and qualification, not of contrast and argument. These poems move us through a sense of continuity and of increasing complication. Clough's assertions are so unassertive, so eroded by nuance and scruple, that there is not much scope for strong antithesis. In the first poem in *Ambarvalia*, for instance, one of the spirits insists that he will do his duty, though when asked if this means that he will participate or stand back from life, he says that he does not know. In 'Bethesda', in which the same spirits lie in sick hope round the pool that might be Lethe or Philosophy, the same spirit now does know, and knows that he will serve 'the world's desires', but has forgotten the word 'duty', now feels that he must do as other men do. The sequel puts the emphasis on fatigue—the spirit and the poet have lived that much longer—and on not knowing. But the first poem was not all that certain, and indeed also said, in one voice, 'I know not' and in another, 'I also know not, and I need not know'. In the sequel the 'I know not' is quoted and repeated, and reinforced in its sad weakness by the poet's 'I saw not, neither know', on which the poem fades out. The conversations between poems do not mark progress: 'Easter Day 11' is 'another voice' and its assertion is posed flatly against the wretchedness of the long and elaborate structure of feeling of the first poem, at the end of which we have moved only reluctantly into a sense of 'reality', like prisoners changing prisons. The second poem presents another view, shows the imagination's activity in entertaining different stances.

II

Although Clough is a fine lyric poet, his central form is of course narrative, and his long poems are built up out of the non-progressive conversation we find in the shorter lyrics. Like the lyrics they accrete contrarieties and qualifications, and do not move towards climax and conclusion. But they are, of course, essentially *narrative* poems in which Clough tries out the different stances, relativities and possibilities in invented action and character, and in impersonated dialogue. *The Bothie*, *Amours de Voyage*, and *Dipsychus* are lyrical narratives, and have the toughness of hybrids. It is important to recognise the lyrical element because Clough is often regarded as a novelist in verse, just as he is often taken as an intellectual, rather than an emotional poet. He is very unlike a novelist, and especially unlike a Victorian novelist. His motion is very erratic, his fluidity and foreshortening and shuttling are all products of an essentially lyrical and musical form, where history is cut down so that feeling is prominent. He is less of a novelist than the other Victorian poets: to go from *The Ring and the Book*, for all its relativism, to *Dipsychus*, is like going from *Stephen Hero* to *The Portrait of the Artist as a Young Man*, from a full view of developed characters and actions to an intense and deliberately obscured selection. Both Browning and Tennyson tell much more complete and coherent stories and have a far greater range of psychological and emotional impersonation, though of course neither is a novelist in verse, and their narrative poems are both more and less than stories versified. 'Tithonus' and 'Œnone' also cut down narrative to emphasise moments of feeling, though these are of course poems where Tennyson can rely on the familiarity of mythological sources. Browning invents more freely, but his favourite monologue form both announces and keeps to its consistent selection. Clough's story-telling is much more disordered and foreshortened than Browning's or Tennyson's. His selections of character are wayward and at first sight arbitrary. He does not tell whole stories (except in *Mari Magno*, by far the least interesting of his big poems) and if we said that he created four characters, we should be exaggerating.

The poems are narratives but they are also lyrical. The lyrical element predominates, though both narrative and lyric express and form his drive towards passionate scrutiny and modification. *The Bothie*, *Amours de Voyage*, and *Dipsychus*, all contain within themselves the reason why they are so and not otherwise, why they are neither pure lyrics nor developed narratives. The distinction Joyce makes in *A Portrait of the Artist as a Young Man* between the three literary stages, lyric, epical, and dramatic, is useful here. Joyce's second stage, the epical, is distinguished from the simple lyric outcry and the impersonalised dramatic form, and fits Clough quite well:

The lyrical form is in fact the simplest verbal vesture of an instant of emotion, a rhythmical cry such as ages ago cheered on the man who pulled at the oar or dragged stones up a slope. He who utters it is more conscious of the instant of emotion than of himself as feeling emotion. The simplest epical form is seen emerging out of lyrical literature when the artist prolongs and broods upon himself as the centre of an epical event and this form progresses till the centre of emotional gravity is equidistant from the artist himself and from others. The narrative is no longer purely personal. The personality of the artist passes into the narration itself, flowing round and round the persons and the action like a vital sea.

In order to see the lyric pressure, we have to say what Clough does with narrative. In *The Bothie*, which is that rare thing, a virile and inartificial pastoral, he outlines a fable about sexual desire and radical discontent. The hero moves through two unsuitable and opposite loves to find his last and right love. Where a novel would thrive on the social and psychological developments, and show each environment and character in some detail, Clough's poem has lyrical not narrative proportions and emphasis. He shows just a little, and indirectly, of Katie, Philip's first love, though he does show the sensual passion, remorse and rejection; he shows nothing at all of Lady Maria, his second love, and describes rather than discusses his feeling for her in a curiously polemic outburst which utters the extreme of feeling for a socially privileged beauty in language and passion that admit their own proximity to irony:

While thou art eating black bread in the poisonous air of thy cavern,
Far away glitters the gem on the peerless neck of a princess,
Dig, and starve, and be thankful; it is so, and thou hast been aiding.
Often I find myself saying, in irony is it, or earnest?
Yea, what is more, be rich, O ye rich! be sublime in great houses. . . .

He can teeter between commitment and irony, because the episode is all done in report, so that we are most conveniently cut off from the lady and the relationship, and, indeed, from any analysis of feeling. All we have is the outburst which does not quite know how to take itself, but does well enough to suggest a social and sexual contrast, necessary to the happy rapid fable and to the treatment of feeling. The poem concentrates on Elspie, and her character and person, socially just right, lovely, intelligent, even bookish (being Scots), are the more plausible for existing in a poem, not in a novel. The three characters and actions of the love-story are usefully foreshortened for the negative advantage of the fable, but also for the positive advantages of expressing sensation and feeling. The natural landscape is much more prominent than character and social contrast and it is there to bring out the needs and strengths and beauty of young desire, 'the natural man revealing'. Trees, glens, granite jambs, water, brightness and a sense of strong movement and able action are all profoundly expressive parts of the poem. The hexameters can rush and throb, while the landscape gives a necessary strength and grace, while the walking and swimming give nakedness, energy, beauty and masculinity. It is these sensations and feelings, not the actions and psychological details, that make the impact and point of the poem. As a fable it is as unlikely and facile and optimistic as some of the tales told in *Mari Magno*, but as a spirited lyric which sympathetically creates the movement, tension and climaxes of sensuality, it is entirely successful.

Amours de Voyage and *Dipsychus* are frankly introverted forms for analysis. In their stories we see character and action rather dimly. In *Amours de Voyage*, character is filtered through an epistolary form in which once again we find foreshortening and distancing. There is some sense of character, but very little detail of personality and relationship. Action is fittingly filtered through the introspective reverie in which Claude thinks out and round and through his passion until action is postponed, inhibited, and impeded. *Amours de Voyage* could not be simply a monologue: it needs enough shift in point of view to establish certain things outside the unreliable sensitive register of Claude's consciousness. It is important to see Mary Trevellyn's changing view of him. This establishes him as having a certain warmth and strength, in what she says about him as a person, and as a solid identity, because she says it, in her independently dramatised point of view. It establishes her too, outside the emotional analysis of Claude's letters: the direct play of her spirit, intelligence, tenderness, and tolerance make the poem larger, more concrete, and sadder than it could have been in an enclosed monologue. There is a sense of the largeness of the world, outside Claude's introspection, of the solid reality of love and this woman. The sense of loss is accordingly greater, though the lyrical concentration on Claude himself, at the beginning, gives the right kind of density and claustrophobia and vagueness: but to have these alone would be to have only the Hamlet of the soliloquies. In *Dipsychus* we are right inside the mind, and the duality of character does not take us very far outside. The disconcertingly narrative nature of detail and character in *Dipsychus continued* brings out clearly the functional sense of imprisonment and doubt in the first part: are there two characters or one? Not that the duality is the only extension of lyric here, there is also the sense of scene, conveyed through the varied and fluent lyric movements—'How pleasant it is to have money' and 'The gondala'—and having something of the local definitions of a narrative poem. There is not only the claustrophobia and doubt of this shut-in life of the tender conscience—talking to itself? to the Devil? to God?—there is also the vagueness and ambiguity of action, the threateningly half-defined rich sensual life of Italian streets and crowds, cafés and hotels, the nudges and solicitations which are just right for a poem in which sexuality is neither healthy, buoyant and joyful, as in *The Bothie*, nor weakly rational and isolated, as in *Amours de Voyage*, but menacing, coarse, violent.

III

What is the relation of intellect to passion in Clough? Walter Houghton quotes Arnold on the intellectuality of eighteenth-century poetry. 'This poetry is often eloquent, and always, in the hands of such masters as Dryden and Pope, clever; but it does not take us much below the surface of things, it does not give us the emotion of seeing things in their truth and beauty' and comments:

> We scarcely need to know that Clough was working within the neoclassical tradition to recognise the connection between these passages and Arnold's criticism of his poetry. For Clough's work is also too intellectual in content and method, too lacking in sensuousness, and therefore deficient in beauty.
>
> (*The Poetry of Clough*, p. 196)

I should like to disagree with this in the strongest possible terms and insist that Clough's poetry is strongly sensuous, both in music and in visual imagery. This category of 'intellectual' poetry cannot be so simply created, by an antithesis between intellectual and sensuous. Clough's processes of analysis and argument are no more 'intellectual' if by 'intellectual' we mean 'merely or primarily intellectual', than are Donne's or Hopkins's. Houghton not only seems to accept Arnold's distinction too readily, but presses on with the case against Clough by employing Coleridge in an over-simplified fashion. Coleridge did not see imaginative poetry, as Houghton implies, as lacking in will and control: indeed, his supreme instance of imaginative art is Shakespeare, and he puts him forward as a case of art

265

formed by will and intellect, of 'judgment equal to genius'. The confusion about Coleridge is part of a rather jumpy argument which moves from Addison to Coleridge and ends with a wrongheaded contemporary review of *Ambarvalia*. Of course Clough writes intellectual poetry, but it is poetry in which the passions and the senses are inseparable from the intellect. Clough is no more a poet in whom logic is strong and passion weak, than he is a novelist in verse. Nor would I agree that this chief gift is that of irony. Houghton is quite right to speak of his rationality, complexity, and plainness, but the heart has its reasons and its complexities, and Clough's poetry is written out of these. Clough has the rare ability to stand back from his strong passion without excess of irony. Where there is irony, it is the very rare kind that can live with strong feeling and does not shrivel it up by ridicule or criticism.

Clough never writes coldly or drily or cynically. His poetry is compulsively argumentative but the argument is a passionate one. In it he does not pretend to be able to extricate thinking from feeling, and he is a truthful poet and a shrewd psychologist because of his inability to do so. Not only is he not a purely intellectual poet, he is not a poet in whose work thinking and feeling can be seen as even temporarily dissociated. In Donne and Marvell we can sometimes see the overlay of argument on feeling: tension can be produced by a loose relationship, a deliberately flouted argument lying loosely on the urgency of feeling, to be torn away or dropped in a climax which goes beyond or below reason. Shakespeare in the sonnets can do something similar, making a plausible argument or persuasion and then suddenly letting it go, so that a feeling is unbared— 'In sleep a king, but waking no such matter'—and the intellectual equations of imagery and argument are withdrawn to show the violent caring that had been restrained up to, and only up to, this point. Such temporary and deceptive uses of argument, such sleights of ratiocination, are not to be found in Clough. He gives us in his art what he was tormented by in life, the endless impositions of thought-and-feeling which is within the experience of most average sensual intellectuals. He does occasionally separate thought and feeling in very thin layers, stripping one off the other. This is what goes on in

Dipsychus, where layer of question is peeled off to reveal not answer but another layer of question: is this the real thing? is this the truth beneath the illusion? is this reason just rationalisation? is the good motive a mask for greed or lust? is this doubt of the good motive a mask for cowardice or sloth?—and so on, in a persistent process of uncovering which comes to an abrupt end. The tender conscience analyses itself tenderly and conscientiously. It has to be followed, valued, and suspected because only its tenderness and conscientiousness can guide us away from coarseness and egoism, only such tenderness and conscientiousness can flatter and delude so well. We may feel impatient with the questionings and reject them as an excessive prolongation of adolescence, as an onion-peeling which we all experience and mostly have to drop because of the sheer pressure of the world's demands. In Clough's case the very conditions which toughen or kill off the tender conscience were prolonged, and not only by the energies of conscience itself. He succumbed in the end, and how unsurprising it is that he should have worked himself to death doing his official duties and helping Florence Nightingale in his spare time: tying up parcels for a good cause is the kind of activity that no tender conscience can fret to shreds, for there is no glory in it. Blanche wrote most effectively the epitaph to Clough's tender conscience:

All the new duties and interests of domestic life grew up and occupied his daily thoughts. The humour which in solitude had been inclined to take the hue of irony and sarcasm, now found its natural and healthy outlet. The practical wisdom and insight into life for which he was distinguished, were constantly exercised in the service of his friends; and the new experience which he was daily gathering at home made many perplexed questions, both social and religious, clear and simple to his mind. In this way, though he did not cease to think about the problems which hitherto had occupied his leisure, he thought about them in a different way, and was able, so to speak, to test them by the facts of actual life, and by the intuitions and experience of those whose character he valued, instead of submitting them only to the crucible of his own reflection. The close and constant contact with another mind gave him a fresh insight into his own. . . . Having thus passed from the speculative to the constructive phase of thought, it is quite certain, from little things which he was in the habit of saying, that, had he been permitted, he would have expressed his mature convictions in works of a more positive and substantial kind.

But it was the conscientiousness and tenderness of the tender conscience that made the poetry. It was the speculative phase in which he constructed poetry.

Speculative is just the word for Clough's poetry, as long as we see speculation as an activity of both heart and brain. It is the word to be put beside Emerson's marvellous phrase for *The Bothie*—'temperate continuity'. It is the speculative element which tempers feeling, the feeling of despair, the feeling of hope, the feeling of loss, the feeling of joy. Clough's poems never give themselves up to feeling, but neither do they distance it. The feeling warms and moves the speculation, and in fact the irony and sarcasm Blanche speaks of are very seldom there untempered. Clough is not a satirist though he very occasionally and very briefly uses pure satire, as in 'The Latest Decalogue'. A profound and sober respect for life holds him back from satire, as it held back George Eliot too. When he parodies epic in *The Bothie* he does so in no rejecting spirit. His mock-heroic has very little in common with Jane Austen's parody of the Gothic novel or with Fielding's mock-heroic: he mocks affectionately and mildly, mediates respectfully between the serious passions which form his subject and the doubt and scepticism to which he insists on exposing them. The feelings are tempered, in all senses of the word: exposed to the temperate reason, and so strengthened, not explained away but not isolated and segregated from critical thought. In *The Bothie* there is burlesque of the epic style and metre and—permitted and defined by the presence of the literary burlesque—the tempering levity to which radicalism and sensuality and their combination are exposed. There is a pervasive puncturing imagery, so often turned against the passions that the poem takes so seriously:

Other times, stung by the oestrum of some swift-working conception,
Heedless of scenery, heedless of bogs, and of perspiration.

And there is the satire of individual characters, as in Hobbes's shot which hits both the hero and (surely) the poem itself:

There shall he, smit by the charm of a lovely potato-uprooter
Study the question of sex in the Bothie of What-did-he-call-it.

It would be only three-quarters of the truth to say that such underminings of his study of sex and imitation of the actions of passions are brought out in their serious intensities by the ministrations of fools and heretics, that the way of Philip is defined by the scepticism and the sensuality of Hobbes and the rationality of Adam. This is pretty obviously the case, but what is also true is that Clough passes the passions through a rational filter and a tempering levity, and forces them to meet logic, scorn and laughter. He knows only too well that one man's grand passion is another's Io-cow. In *The Bothie* the temperate levity is high-spirited, almost boisterous, a needed and relating spirit for the physical rush and buoyant spurt of the central passion. It is not, by the way, a matter of local effects: *The Bothie* creates a very elaborate structure of feeling in which the natural landscape and sense of physicality prepare us for both the fear and the powerful celebration of sensuality towards the end, just as the levity and mock-heroics, in form and debate, have so toughened the feelings that at the very end, in Hobbes's letter, the poet can risk scepticism in the Rachel/Leah image. The irony strengthens rather than undermines the final pastoral salute to a new society, to marriage, work and fertility.

In *Amours de Voyage* the levity is placed within the central character, and far from tempering a violent sensuality and questioning an affirmative ending, its temperate effect is undermining, and from within. The passions are not shown in violent physicality, though as always, Clough's presentation of sexuality is powerful and original. It is not the naked energy of *The Bothie* or the bizarre tumescence of 'Natura Naturans', (which surely has a claim to be the most successfully sensual Victorian poem) but the tug away from and towards sexuality:

Lo, with the rope on my loins I descend through the fissure; I sink, yet
Inly secure in the strength of invisible arms up above me;
Still, wheresoever I swing, wherever to shore, or to shelf, or
Floor of cavern untrodden, shell-sprinkled, enchanting, I know I
Yet shall one time feel the strong cord tighten about me. . . .

269

The levity of Claude is admittedly defensive, though it extends beyond the exploration of amorous sensation and conflict, its wry mock taking in Malthusian doctrine, 'emasculate pupils and gimcrack churches of Iesu', his own coxcomb exultation, Parisian *millenia*, and the British female. There are only snatches of levity, no long passages, no concentrated satire: the wry mock is much closer to the wary feeling, and both are seen as parts of the same temperament and mind. In *Dipsychus* the tempering is perhaps most centrally and conspicuously a part of the total form: the mocking Spirit uses mockery for his argument, and there is initially the huge gap between his crudeness and total detachment—he *is* the satirist who flouts and inhibits feeling—and the torturing sincerity of the tender conscience. The levity also exaggerates sensuality and ambition and the desire for money so that we see them—how?—either as reckless, carnal, coarse, greedy *or* as magnified and distorted by the tender conscience. The poem unfolds and expresses the difficulty of deciding between the sanity of laughter and its deadliness. The mocking spirit is the other side of the tender conscience, tenderness can curdle into sour rejection, and laughter can tolerate and reject. Like E. M. Forster, Clough saw that the sense of humour can be deadly to the feelings, and also pointed it out to an age in danger of overvaluing humour. Yet intensities must be curbed, noonday light is drier and truer than moonlight, and the feelings never exposed to laughter can hardly survive. The sense of humour must not be overvalued or undervalued.

At the heart of Clough's poetry, are the various stances, which shift, which ask and answer, which dovetail and contradict, which may be polarised, which may seem to mask each other, which are poles apart or dangerously close to each other. They are most brilliantly and profoundly ordered and disordered in *Dipsychus*, which combines the analysis of *Amours de Voyage* with the irony of *The Bothie*. There is the contemplative mind, standing back from sexual desire, from wordly coarseness, from ambition and greed of all kinds. It stands back in meditation, a poet's and a scholar's meditation, studious and purely seeking. The concept of love contemplated purely, is imaginative not imaginary, ideal but not above matter:

I hold heart can beat true to heart

and

> Love the large repose
>
> Restorative, not to mere outside needs
> Skin-deep, but thoroughly to the total man.

The contemplation is actual, not ideal, though hard to keep up:

> There have been times, not many, but enough
> To quiet all repinings of the heart;
> There have been times, in which my (tranquil) soul
> No longer nebulous, sparse, errant, seemed
> Upon its axis solidly to move,
> Centred and fast; no mere chaotic blank
> For random rays to traverse unretained,
> But rounding luminous its fair ellipse
> Around its central sun.
>
> <div align="right">(<i>Dipsychus</i>, Scene X)</div>

Indeed, the sense of actuality is the important thing. His ideal is not only something within experience and experienced, but notable for its concreteness and definiteness: it affronts that feeling of thinness and unreality which accompanies contemplation out of touch with the human: and works through the solid images which are so important in this poem. The contemplation is aesthetic:

> O beautiful beneath the magic moon,
> To walk the watery way of palaces!
>   O beautiful, O'ervaulted with gemmed blue,
>   This spacious court, with colour and with gold,
> With cupolas, and pinnacles, and points,
> And crosses multiplex, and tips and brass. . . .

But it takes in humanity, too, and is very Wordsworthian in the movement from the inhuman to the human, 'this gay flickering crowd' and what 'seemed more profound', the sense of 'the whole mass/O' the motley facts of existence flowing by'. Then comes doubt: 'Hints haunt me ever of a More beyond', but next, instead of moving backwards towards an ideal, we suddenly and startlingly question contemplation's sufficiency, and wonder if 'what I call sin' is 'a painful opening out/of paths for ampler virtue'. Contemplation is suspected as habitual and old, 'the easy-chair of use and wont', but suspicion gives way to the suggestion that waiting may be a waiting for the ideal, for 'a necessity for God', and we move back again to the credit side of contemplation. Argument depends on feeling: we have to feel the sense of ignobility in the contemplation of the scholar and the aesthete and friends, and the sense of certainty, 'my soul secure in place,/And the vext needle perfect to her poles'. The double self is set out over and over again, in analytical terms then in detailed and close examples of opposite feelings, and last, argument shrunk and crushed to enactment, in two almost sickeningly polarised images, the one of an aimless and hopeless threading in the byways of the town, the next 'in a moment' crowning the Campanile's top, 'looking down'. This is a fine instance of the movement of poetry: the gradual narrowing from full argument, to briefer form, to images alone. The conflict and uncertainty are acted out in the structure in which we turn with no link from 'the vext needle perfect to her poles' to the next movement of the vext needle. The image of the needle is picked up indirectly in 'thread the winding byways' and the image of the pole transformed into 'the Campanile's top'. There is continuity but also a physical and imagistic swing. This is only a passage, too, in a large and elaborate pattern of variations on this oscillating movement. Dipsychus decides to accept the double life in which he is true to neither life, and the decision is expressed in an unironical religious image, in which he thinks the workday week is made bearable by the one day in seven, and must be borne for fear of losing the pure solace of that one day. This argument is taken up by the Spirit, who plays with the sabbatical image and turns it into

> Once in a fortnight say, by lucky chance
> Of happier-tempered coffee, gain (great Heaven!)
> A pious rapture: is it not enough?
> O that will keep you safe. Yet don't be sure—
> Emotions are so slippery.

The sabbatical security can be weak, cowardly, fatigued, can in the end be seduced into the wrong kind of action, end up with a chambermaid. The violent rough language of contempt and warning is set against the mild sublime of that sabbath peace, and 'emotions are so slippery' is another instance of this argument in feeling: the Spirit argues but uses sarcasm, laughter, contempt, and to Dipsychus whose vacillations of image have already shown the slipperiness. This is the best against the worst, but the relationships are complex, and we move to the lowest point from the highest through several swings and shifts. 'The lowest point': the formulation just cannot be made in these terms. Dipsychus is not Marlowe's Faust, and he only resembles Goethe's insofar as his final 'redemption' is made possibly co-terminous with his fall. Is the lowest point the highest after all? The Spirit points out to Dipsychus that just as the Devil can quote Scripture so God can masquerade and use the Devil. But it is the Spirit that says so. Dipsychus tells the Spirit that he is crudely misled in thinking such pacts are binding, but Marlowe's Faust said something similarly brash in 'I think hell's a fable'. The suggestions are resonant, but made by powerful interests which twist and modify, so that we do not know: 'perhaps he wasn't a devil after all. That's the beauty of the poem; nobody can say'. We see the possibilities vibrate, as relativism and interest undermine assertion, and we do not even know whether to express doubt in God's name or in the Devil's. Clough is too impassioned and too uncertain to be praised as an ironist. To call him an 'intellectual' poet is as misleading as to call him a verse-novelist. He is a feeling analyst, a writer of lyrical narrative, an ironist who moves beyond irony, an intellectual both sensuous and passionate.

Belief and unbelief are accommodated in the scepticism *and* in the hopefulness at the end of *Dipsychus*: it may be easier to see the defeat of the Devil (if he is one) if belief is admitted or flouted. If you lost or kept faith the habit of self-scrutiny made its pressure felt, especially at Arnold's Rugby—though we must observe Clough's warning to his uncle in the Epilogue, 'You must not refer it to Arnold, at all at all' and 'I ascribe it to the spirit of the time. The real cause of the evil you complain of . . . was, I take it, the religious movement of the last century, beginning with Wesleyanism, and culminating at last in Puseyism. This over-excitation of the religious sense, resulting in this irrational, almost animal irritability of conscience, was, in many ways, as foreign to Arnold as it is proper to—'. Characteristically, the sentence is left unfinished as his uncle's levity interrupts. Clough's argument here is also a declaration of bias and interest. The tenderness of conscience was of course not just a matter of the over-excitation of the religious sense, with the special difficulties of the humanist's ethic which faced the ex-Christian. It is also a function of sexual problems: Philip's problems and Claude's and Dipsychus's and Clough's. Sexual choice and conflict in and out of marriage both seemed and was different. Clough's anguished discriminations between a bestial love which he recognises in 'Love and Reason' as still better than beastly for being human, a love which can enlist Reason on its side, and a love 'that itself was Reason' have the special cutting edge of his own time, without being entirely blunted a century later. The problem of work and money was also a pointedly Victorian one: Clough had to choose first between a conscienceless financial security in Oxford and an honest hand-to-mouth existence after he gave up his fellowship. Then he had the choice between an uncommitted freelance insecurity as a celibate and a dull office job in order to keep a wife. Religion and economics and sex wove a complex web for Clough: the tender and over-excited conscience had real enough problems. The poetry is not only the deeply moving record of intelligent passion but a document of its time, capable of considerable detachment but, as I see it, never losing the attachment to the personal.

NOTES

[1] Mr. Gollin, in the review already mentioned (*Victorian Studies*, X, March 1967), disagrees with Veyriras's reading of the poem as an expression of poignant suffering and tells us that it is 'a consoling statement about anachronistic suffering'. I read the poems as a movement from poignant suffering towards consolation, and this movement is what I would call typically Cloughian: the sense of doubt's suffering is eroded but not removed by the consolations of rationality, and the poem's complex feeling is dynamically melancholy, sympathetic and tough.

12

AMOURS DE VOYAGE: THE AQUEOUS POEM

John Goode

'Here in Rome, we may not be moral mediocrities'
(Mazzini to the Roman Assembly, 1849)

'And there is no high-road to the Muses'
(*Homage to Sextus Propertius*)

I

Clough has been given a good deal of attention in recent years, but most of it seems to me to be of the wrong kind. Above all it shows a remarkable timidity of evaluation. Paul Veyriras *begins* his vast recent study (Paris, 1964) by disowning any great claims for Clough. 'Sa poésie,' he writes, 'n'a pas l'ampleur qu'on exige des chefs d'oeuvre.' John Jump calls *Amours de Voyage* 'a minor masterpiece', and so does Walter Houghton who places it a little lower than *In Memoriam*, *Empedocles on Etna* and *The Wreck of the Deutschland*. Such phrases and comparisons seem pretty uninviting to me. And if Clough does foreshadow Eliot (as Houghton claims), this really entitles him to no more than a paragraph in a history of Eng. Lit.

Obviously I think much larger claims have to be made, at least for *Amours de Voyage*. The fact that they haven't is due, I think, to the irrelevance and inadequacy of most of the scholarship. Too often even now the attention to the poetry is secondary to attention to the man who is seen to be little more than a set of conditioned reflexes vibrating in an eminently Victorian frame of mind. Chorley, Veyriras—and even Houghton—are cases in point here. Exposition of the poetry encourages this because it fails to come close enough to the language of the poem itself. And this too reduces the poem to a routine, if pleasantly witty, piece of honest doubt. Whereas it must be obvious to anybody who has read the poem that it is the product of a radically different kind of mind from those which produced *In Memoriam* or *Empedocles on Etna*. Not that I want to sell Clough on the cheap by claiming some specious 'modernity' in his poetry. The comparison with Eliot is just as damaging as the undiscriminating juxtaposition with Arnold and Tennyson. For although Clough's dominant mode is, like Eliot's, an ironic one, it is, as I shall try to show, serving a very different, even antithetical, function. It is impossible to discuss Clough by lifting him out of the 1840s, but this doesn't mean that we should bury him in it. For the irony is extremely important, and it suggests a relationship to the reality which he shares with Tennyson and Arnold which is not their relationship.

To talk about difference any longer would be evasive. I mean superiority. The claim that must be made for *Amours de Voyage* is not just that it is a masterpiece, but a major masterpiece; indeed for me *the* major masterpiece of high Victorian poetry. Naturally I can't conclusively prove this in an article on this scale, but after all the evasions, it seems time for somebody to be quite flagrant.

What I *can* hope to show is that *Amours de Voyage* demands the attention that we pay a great poem. And this means being aware of the fullest implications of its texture and its form. It isn't difficult to see why this has never happened. Everybody is conscious that Victorian poetry is overshadowed by the novel in its own time and by Romantic and Modern poetry in its historical position. This means that critics are anxious to assimilate qualities of the novel to some poems (as indeed were some of the poets) and *Amours de Voyage* is a likely victim because it has at its centre a 'character' carefully defined both socially and intellectually. Alternatively, Claude is a persona, like Eliot's Prufrock, recording with ironised objectivity the poet's own alienation from the contemporary world. Neither of these claims is false; both of them are inadequate. For we very quickly realise that Claude has nothing like the depth and complexity of, for example, Lydgate, or even Sir Willoughby Patterne. And, seeing Claude as an early Prufrock, we are likely to notice that Eliot's interior monologue has much more

economy and honesty than a poem which is capable of 'Honour
to speech! and all honour to thee, thou noble Mazzini!' Seen
as a possum *avant la lettre*, Clough trails pretty large clouds of the
ineffectual angel.

However, a reading of the poem unhampered by the habitual
anxieties of the Victorian poetry specialist, will also reveal the
inadequacy of such interpretations. For the most obvious
quality of the poem is the richness of its verbal texture. Claude
isn't primarily important as a 'character' (the absurdity of
Veyriras's complaint that George, Georgina and Mary are
insufficiently delineated should warn us against that kind of
reading); he is a writer of letters. Nor is the poem an interior
monologue, the letters are to particular people. And what we
should be most conscious of is not the narrative of events or the
revelation of character, but the patterns of words. I shall say
something about the rôle of Claude later, but what must be
immediately obvious is that the language and image patterns
of the poem transcend his own social limitations. In order to
understand the radical significance of the thematic content of
the poem, we must attend to such patterns first, without reference to Claude. Only then will we be in a position to understand the radical significance of the poem itself.

II

The central preoccupation of *Amours de Voyage* is a search for
continuity. This grows from a need to establish a viable relationship between self and world, but, more importantly, it
demands a resolution of the conflict between the two empirically
verifiable attributes of self, eyes and shadow—the self as perceiver and subject ('Though but to see with my eyes . . .') and
the self as phenomenon and object of others' perception ('Do
I look like that? You think me that: then I *am* that'). What
makes this tension so radical is that there is no assumed
substantial self to be the source and thus the link between the
attributes. The continuity with the outer world has to be effected
on the basis of perception or of seeming rather than of 'being'.
As we shall see, eyes and shadow propose different kinds of
continuity which are rejected: through the perception of the

real Rome, the eyes find continuity in time, but the social being which gives the eyes presence traps the spectator in isolation; through the acceptance of social identity, the shadow finds continuity in space through love, but this too comes to seem factitious, the uprooting of personality from time through the social lie about marriage.

The 'substantial' self disappears in Clough's work because, from the beginning, though it is so important in the preservation of an identity separable from the impinging social world, it is never more than an ambivalent metaphor. We can see this very clearly in the sequence of poems called *Blank Misgivings of a Creature moving about in Worlds not realised* (1839–1841). In IX, Clough prays for preservation from absorption in the outer reality:

> Let me not feel, nor be it true,
> That while each daily task I do
> I still am giving day by day
> My precious things within away,
> (Those thou didst give to keep as thine)
> And casting, do whate'er I may,
> My heavenly pearls to earthly swine.
>
> (*Poems*, p. 33)[1]

Clearly there is here an inner sanctuary of self which is separate from the external world, but which mediates with that world ('while each daily task I do'). But even this bald antithesis is ambiguous. The inner sanctuary can only be defined in terms of a metaphor of which the vehicle is God. Throughout the sequence we are conscious only of negations of self (either the anti-self of the social mask or the pre-self of 'kind maternal darkness'). The landscape of self in IX is 'by hedge or tree unbroken' and is given meaning only by a few grey woods which in their 'unaltering impotence . . . enhance the sovereign dulness'. It is a blank world, carrying 'nothing into reality' which only a vague and unnamed power beyond self can concretise into an image ('heavenly pearls').

But in *Amours de Voyage* there is no God, and therefore no available metaphor of self. What Claude finds in Rome is not the Christian image of heavenly pearls,

Aspirations from something most shameful here upon earth and
In our poor selves to something most perfect above in the heavens,

but a 'positive, calm, Stoic-Epicurean acceptance'. Immediately
after this the possibility of the shadow being all there is of
substance is most nakedly confronted:

Curious work, meantime, re-entering society: how we
Walk a livelong day, great Heaven, and watch our shadows!
·What our shadows seem, forsooth, we will ourselves be.

(I. 83–85)

This is the point from which the sense of continuity has to
begin, and it conditions even the apparent antithesis of the
societal self, the self as seer. For Claude's eyes are not the eyes
of the Emersonian soul but the eyes of a social being, the
English tourist. Emerson wrote: 'Travelling is a fool's paradise',
and it is his voice which whispers in the prologue to Canto
I. Tourism is an aspect of social man's failure in 'self-
culture', and it is important that what most characterises
Claude as seer is the social image, 'Murray as usual under my
arm'. Murray defines Claude, even provides some of his comments on Rome.

⋅ Even so it would be wrong to see Claude's encounter with
Rome as nothing more than a revelation of his lack of self-
reliance. For initially it does provide for the possibility of the
spectatorial self seeking a relationship with the external
through a continuity in time ('*wherin gods of the old time
wandered*'). It may seem odd to insist on this when the search for
the more perfect earth is immediately countered in Letter I
with 'Rome disappoints me much'. But careful discriminations
need to be made here. Claude's word 'rubbishy' is not just pre-
tentious, it is also precise. What disappoints him is the visible
past available to the socially defined tourist. Its emblem is the
Monte Testaceo which suggests the very opposite of continuity
in time. The past seems to bury the present:

All the foolish destructions, and all the sillier savings,
All the incongruous things of past incompatible ages,
Seem to be treasured up here to make fools of present and future.

(I. 21–23)

It is important to insist on the clutter, the heaped-up rubbish which makes nonsense of the relationship between past and present: 'Things that nature abhors, the experiments that she has failed in'. Thus visible Rome operates against the central image of continuity in the poem—growth, the communication of past and present through a continually present nature:

> Somehow a tyrannous sense of a superincumbent oppression
> Still, wherever I go, accompanies ever, and makes me
> Feel like a tree (shall I say?) buried under a ruin of brickwork.
>
> (I. 36–38)

The solidity which has no splendour suffocates the soul in search of identity through the sense of history because the spirit of more perfect ages does not shine through it. It is brickwork not marble, it endures but it does not reflect. And this is because it embodies human failure not human ideals. Of the Coliseum, Claude writes:

> Doubtless the notion of grand and capacious and massive amuse-ment,
> This the old Romans had; but tell me, is this an idea?
>
> (I. 46–47)

Nevertheless it is not as simple as this. The opening establishes an ambiguous relationship with Rome which becomes in the course of the first Canto a discriminating one. Houghton calls Claude's attitude to Rome vacillating, but I think that there is a straightforward progression. Visible Rome is rubbish, 'but I shrink and adapt myself to it'. It cannot be dismissed so easily, it inevitably impinges on identity, and though Claude recovers from this momentary shrinking to reassert his separateness from the seen world in the flamboyant inversion of the claim made about Augustus at the end of Letter II, a spirit of more perfect ages does emerge. At the end of the Canto, the question is not rhetorical:

> Do I sink back on the old, or do I soar from the mean?
> So through the city I wander and question, unsatisfied ever,
> Reverent so I accept, doubtful because I revere.
>
> (I. 282–284)

The reverence grows out of the perception of the true and false

Romes. Even at the disillusioned opening Claude concedes that 'only the Arch of Titus and view from the Lateran please me'. The Arch of Titus belongs to the Rome of aggressive paganism (it is linked with the conquest of Jerusalem). From the moment at which Claude discovers not Christian neurosis but the Stoic-Epicurean acceptance, he is able to discriminate between the Horatian wisdom (in I. VIII, he celebrates the pagan survival with a version of lines from the Odes) and Jesuit repression. It is Loyola who becomes the focus of the superincumbent oppression:

> Innocent, playful follies, the toys and trinkets of childhood,
> Forced on maturer years, as the serious one thing needful ...
>
> (I. 80–81)

There is nothing distasteful about Claude's attack (as Houghton claims)—it is perfectly consistent with the interplay of growth and fixity which have already been established. 'Forced on maturer years' is a denial of growth, and the Jesuit responsibility for piling up rubbish (the Gesu, for example) and for 'overcrusting with slime' the true Rome fits in with this pattern. Through the rubbish and slime (Christianity), the continuing spirit of Rome emerges in the celebration of pagan monuments, the Pantheon (Dome of Agrippa), the immutable *manhood* of the marvellous twain (the Dioscuri), and the Vatican marbles. Inevitably bound up with this spirit is the spirit of the Renaissance (the Pantheon provides the link: Raphael is buried there, and Michelangelo's dome, St. Peter's, 'had hung the Pantheon in heaven'). Thus the epilogue to Canto I looks to Alba, birthplace of Romulus.

Of course this is not an unqualified illumination. It is rather a progression from disillusion through discrimination to a hesitant reverence. '*Do I sink back on the old, or do I soar from the mean*' probes questions which are unanswered in Canto I. 'I shrink and adapt myself to it' remains ambiguous because reverence may be immersion, the denial of growth; Emerson said of the tourist, 'he carries ruins to ruins'. But if the doubts are unanswered, they are not unanswerable. Claude precisely defines the condition on which Rome can become a soaring from the mean in Letter X: 'Utter, O some one, the word that

281

shall reconcile Ancient and Modern'—which demands a flow of time through the present into the future. The local 'some one' is Michelangelo, but we are already conscious that the Renaissance, as well as pagan Rome, is separated from the Modern by the Lutheran flood and the Loyolan slime. The reconciling word which gives continuity to the spirit of perfecter ages is the rhetoric of the historic defence of Rome. Looking back on 1849, Mazzini was to write: 'It was necessary that all should learn how potent was the immortality stirring beneath those ruins of two epochs, two worlds. I did feel that power, did feel the pulsations of the immense eternal life of Rome through the artificial crust with which priests had covered the great sleeper, as with a shroud.'

The sense of historic continuity in the historic act is important in the poem and we shouldn't be in too much of a hurry to point out the irony of non-commitment. In an unused but uncancelled passage in the main early draft of the poem,[2] this sense is explicit:

> Yet Politics, I will confess it,
> Yes, my political friends, I recant and acknowledge, have something
> Generous—something organic Creative and Art-like in them.
>
> (*Poems*, p. 516)

Even here, of course, the assertion is ironically questioned: 'Politics, Art and Love—and the greatest of these is the purest'. But what is important is that it is possible to see the historical moment, the political act, as 'organic Creative'. Claude echoes the rhetoric of revolution.

Of course, the identification is only spasmodic and always absurdly sentimental ('Victory! Victory!—Yes! ah, yes, thou republican Zion'). However, this isn't a simple matter, because there is a complex relationship between subjectivity and objective truth in Claude's response. Of the French Revolution in 1848, Arnold wrote to Clough: 'Certainly the present spectacle in France is a fine one: mostly so indeed to the historical swift-kindling man ... Even to such a man revolutions and bodily illnesses are fine anodynes when he is agent or patient therein: but when he is a spectator only, their kind effect is transitory.' Clough isn't capable of such predictably complacent irony (though in II. VI, Claude seems to be), but he is conscious of the historical vacuum of the tourist who can be no more than reporter. The verse of II. V, which records 30 April, exactly captures the interplay of presence and isolation:

Twelve o'clock, on the Pincian Hill, with lots of English,
Germans, Americans, French,—the Frenchmen, too, are protected,—
So we stand in the sun, but afraid of a probable shower;
So we stand and stare, and see, to the left of St. Peter's,
Smoke, from the cannon, white,—but that is at intervals only,—
Black, from a burning house, we suppose, by the Cavalleggieri;
And we believe we discern some lines of men descending
Down through the vineyard-slopes, and catch a bayonet gleaming.
Every ten minutes, however,—in this there is no misconception,—
Comes a great white puff from behind Michael Angelo's dome, and
After a space the report of a real big gun,—not the Frenchman's?

(II. 115–125)

The verse is vividly pictorial: the smoke, the gleaming bayonets and, rhythmically, the cliff-hanging 'and' of the penultimate line enact the movement and suspense of the battle with controlled narrative precision. But the accumulation of detail in the opening lines enacts a precise perspective too; Claude sees, but he sees from the Pincian, the favourite resort of the Northern tourist (who has been zeugmatically linked with Oudinot in the last line of the prologue to Canto II). And he stands among foreigners, including, ironically, Rome's enemies. Thus the whole passage is governed by the paralytic verbs of the trapped spectator: 'So we stand and stare, and see', 'And we believe we discern', 'in this there is no misconception'.[3] The subjective disjunction implied here becomes more explicit in the following letters. II. VII makes it clear: 'So, I have seen a man killed! An experience that, among others!' 'Experience' is loaded with irony, for it is one which is seen and not lived. The hexameter allows for the juxtaposition of event and comment which undermines the event's immediacy and thus its meaningfulness. Later in the letter, Claude's paralytic isolation becomes farcically complete as he realises that, being dressed in black, he might be mistaken for a priest and so runs away from the crowd. The spectator is paralysed by what he *seems* to be, by his social shadow.

Thus, because he is a tourist, for Claude, the spirit of more perfect ages abiding in the historical event is an illusion. The perceptual self discerning the true Rome is unable to participate in the spirit's temporal continuity. Claude is able to share the rhetoric (the *Marseillaise*, for example) but not its realisation. But the irony is more complex than this. For the defence of Rome, as Mazzini admitted to Clough, was not undertaken in the hope of success, but in order to create a national consciousness. The flamboyant heroism throughout the siege was really a dramatised rhetoric itself. Claude's bitter '*Sanguis martyrum semen Ecclesiae*' is not inaccurate.[4]

The disengagement from the defence of Rome is not a refusal to act, but an awareness of the limitations of a particular rhetoric.

The farewell to Rome in III. XI, is, then, a rejection of a particular rhetoric, the 'ancient lyrical cadence' of Tibur and Anio, through an elaborate celebration and firm limiting. The opening lines (III. 214–219) evoke it only to comment on its unreality ('so not seeing I sang'). It is evoked a second time in terms not of literary convention but of narrative actuality ('here as I sit') but presence elicits rejection: 'so seeing and listening say I . . . Tivoli beautiful is' only returns Claude to the unreality of the original invocation. So that the valley and villa of Horace is not the place to say farewell, but the Montorio, the key point for which the French troops were aiming in their last assault on Rome. The closing lines of the letter, bitterly but accurately, judge the spirit of eternal Rome, concretised in the Republic, to be merely a rhetorical illusion:

But on Montorio's height, looking down on the tile-clad streets, the
Cupolas, crosses, and domes, the bushes and kitchen-gardens,
Which, by the grace of the Tiber, proclaim themselves Rome of the
    Romans,—
But on Montorio's height, looking forth to the vapoury mountains,
Cheating the prisoner Hope with illusions of vision and fancy,— . . .
Waiting till Oudinot enter, to reinstate Pope and Tourist.

(III. 233-39)

The leisurely, end-stopped lines, the repetitive evocation of proper names, the accumulative Horatian rhetoric of the first twenty lines of the letter give way to the harsh enjambement and the perfunctory, generalised and plural catalogue of nouns, returning us again to the clutter of visible Rome. 'Proclaim themselves Rome of the Romans' clashes satirically with the last line (with its list of foreigners—barbarian invader, inheritor of the barbarian Spaniard, and barbarian tourist); the clash draws attention to the ambiguity of 'proclaim'. The Horatian wisdom and the spirit of more perfect ages depend on not seeing. Looking means seeing the defeat of Rome, and the word which links ancient and modern is merely declamation, doesn't relate to the actual: 'this Church is indeed of the purely *Invisible*, Kingdom-come kind'. The prologue to Canto III, it is true, momentarily offers a traditional refuge in an aesthetic contemplation of Rome but this exposes itself. 'Yet, at the worst of the worst, books and a chamber remain'—we are thrust back to the whisper of doubt in the prologue to Canto I. The spirit of Rome can only live in its history—and its history is declamation.

Thus in Canto III, there is an increasing focus on the spatial continuity of love. Rome delusively offers continuity through the perceptual self; love begins in the social self, the shadow. I. XII moves from a jocular image of absorption in the language of the mercantile Trevellyns ('But I am in for it now—*laissez faire*, of a truth, *laissez aller*') into a series of images of sexual involvement (island of Circe, labyrinth, fissure). It is important to insist on this because critics have by and large tended to sentimentalise the theme of love in the poem. Naturally we are reminded of the *Roman Elegies*, in which, from the outset, Rome is meaningless without love: 'Oh, Rome, though you are a whole world, yet without love the world would not be the world, nor would Rome be Rome'.[5] The same point is made ironically in I. VII where Claude compares himself first to critical Iago, and then to 'poor critical coxcomb Adam'. The exact echo of Genesis II. 20 ('But for Adam there is not found a help-meet for him') highlights the tension between the self as perceiver and the self as social animal. Adam the namer, Claude the topographical poet, is detached from the creation he celebrates (even if critically). Love offers the means of connection, as it does in Goethe.

But the *Roman Elegies* celebrate a very different kind of love. It is sexual, casual (the girl is a whore), and its object is Roman ('Und der Barbare beherrscht römischen Busen und Leib'). In *Amours de Voyage*, 'we turn like fools to the English'. Initially the communication is social, and Claude's connection is primarily an overcoming of class snobbery. If Goethe makes Rome meaningful through the lineaments of gratified desire, Claude merely finds a 'serene co-existence', a necessity simple, but one which can only be elaborated in a sentimental rhetoric:

Meat and drink and life, and music, filling with sweetness,
Thrilling with melody sweet, with harmonies strange overwhelming,
All the long-silent strings of an awkward, meaningless fabric.

(I. 172–174)

Claude himself assesses the rhetoric immediately by realising that the necessity simple could be fulfilled by nephews and nieces (the rationalisation here is significant: society isn't fair to Uncles, so they must fall in love). But it is important to note that it is the language which is treacherous. Claude muddles his metaphors: the long silent strings begin as strings of a piano which the harmonies strange of the female presence bring to life; but they end as the threads of a fabric which is incomplete (so that we move from musical strings to a warp and woof image). Thus the image changes from music/silence to meaning/ meaninglessness. Treacherously (because illogically) love (the love Mary offers) becomes more integral to being.

Claude is sliding from one cliché to another here, and this is bound up with the ambiguity of love in the poem. If we are conscious of Goethe (and we are obviously meant to be) we can see that Claude is not wrong to be indecisive about Mary: his mistake is to turn to the socially integrated English, when he really needs a Roman whore. 'Juxtaposition' accumulates ambiguities. The word on one level obviously associates with Goethe's sixth Elegy, which is a panegyric of the Goddess Opportunity (*Gelegenheit*) who is a goddess of the accepted moment. But Clough takes the word beyond its sexual con- notations to something more sinister. 'But Allah is great, no doubt, and Juxtaposition his prophet' is more than an exasperated joke. 'Islam', Carlyle had said, meant 'that we must submit to God', so that it can become related to the social lie about marriage, the institutionalisation of a passing instinct through the myth of providence. It thus becomes associated with 'affinity' which can mean simply 'marriage'. The progression which Eustace initiates, and which becomes the agent of factitiousness, is 'juxtaposition', 'affinity', 'obligation', 'marriage'. Claude's hesitations are thus in the interests of truth. The socialisation of love is a lie. Juxtaposition is transitory: Mary in absence becomes 'a pale blank orb which no recollection will add to'. Affinity is extra-personal and pre-social. Lyell uses the word to describe the relationship between gradually differentiated species from a common stock, so that as soon as Claude is given the word in III. VII he explores its meaning in a recession through the stages of evolution, from mammals, through reptiles, to rocks and stones. The affinity of social love is no less a denial of self, than the affinity of biological origin, and it is more absurd because it is a lie. Claude ends the letter with a momentary desire to return to 'that perfect and primitive silence'—the pre-self is real, and anti-self ('duty') is hypocritical. The rhetoric of Victorian love is as factitious as the rhetoric of Italy.

There is a third mode of continuity in the poem which postulates a definition of being independent of the perceptual and the social selves. As we have seen immortal Rome is a tourist's delusion, and love a conventional lie: both lead back to the social self, the shadow without substance. Both are ultimately measured against a romantic image of self through growth. The most explicit introduction of this theme is in one of the first letters about love:

> There are two different kinds, I believe, of human attraction:
> One which simply disturbs, unsettles, and makes you uneasy,
> And another that poises, retains, and fixes and holds you.
> I have no doubt, for myself, in giving my voice for the latter.
> I do not wish to be moved, but growing where I was growing,
> There more truly to grow, to live where as yet I had languished.
> I do not like being moved: for the will is excited; and action
> Is a most dangerous thing; I tremble for something factitious,

Some malpractice of heart and illegitimate process;
We are so prone to these things with our terrible notions of duty.

(II. 266–275)

The modulation of tone here is so precise that we can no longer
ignore the function of Claude, and it is in connection with the
theme of growth that Claude's rôle becomes most important.
Clough firmly places him with 'and action/Is a most dangerous
thing' in which the hesitant voice of the enjambement leads
one to expect an important statement which materialises, in
the downward curve of the intonation, as a hurry-scurry piece
of evasiveness. But a careful equilibrium is created by the
accuracy of the last line. It is an accuracy of social observation
('*we* are so prone') which contrasts with the pompous emptiness
of the philosophic generalisation. The available social context
has terrible notions of duty: we think of Eustace, of George, even
of Mary who accuses Claude of being 'not quite fair to the
party' and who is deeply conscious of the social advantage of
only letting Claude know what it is 'right' to let him know.
This balance allows us to take seriously the image of growth
against which Claude is opposing the atrophy of convention.
The attraction which disturbs and unsettles, is the kind offered
by the socially defined Mary because it is bound up with the
factitious choice of conventional action in the hope that it will
furnish belief. Literally she *moves* him, and the comic justice of
Canto IV punishes Claude with a frantic, meaningless pursuit.
But punishes him partly, surely, because he has given in to the
factitious at that point. The parody of *Julius Caesar*, 'there is a
tide, at least, in the *love* affairs of mortals', places the pursuit
as a kind of sexual opportunism: marriage might show a profit.

But in the passage I've just quoted, the marital lie is firmly
placed against the imagery of growth. 'To live where as yet I
had languished' suggests the casualness of *Natura Naturans* in
which a momentary sexual encounter releases Spring. The
pressures which drive Claude from Eden in the following letter
are the pressures which institutionalise time through marriage:
'Bid me not venture on aught that could alter or end what is
present'. I don't see how Houghton can talk of Claude's fear of
sex. What he fears is the factitious rhetoric of institutionalised
love; 'let love be its own inspiration'.

288

Only in the last Canto does Claude associate his relationship with Mary with the possibility of growth:

I, who refused to enfasten the roots of my floating existence
In the rich earth, cling now to the hard, naked rock that is left me.
(V. 66–67)

This certainly ironically rebounds on Claude. His refusal to accept the social lie inevitably becomes a refusal to accept natura naturans as well. But the ironies are more complex than this. The shrewdness of social observation comically recoils, but it does so because of Claude's philosophic inadequacy. In the passage I have just quoted from Canto II, we note the familiarity of the verbs describing the attraction which is natura naturans: 'poises and fixes and holds you'. It sends us back a hundred lines to the passage in which Claude meets the crowd which is about to murder the priest:

Gradually, thinking still of St. Peter's, I became conscious
Of a sensation of movement opposing me,—tendency this way
(Such as one fancies may be in a stream when the wave of the tide is
Coming and not yet come,—a sort of poise and retention);
(II. 172–175)

In Canto III, the image of growth is rejected by the opposing imagery of chaos ('Let us not talk of growth; we are still in our Aqueous Ages'). But we can see that the image of growth has built into it the rhetoric of chaos, (the unruly mob, the tidal wave). By an accident of language arising from Claude's own factitious acceptance of 'growth', the association of Mary with growth in V is already nostalgia for an image that never was, for a rhetoric which contains its own contradiction. The rootlessness of Canto IV is not a confrontation with his mistakes. The metaphor of growth with that of eternal Rome and love is cast on to the Testaceo.

Unless we admit that this is what is happening, the end becomes incoherent, whereas it is the enactment of incoherence. Claude in Canto V searches desperately for any means of continuity, reaching the depths of intellectual depravity when he finds comfort in a barrel-organ in Florence. Truly, he is not broken: the factitious comforts are rapidly rejected. Houghton rightly emphasises the importance of knowledge at the end of the poem. But we should recognise how limited the discovery is. The celebration of knowledge receives exactly the same ironic inflation as the other moral codes which are rejected: 'Faith, I think, does pass, and Love; but Knowledge abideth', and the letter ends with the transition from celebration to deflation which is the established modal movement of the poem: 'Eastward, then, I suppose, with the coming of winter, to Egypt'.

The knowledge that Claude finds it possible to believe in has nothing to do with routine Victorian refuges in knowledge (sweetness and light or positivism, for example). The least ironised affirmation comes immediately after Claude has seen through the falsity of religious comfort:

> What with trusting myself and seeking support from within me,
> Almost I could believe I had gained a religious assurance,
> Found in my own poor soul a great moral basis to rest on.
> Ah, but indeed I see, I feel it factitious entirely;
> I refuse, reject, and put it utterly from me;
> I will look straight out, see things, not try to evade them;
> Fact shall be fact for me, and the Truth the Truth as ever,
> Flexible, changeable, vague, and multiform, and doubtful.—
> Off, and depart to the void, thou subtle, fanatical tempter!
>
> (V. 95–103)

We can see how far Claude has gone beyond 'honest doubt'. There is *no* moral basis, not even self-reliance. In the following passage, Claude foresees himself admitting the fanatical tempter again in the face of death ('When the pulses are weak, and the feeble light of the reason/Flickers, an unfed flame retiring slow from the socket'). So that there is not even the morality of disbelief, since that too will perish before the ultimate absurdity. At the same time, this is a positive statement, because Claude uses the verb 'rest on' to describe his relation to the moral basis. Thus he pins it down as a psychological need: the initial search for continuity is itself specious. And what he is thrust back on is the mere flux of the phenomenal. There is no continuity through memory, as in Tennyson, no consistency through stoic withdrawal as in Arnold, not even growth as in Wordsworth. Merely total empiricism: Clough has retreated from the reconstructive rhetoric of Romantic and Victorian poetry to the chaos of the multiform, to the honesty of David Hume.

III

Amours de Voyage is an experimental poem with no real precedent in English. Even its relationship with the *Roman Elegies* is, as we have seen, by no means imitative (though Goethe obviously gave Clough the idea). To some extent, Goethe is to Clough as Virgil is to Pope. His poem is a referential ideal, in which Rome is discovered through love, ironically played off against the actual possibilities available to an intellectual Englishman. *Amours de Voyage* is in itself an ironic title: it is Goethe, not Claude who has an 'amour'. Yet the poem is much more than a decreative inversion (the strangling of romantic love by 'romantic' marriage), and it moves not towards total antithesis (as Book Four of the *Dunciad* does) but towards moral anarchy.

One wants above all to use the word 'wit' about Clough's best poetry, and by this I mean that we are aware of a sophisticated verbal mode of discrimination among values. It is not insignificant that Clough should have had so much admiration for the eighteenth century, for he alone among the most important Victorian poets is capable of maintaining the same detached ironic interest in language as an index of cultural values that Swift and Pope had. Yet there are obvious and vast differences. Pope's detachment is bound up with an assurance about the values among which he is discriminating (I don't mean this in a *simpliste* way, but in the sense that he knows that the languages which he is exploiting relate to systems of value which are coherent and stable). Clough doesn't have this assurance because by the 1840s the stability of relationship between language and meaning has disappeared. Thus in 'Duty—that's to say complying' there is a tension between two levels of irony. For the first 38 lines, we have an accurate and straightforward satire based on the antithesis of ideal and actual meanings of 'duty'. The final couplet, however, introduces a different tone:

Moral blank, and moral void,
Life at very birth destroyed,
Atrophy, exinanition!
Duty!—
Yea, by duty's prime condition
Pure nonentity of duty!

(*Poems*, p. 28)

The breakdown of metrical control, the enacted incoherence,
throws doubt on the irony of the opening of the poem. The firm
moral sense is there, but the assurance of communication has
gone. And this takes us beyond the exasperated indignation of
the single-word fourth line to the insoluble ambiguities of the
fifth and sixth. Is Clough still contrasting real and actual
meanings of 'Duty', or is 'Duty' itself a nonentity? How can a
word which was originally something, however distorted,
become pure *nothing*? We are thrust back on the literal meaning
of the first line through a double irony. Thus the motive of
Clough's irony is, like Pope's, related to the awareness of the
threat to language as an accurate medium of communicating
values. But its discovery is radically different: in the historical
context, language itself is suspect.

In a more complex way, this sense of both the urgent need
for an ironic verbal discrimination and of its impossibility
dominates the experimentalism of *Amours de Voyage*. Light dies
not only at the uncreating word of dulness but also of wit. This
is why it is so important that Claude writes letters, because what
matters is not experience itself, but the verbalisation of experience. The letters of Georgina and Mary offer a different,
'witless' language which challenges Claude's. Equally important
is that the letters are one way. Originally Clough had one letter
from Eustace, but rightly he abandoned it because it would
have established a dialogue which would have distracted our
attention from the act of verbalisation. In Canto V, Eustace
even becomes an unknown God, and there is a good deal of
comedy arising from Mary's letters to Miss Roper which spend
a lot of time repeating Miss Roper's information, so that Clough
goes out of his way to alert us to the *self*-exposure of the language.
From this need, too, arises the social definition of Claude. He
has to be '*very* clever' (though not very original) because he is to

celebrate the available languages of coherence. Equally he has to be very inexperienced because he is to measure these languages against multiform fact. So it is that Claude is in pursuit, very often, of the phrase which will cope with what he is learning:

> Mild monastic faces in quiet collegiate cloisters:
> *So let me offer* a single and celibatarian *phrase* . . .
> (III. 182–183: my italics)

Thus his way of coping with the superincumbent oppression of Rome is to offer a witty inversion of the bricks-and-marbles dictum; thus, at the moment of disillusion, he constructs a formal elegy for Manara and Medici and comments: 'All declamation, alas! *though I talk*'.

The primary attention to language explains the 'hurry-scurry anapaests' as well. Clough needs a metre which can accommodate and judge available rhetorics within the line. A simple example is '*Dulce* it is, and *decorum*, no doubt, for the country to fall'. The main structure exactly follows the Latin syntax through the postponement of 'pro patria mori' to the end of the line. But by splitting up 'dulce et decorum est', Claude adjudicates between the two virtues: dulce, yes, decorum, perhaps. Thus the possibility of the aphorism's factitiousness is built into an almost exact evocation: a tension is established between a subjective need and an objective value. Obviously too, 'no doubt' establishes an intonation of modern collo-quialism which interrogates the objective availability of the Horatian language. The juxtaposition of the colloquial and the Latin makes the *latinate* syntax of the end of the line ambivalent. The irony works both ways: the aphorism is made to seem pompous through the casual deflation, and the undergraduate intonation is made to seem unheroic. The narrative bears this out: Claude is comically unheroic, but the heroism is merely rhetorical. Only the hexameter could have achieved this complexity. A pentameter would not have allowed for the necessary expansion, and an iambic could not have balanced the rhetorically placed 'it is' against the conversational 'no doubt'. Naturally the verse doesn't regularly work in this way, but it always works to the same end which is the self-exposure of language. Pope uses the heroic couplet to discriminate the antithesis of language and actuality: Clough uses the hexameter to discriminate the conflict of languages.

It is this which makes the poem a great one. Formally, it is not merely experimental, it is an experiment. Its expansiveness gives us the opportunity to watch available languages, metaphors and intonations work themselves out and mutate into something else. At the beginning of Canto III, for example, Claude narrates quite historically his discovery of the imagery of the Aqueous Ages first on the boat and then looking at the Triton in Rome. 'Let us not talk of growth; we are still in our Aqueous Ages' is an improvised epigram growing out of the collision of Genesis and Evolution in a context of organic being and flux (the collision is only made explicit in an unfortunately omitted passage). A little later he elaborates on the improvisation through a formal restatement of alternative images:

Not, as we read in the words of the olden-time inspiration,
Are there two several trees in the place we are set to abide in;
But on the apex most high of the Tree of Life in the Garden,
Budding, unfolding, and falling, decaying and flowering ever,
Flowering is set and decaying the transient blossom of Knowledge,—
Flowering alone, and decaying, the needless, unfruitful blossom.
    Or as the cypress-spires by the fair-flowing stream Hellespontine,
Which from the mythical tomb of the godlike Protesilaüs
Rose sympathetic in grief to his love-lorn Laodamia,
Evermore growing, and, when in their growth to the prospect attaining,
Over the low sea-banks, of the fatal Ilian city,
Withering still at the sight which still they upgrow to encounter.
    Ah, but ye that extrude from the ocean your helpless faces,
Ye over stormy seas leading long and dreary processions,
Ye, too, brood of the wind, whose coming is whence we discern not,
Making your nest on the wave, and your bed on the crested billow,
Skimming rough waters, and crowding wet sands that the tide shall return to,
Cormorants, ducks, and gulls, fill ye my imagination!
Let us not talk of growth; we are still in our Aqueous Ages.

                                                      (III. 79–97)

Clearly, the first two paragraphs express the transience of growth in terms of knowledge and love respectively. The first image ironises Genesis by making knowledge (which involved the fall) the high point of life, and ironises knowledge by making it a parasitic, fruitless and futile failure of growth to become anything more than process. The second, classical image makes the same point about love which also grows without achieving its end. But this image too relates to Wordsworth's *Laodamia* in which the trees are emblems of nature's participation in grief. The differences are immense. Wordsworth's last line fixes the process in a synoptically grasped pattern by containing it in the interplay of nouns: 'A constant interchange of growth and blight'. The 'interchange' is acted out in Clough, and what we have is not a contained pattern, but the syntax of a vicious circle. This is obvious from the refusal of the process to go beyond its continuing verbs ('withering' being a participle, and 'to encounter' being an infinitive). Rhythmically, the repetition of 'still' makes for a buffeting to and fro within the line. The finality of the necessarily heavy stress on 'upgrow' leaves the rest of the line to die out like a loosely swinging rope. Thus, within the hexameter, Clough enacts the moral anarchy of the image's refusal to achieve its purpose. The same is true of the first image, in which the repetition of 'flowering . . . decaying' keeps the flower of knowledge in futile and incomplete movement. Both images are condemned to a Sysiphus-like striving after what they always just miss.

The elaboration is necessary because what is emerging is not just the inadequacy of love and knowledge, but the failure of the rhetoric of growth to achieve any finality. The 'Not . . . or . . . but' structure of the passage has no logical justification, but arises from the refusal of the first two images to focus properly. The literary images of growth press forward through their self-exposure to the natural image at the end. This is an image without fixity, without pretensions to coherence. There is no attempt to control the subjective distortions: 'Ye that extrude from the ocean your helpless faces' is viable only as a visual illusion, and the violently active verb taken with 'helpless' implies an unresolved ambiguity in the relationship between freedom and necessity. In the anarchy of the sea, there is no defined and stable distinction between inner and outer. 'Cormorants, ducks, and gulls, fill ye my imagination' takes us into a nightmare world of invading flux. The important point, however, is that this is arrived at through a dramatic interplay of traditional metaphoric vehicles of coherence. Language itself is treacherous.

This is why comparison with Eliot is so irrelevant. In Clough there is no grasping of surviving fragments of tradition in a culturally sterile world. The tradition itself is what overwhelms and betrays: culture is a lie, anarchy the only truth. Any less elaborate structure would have been inadequate to enact the poem's radical discovery. Any more formal discipline would have been factitious (which is what we may feel about *In Memoriam* after all, and even *Empedocles*). Clough creates a form which gives 'the strange disease of modern life' a local habitation and a name. The disease is a disease of language, the available rhetorics are shipwrecked on the ocean of protracted exposure. Many images are called, but in the end there are few left to be chosen. Only a form which is in itself an experiment, which is prepared to float language and watch it become what it didn't set out to be, could have achieved this. For an aqueous age, Clough creates an aqueous poem, and I don't know of any English poet who has achieved so accurate an instrument of ironic openness. It is no use reviving Clough on a margin of minority. *Amours de Voyage* ought to be given major currency.

NOTES

[1] Quotations from Clough's poetry are from *The Poems of Arthur Hugh Clough*, Oxford 1951. For poems other than *Amours de Voyage* page references are given, as are references to variant readings recorded in the notes. For *Amours de Voyage* reference is to Canto and Line number.

[2] Even a critique which has no pretensions to being scholarly has to make difficult decisions about the text of *Amours de Voyage*. Much of the variant material would obviously just clutter up the poem and Clough was clearly right to repress it in 1858. But knowing what we do about Clough's later years, are we right to trust him as an editor? Some passages seem to be rejected on grounds of prudence, and it is therefore necessary to exercise a local discretion.

[3] It is worth comparing this passage with the accounts in Henry

James's *William Wetmore Story and his Friends*, pp. 133–155, which give exactly the same impression of excitement and remoteness.

4 Trevelyan vividly re-creates the splendidly Romantic heroism of the Romans in *Garibaldi's Defence of the Roman Republic* (1907).

5 David Luke's translation (*The Penguin Goethe*, p. 91). The German is:

Eine Welt zwar bist du, o Rom; doch ohne die Liebe
Wäre die Welt nicht die Welt, ware denn Rom auch nicht Rom.

13

G. M. HOPKINS: VICTORIAN

A. R. Jones

I

G. M. Hopkins's reputation, like that of Thomas Traherne and William Blake, is almost entirely posthumous. Unpublished during his lifetime, Robert Bridges withheld the publication of his poems until he felt the public was ready for them. The first edition of the poems was published in 1918, twenty-nine years after the poet's death, and the editor in his 'Preface to Notes' shows Bridges to have been in some degree remarkably unsympathetic towards the poems and to have undervalued the poet to a surprising extent. He charges Hopkins with 'faults of taste', 'artistic wantonness', and 'faults of style' which, he says, 'a reader must have courage to face, and must in some measure condone before he can discover the great beauties'.[1] Bridges does not conceal his lack of sympathy for the way in which Hopkins outraged all sense of literary decorum particularly by his obscurity which, he says, confuses the reader, and by his oddity, which provokes the reader's laughter. He limits his preface to categorising and explaining Hopkins's style in the hope that readers may be prepared for the poet's mannerisms and therefore more accessible to the appeal of his 'rare masterly beauties'. He does not mention the problems raised by Hopkins's subject matter or the peculiar nature of his habits of mind. The edition was a small one, 750 copies only, and after ten years it still was not exhausted; but then, in 1930, a new edition was published with an enthusiastic and less pedantic introduction by Charles Williams and the Hopkins cult was born. This edition very rapidly went into ten impressions and a third edition, edited this time with both care and enthusiasm by W. H. Gardner, was published in 1948 and has been in print and continually reprinted since.[2] Hopkins's reputation, however, was firmly established by Charles Williams's edition and the poets and critics of the 1930s appear to have developed a more or less uncritical enthusiasm for his work. C. Day Lewis, in that strange manifesto he produced for the 1930s' poets, *A Hope for Poetry*, eagerly accepts Hopkins, together with Wilfred Owen and T. S. Eliot, as one of the trinity who led poetry out of the darkness of Georgianism into the light of Auden and Oxford. Hopkins attracted imitators who admired him to the extent that the poetry they produced often now reads more like parody than imitation. The critics, for the most part, agreed with the poets; 'a major poet', F. R. Leavis judged him, 'the one influential poet of the Victorian age, and he seems to me the greatest'. Whether he is indeed 'the greatest', at least F. R. Leavis remembered that he is a poet of the Victorian age, an obvious enough fact but one that was in danger of being over-looked. Michael Roberts began his influential anthology, *The Faber Book of Modern Verse*, with thirteen of Hopkins's poems, including the whole of *The Wreck of the Deutschland*, while W. B. Yeats is represented by eight poems and T. S. Eliot by five. If his anthology is any criterion, then, modern poetry is more indebted to Hopkins than to Yeats and Eliot combined. Although the anthology selection encourages this view, Michael Roberts in his introduction makes it clear that although he believes that Hopkins 'differed from most of the English poets of his time', there is 'no strong discontinuity' between him and, for example, Doughty. He values Hopkins chiefly as a technical innovator in poetry but also for what he calls his 'intensity' and the way in which 'working in subterranean fashion, he moulded a style which expressed the tension and disorder he found inside himself'. Roberts predicted that more and more modern poetry would appeal directly to the sub-conscious mind and he is characteristic of the 1930s' attitude towards Hopkins in directing attention both to his stylistic and linguistic experiments and to the psychological conflicts and complexities expressed through them. Louis MacNeice, for example, having warned his fellow-poets of the dangers of imitating Hopkins too closely, remarks that 'both his rhythms and his syntax were peculiarly appropriate to his own unusual circumstances and his own tortured but vital personality'. In using words such as tension, disorder, tortured, and so on, to describe Hopkins's poems, both Roberts and MacNeice are insisting on a psychological level of interpretation; a level that suggests to them that Hopkins's was an essentially modern though abnormally frustrated sensibility struggling to realise a profoundly human sensuousness within a religious discipline that denied its utterance. In melodramatic terms (the 1930s' poets often resolved their conflicts by simplifying them to the point of melodrama), Hopkins's poetry was often seen as the obscure but moving expression of suffering humanity trapped in the dark prison of a harsh and life-denying regime; the voice of oppressed mankind everywhere (but particularly in Europe under Fascism); a poetry of powerful sensuousness that embodied the freedom of the world of spirit and imagination denied him in the world of Victorian materialism and/or in the world of Roman Catholicism. The poet and the priest were in deadly opposition; the man and the age entirely incompatible; therefore, because these elements were opposed, they must be distinct—it was argued—so the poet could be discussed without reference to the priest, the man without reference to his age. This attitude still persists to some extent even after the publication of his letters and notebooks and in spite of the studies of Hopkins undertaken, in particular, by Father D'Arcy and Father Peters. In the light of this material and of these commentators' work it is difficult to sustain any attitude other than that Hopkins' poetry springs from intensely held, *doctrinal* beliefs, and that, far from being in revolt against Victorianism and Victorian poetry, his work is the culmination of certain central Victorian preoccupations. Far from rejecting his vocation or his age, his poetry is an expression of them and cannot be understood without reference to them.

II

Hopkins was acutely aware of contemporary poetry and he returns time and time again to the discussion of individual works and authors and is constantly measuring himself and his own poetry against theirs. As a poet, after all, he shared their problems and was particularly concerned with the question of the language and form appropriate to poetry, one of the dominant concerns of his time, as well as with the discussion of an appropriate aesthetic. He drew largely on Pater and Ruskin for the theoretical basis of his ideas and on the Romantics, particularly Wordsworth and Keats, on Tennyson and Browning but particularly on the Rossettis, both Dante and his sister Christina, to learn how this aesthetic could be embodied in poetry. His comments on the work of contemporary poets show an acute realisation that he shares common problems with them at the same time as he realises that they have not solved them. He tended to judge their achievement in relation to their language as in his well-known comment on Browning's use of language as 'a way of talking with the air and spirit of a man bounding up from table with his mouth full of bread and cheese and saying that he meant to stand no blasted nonsense'. Hopkins's poetry does not, of course, belong to the great creative years of the middle decades of the century but to the late 1870s and the 1880s, the age of Pater, Rossetti and Swinburne, of Newman and Pusey; on the one hand, of the growth of the aesthetic ideal, an awareness of something like symbolist techniques, and on the other, of the religious revival, the regrouping and re-thinking of religious attitudes following the bewilderment and doubt of the middle decades. Hopkins belongs firmly to his period; his adherence to the doctrine of the aesthetic ideal is absolute and he followed the religious reaction of his time from low-church Protestantism to high Anglicanism and, under Newman's influence, from high Anglicanism to Roman Catholicism. (By 1851 Newman, Faber and Manning had gone over to Rome and it is estimated that by 1853 no less than four hundred Anglican clergymen had followed them into the Roman Church.)[3] Hopkins thus shared in the literary mediaevalism of the Pre-Raphaelites and the religious mediaevalism of the Oxford Movement and was able to bring the two together. The poets and thinkers of the 1870s and 1880s tended to reject the middle way, the compromise of earlier decades, and in all areas of thought and life moved out to take up extreme positions; thus Hopkins became not only a Catholic convert but a Jesuit. In his poetry, curiously, the

antitheses of Victorianism, all those conflicting and contradictory forces, that seemed to be pulling Victorian poetry in so
many different directions, are brought together and in one way
or another resolved. Thus he bridged the chasm between the
real and the ideal that in so much of the poetry of Rossetti
produces a dream-like and often sensational confusion between
the flesh and the spirit; he restated the vital, romantic relationship between man and nature; he extended the Pre-Raphaelite
technique of building up vivid, detailed, allegorical pictures in
such a way as to change what in Rossetti often verges on the
precious and is static and ornamental, to a picture that is
living, powerfully and urgently expressing its spiritual significance. Most important of all he managed to establish a vital
relationship, however rhetorical, between the language of
poetry and the language of speech. What in his contemporaries'
poetry is stilted, artificial and decorative, in his poetry becomes
organic and functional. In his use of language he strongly
recalls Pater's architectural analogy in his essay on 'Style';

> For the literary architecture, if it is to be rich and expressive,
> involves not only foresight of the end in the beginning, but also
> development or growth of design, in the process of execution, with
> many irregularities, surprises, and afterthoughts; the contingent
> as well as the necessary being subsumed under the unity of the
> whole.
>
> *Appreciations with an Essay on Style* (1889; ed. of 1910)

Hopkins was, of course, fascinated by architecture and in com-
menting on his own work frequently uses the term design to
describe the essential structure of his poems. The analogy
between his poems, as structure, and Victorian Gothic architecture has been drawn by Kenneth Clark in *The Gothic
Revival*[4] when in a discussion of the architect William Butter-
field he notes;

> But the reason why he [Butterfield] administers so many shocks to
> the sensitive eye is more like that which has induced some modern
> musicians to shock the sensitive ear—a kind of ruthlessness, a
> determination not to let mere taste and amiability interfere with
> conviction. He is the first master of discordant polyphony. And he
> is worth comparing with Gerard Manley Hopkins in his clash of
> interrupted rhythms, no less than in the indigestibility of his detail.

Certainly in so many ways Hopkins's style seems the verbal equivalent of Victorian Gothic architecture. Antiquarian, mediaevalist, fastidious and erudite like so many of contemporary philologists he attempted to return to the native sinews of the language and escape from the effeminate, foreign domination of Latin and the Romantic languages. Like the architects of the Gothic revival his style was nothing if not eclectic but like them he reached back beyond the Reformation to the time when England was Roman Catholic and found in the Middle Ages a new ideal in language, in religion and, with his admiration for Duns Scotus, in philosophy. He paid painstaking attention to minute details of etymologies and to the exact shade and hue of individual words though his poetic rhythms and structures are violently contorted, wild flourishes, vigorous contrasts and balances, and copious rhetorical gestures. He uses his theory of 'sprung-rhythm' with its 'outriders' in much the same way as the neo-Gothic architect used gargoyle, buttress, and ornate decoration; the energy the poem generates is often the result of friction between the texture of the poem and its meaning, or of the pressure necessary to subdue the texture in order to reveal the poem's structure. In so many of the poems the texture is decorative, not functional, and in calling attention to itself detracts attention from the poem, but such a process would be quite acceptable to an age in which railway stations were designed as cathedrals and the only really functional public architecture, of the Crystal Palace, was produced by a gardener accustomed to building greenhouses. Like the Pre-Raphaelites in painting, Hopkins aimed at realistic fidelity to detail though the linguistic texture of his verse achieves that kind of grotesque style that Bagehot describes as one of Browning's characteristics and that is visually such a prominent feature of neo-Gothic. He accepted Pater's dictum that all art tends towards the condition of music and like his contemporaries was aware that Goethe had described architecture as 'frozen music'.[5] Beauty was that abstract quality that transcended the concrete realities of sensuous life and existed in a series of harmonious relationships. In an essay he wrote as an undergraduate for Pater, his tutor, he says;

Beauty lies in the relation of the parts of a sensuous thing to each other, that is in a certain relation, it being absolute at one point and comparative in those nearing it or falling from it. Thus in those arts of which the effect is in time, not space, it is a sequence at certain intervals—elementarily at least.

Hopkins adheres to this Pateresque theory of beauty and is conscious of it in the way he employs abrupt and contrasted images as point and counterpoint within a musical phrase or sequence in such a way that although the rhythms are essentially broken, a harmonious relationship between ideas and rhythms has been established. But central to the belief of Hopkins as a priest and to his practice as a poet is the concept of the word, and the word, we recall, was God; ideas are the word, in poetry images are the word realised in terms of sensuous perception. Nature and the world of sensuous objects, the image of life we perceive is 'charged' with God, is 'news' of God. He relates all this to the philosophy of the Franciscan Duns Scotus who places such stress on the unique, individual essence of things—as opposed to the Thomist emphasis on their generic attributes—which is why Hopkins, though discussing abstract relationships, always insists on concrete, sensuous images and very careful, very precise analogies. He coined the peculiar terminology of 'scape' and 'inscape', 'stress' and 'instress', to describe the process whereby through close study and careful analysis, objects, sensuously perceived, would give up the spiritual reality that lies beyond their appearances. Thus the idea of beauty that he took from Pater and the world of secular aesthetics is used by Hopkins within a framework of reference that is specifically religious. If his concept of nature is strongly reminscent of the neo-Platonists of the seventeenth century, for Hopkins it belongs to the world of Catholic, mediaeval theology. Though he shared with Rossetti and his contemporaries their concern with the idea of beauty, as indeed he shared so much else, he differed greatly in the way he developed the idea and the purposes to which he harnessed it, for the area of human experience on which he drew is severely limited. If he succeeded where his contemporaries failed, he did so by restricting the area of his poetry severely; even as a 'religious' poet compared with other 'religious' poets, such as

Crashaw, Vaughan, Herbert or even T. S. Eliot in the *Four Quartets*, not to mention Donne or Blake, his range is surprisingly narrow and his interests peculiarly doctrinaire.

III

There is no doubt that, in so far as Hopkins destroyed the poetry he wrote before he joined the Society of Jesus, he must have felt some conflict between the service of God and the service of art, though this feeling does not seem to have lasted beyond 1875. He admitted to R. W. Dixon that;

What I had written I burnt before I became a Jesuit [1868] and resolved to write no more, as not belonging to my profession, unless it were by the wish of my superiors; so for seven years I wrote nothing but two or three little presentation poems.

In fact, of course, a number of the early poems have survived in one form or another, although they add little to his reputation or to what we could have learnt from his later poems. They are for the most part written in the prevailing mode of Pre-Raphaelite lushness and establish themselves as being primarily concerned with the idea of religion, a rather awkward alliance between Keats and Herbert. 'Easter Communion', for example, is a confidently written sonnet that betrays a certain priggishness in the poet's attitude as he establishes a direct relationship between self-denial and punishment, on the one hand, and reward and enlightenment, on the other. His reference to secret self-flagellation and hair-shirts seems to indicate a curious kind of masochistic fantasy and a fantasy that was to return in the later sonnets when after self-sacrifice and suffering, the reward is withheld. The homely restraint of Herbert echoes in lines such as

> God comes all sweetness to your Lenten lips

but this chaste quality runs to over-indulgence in Keatsian images such as,

> God shall o'er-brim the measures you have spent
> With oil of gladness;

—which must recall the notable use of 'o'er-brimm'd' in

306

For Summer has o'er-brimm'd their clammy cells.

The sensuous qualities of the verse appear to run counter to the ascetism of the attitude it embodies and this is even more obvious in 'The Habit of Perfection' which, while rejecting sensuous experience in favour of spiritual illumination, none the less manages to celebrate his love of the natural world and of sensuous pleasures. This parallels in some ways the early Milton of the Nativity ode in which he celebrates the death of the pagan gods with a luxuriance that bestows on them a vivid and dramatic life. Hopkins in these early poems refuses to separate abstract idea from concrete experience and the attraction of the poems is in the power of their sensuous texture not in their often remarkably unattractive ideas.

The Wreck of the Deutschland was written in the winter of 1875 while Hopkins was at St. Beuno's College, North Wales, and breaks his seven years self-imposed silence as a poet. It was in fact written at the suggestion of the College's rector and at a time when Hopkins was both a 'theologian' and was learning Welsh and interesting himself in Welsh poetry; one MS copy of the poem is, according to W. H. Gardner, signed 'Brân Maenefa', a bardic signature. Apart from writing a Welsh version of 'O Deus, ego amo te', one original poem in Welsh, also signed 'Brân Maenefa', has survived. This poem is entitled 'Cywydd' the Welsh name for a peculiarly traditional form of seven syllabled lines. Unlike his version of 'O Deus, ego amo te', the cywydd includes cynghanedd, the traditional system of stress, alliteration, assonance and rhyme which is the most difficult in the language. W. H. Gardner notes that Hopkins's use of cynghanedd is incorrect except in two of the eighteen lines of the poem although he has approximated to this system throughout and there can be little doubt that Hopkins's study of the Welsh language and of Welsh traditional poetic forms explains why *The Wreck of the Deutschland* is so sensationally different in rhythm and linguistic form from anything he had written earlier and why the characteristic Hopkins style should appear fully developed in that poem without any apparent prior experimentation. Clearly he is adapting traditional Welsh forms and linguistic patterns. Moreover, it is interesting to notice that in 'Cywydd' he looks forward to the time when the Catholic religion will be re-established in Wales in much the same way as, at the end of *The Wreck of the Deutschland*, he hopes for the return of England to Roman Catholicism. Both in form and content, the Welsh poem clearly precedes and foreshadows *The Wreck of the Deutschland*. He was being initiated into the missionary spirit of the Jesuits; the original objective of the Society was to counter the religious reformers of the sixteenth century, and was, also, at some other level, haunted, he said, by the echoes of a new rhythm. The most obvious feature of the poem is its technical innovations; it is clearly an experiment in poetic technique of great daring and originality though as a narrative it is extremely confused, the linguistic texture completely swamping the poem. Father Peters categorises the technical devices of the poem in detail describing Hopkins's omission of articles (there is no indefinite article in Welsh, it should be noted), his use of personification and impersonation, his frequent interjections of 'ah', 'oh', or 'O', and the way in which Hopkins attempts to sustain a language of co-ordination rather than one of subordinate clauses and phrases mainly by the use of colons and dashes (he counts 21 colons and 24 dashes). He describes also Hopkins's use of conversational idioms side by side with revived saxon terms and the way in which he controls assonance, internal rhyme and alliterative patterns. There is little to add to his description of the poem's technique though we may wonder whether this complexity of form is appropriate to the poet's statement. Certainly in those passages of the poem that are purely descriptive the language does vividly re-enact the dramatic events. But although the poem originated in Hopkins reading a newspaper account of the disaster, and in describing this event in stanzas 12–17 he keeps very close to the factual details; the poem is essentially a religious meditation on the relationships between man and omnipotent God. The ship is used traditionally as a symbol of the life and destiny of man but whatever the poem is, it certainly is not a lament for suffering humanity but rather a triumphant celebration of God's power, revealed in terror and mystery. The nun as witness is martyred, the crucifixion is re-enacted and man is re-born, spiritually at least, through

Grace. The meditation in 'Part the First' of the poem, in which Hopkins describes his own dark night of the soul and how he was eventually brought by Grace through suffering and doubt to light, finds its dramatic analogy in 'Part the Second' in that the two parts are complete in the symbols of shipwreck, storm, suffering and eventual salvation. The necessity of a faith as pure as the nun's cry of faith is insisted on for then and only then will the mystery of God's majesty be revealed in the storm as in the heavens. The concluding stanzas make it clear that this faith must also be of Roman Catholic orthodoxy, that the wreck and the martyrdom are a sign to Protestant England to return to the Catholic faith. The faith on which the poem insists is, of course, specifically Catholic, in its conclusion and in its reference to Luther, 'beast of the waste wood', who is associated with Cain. But movement from darkness to light described by Hopkins in 'Part the First' and paralleled by the shipwreck in 'Part the Second' is a movement towards Grace in specifically Jesuit terms. The temptation is always to interpret in general terms what Hopkins intended to be read in precise particulars. We are not here concerned with the nineteenth century debate between doubt and faith, between materialism and religion, but with a particular and particularly doctrinal kind of faith that is shared by Franciscan Nuns and a Jesuit priest schooled in Loyola's *Exercitia*. In any case, Hopkins is singularly unconcerned with the human implications of the disaster, though he realises there were two hundred souls aboard the ship including women and children. There is one chilling image of the courageous man who went to the help of one of the distressed women passengers, but

> He was pitched to his death at a blow,
> For all his dreadnought breast and braids of thew:
> They could tell him for hours, dandled the to and fro
> Through the cobbled foam-fleece. What could he do
> With the burl of the fountains of air, buck and the flood of the wave?

In making the man symbolic of natural man powerlessly crushed by the majesty of God's storm, unsupported by the light of grace, Hopkins achieves a fine image of human impotence but in so doing loses the tragic human implications of the man's futile heroism. In the end because of his pre-occupation with the terror and majesty of God, Hopkins loses sight of man, and in concentrating attention on the spiritual agony of the nuns and the symbolic aspects of the event, overlooks the community of human suffering represented by the passengers and crew. He has, indeed, divested himself of the love of created beings and, to misquote T. S. Eliot, the gain to God is a loss to man. (This unconcern for human values is clearly brought out by the casual first line of *Felix Randal*:

Felix Randal the farrier, O is he dead then? my duty all ended,)

The passionate and dramatic urgency of Hopkins's language is deployed to carry a meditation on the relationship of priest and God and of martyr and 'martyr-master' which is contained within a special and doctrinal frame-work of reference.

Other shipwrecks have had their influence on literature, the sinking of the *Abergavenny*, for instance; but perhaps the shipwreck that is best compared with *The Wreck of the Deutschland* is that which resulted in the death of Edward King, the occasion of Milton's *Lycidas*. Milton sees the death of King not merely as an unfortunate accident but as a positive act of God in much the same way as Hopkins views the death of the nuns. But Milton's poem proceeds by questioning God's ways and pursuing an enquiry into the nature of evil and attempting to reconcile evil with God's providence. The poem is conducted, at a personal and universal level, always in human terms; the emotional and intellectual conflicts are enacted poetically in such a way as to involve the reader, in spite of the pastoral convention. It would be hard to imagine Hopkins admitting to the wish, however playful, to 'sport with Amaryllis in the shade', or realising poetically the violence of nature and the insignificance of man in quite the terms in which Milton imagined the body of Lycidas at the 'bottom of the monstrous world'. Milton's poem ends quietly with the conviction of vision but his poem is rich in human implication and dense with human doubt and suffering. Technically, of course, it is a very much more varied performance than Hopkins's poem, moving from one contrast to another, including lyric and satiric elements, it is continually changing pace and tone.

Hopkins maintains the rhetoric of his poem on one breathless level throughout. His poem offers a vigorous dialectic, it is erudite and academic, even startlingly original in its diction and rhythms; it moves from ecstasy to hysteria, from agony to the glory of martyrdom but nonetheless remains sacramental rather than religious in any broad sense. Like Milton's *Penseroso*, Hopkins regarded man as a passing spectacle. There is not in this poem any evidence of a conflict between the poet and the priest but rather the poet is too much the priest. In spite of the remarkable linguistic texture of the poem, like so many of Hopkins's poems, it is wholly public and rhetorical in tone, written, as he said, to be read aloud in the bardic, oral tradition. Although he never succeeded in his ambitions to write a drama, the rhetoric of his poems needs dramatic production, or, at least, needs to be declaimed dramatically. With the possible exception of what Bridges called the 'terrible posthumous sonnets' his poems are best projected in a declamatory manner; so many of them seem to have been written at the top of his voice and he appears to have relied on a system of musical notation marking the voice stresses rather than on orthodox punctuation, marking the units of sense. His poetry is particularly dramatic in its abruptness and in the sudden changes of rhythm and transitions from one image to another; Hopkins in so many ways echoes Browning although he lacks Browning's psychological awareness and does not attempt to mediate his poetry through *personae*. Even if projected dramatically, Hopkins's impulse is always lyrical. What his verse lacks is the flexibility that characterises Browning or even Clough who learnt, particularly in *Amours de Voyage*, to control the long-line in such a way as to modulate its tone from the easy, relaxed conversational to impassioned, urgent statement, and to do so without the obtrusive machinery of alliteration, assonance and internal rhyme on which Hopkins relied. Yet in his use of language, however self-consciously, Hopkins does manage to convey a sense of almost physical tension and movement. He admired soldiers and manual workers perhaps for the same kind of reason that Yeats admired men of action because they embodied his anti-mask. In his studies of manual workers he still remains a spectator and the impression he conveys in his portrait of Harry Ploughman, for instance, is purely physical, a vivid realisation of strength and the beauty of the man's body as, fully extended, his whole strength is concentrated in the act of ploughing. His attitude towards Felix Randal whose spiritual strength grows as he becomes physically weaker is of priest to parishioner, confidently patronising in the tone of,

Thy tears that touched my heart, child, Felix, poor Felix Randal;

His relationship with the bugler who takes his first communion and with the soldier is also that of a priest except that in both poems Hopkins betrays, perhaps, an unexpected note of Kiplingesque patriotism which he dignifies by drawing analogies between the soldiers and Christ who

> For love he leans forth, needs his neck must fall on, kiss,
> And cry 'O Christ-done deed! So God-made-flesh does too:
> Were I come o'er again' cries Christ 'it should be this'.

It is not surprising that a follower of Loyola should think of Christ in military terms but it is possibly unexpected to find Hopkins indulging a sentimental kind of Victorian patriotism and lending it his religious blessing. Hopkins responded best to subjects of the natural scene or subjects taken from classical mythology and is most vulnerable in so far as his weaknesses are most exposed in those poems concerned with men and the life around him. Taken altogether it is the narrowness of his range that is most striking; he returns time and time again to themes first introduced in *The Wreck of the Deutschland* just as in that poem his poetic technique, his characteristic devices and mannerisms, appeared for the first time and appeared fully developed.

IV

Between 1875 and his death Hopkins in a most assured manner embarked on the brilliant linguistic and metrical experimentation with which his name is securely associated. *The Wreck of the Deutschland* in many ways introduces the framework of these experiments and what is introduced, often extravagantly, in that poem is mined and refined by Hopkins in his later poetry.

His attitude towards the purity of the language hardens, sometimes to the point of pedantry, and in his desire to return to the native sinews of pure English diction he links himself with those other, now faintly ridiculous, nineteenth-century philologists who, wishing to cleanse the language of all alien influences, preferred clumsy native compounds to those words derived from Latin or other foreign sources; they studied 'speechcraft' rather than grammar. Their programme of linguistic reform suited Hopkins's mediaevalism well; the native traditions in language as in so many other fields were, he believed, perverted at the time of the Reformation. This mediaevalism of his was, of course, one of the prevailing characteristics of Victorianism generally and was given its most obvious form in the wholesale revival of Gothic ideals; in Ruskin's aesthetics, in Morris's politics and in Scott's architecture. Even in his interest in and study of Welsh culture he joined all those who between Matthew Arnold and W. B. Yeats interested themselves in Celtic languages and cultures and who delighted in the revival of what they considered to be pristine vision. Hopkins is typical in so far as he combines an austere sense of traditionalism with extreme and revolutionary boldness and it is not therefore surprising that his boldest experiments with form and language were conducted within the traditional sonnet form that he developed in the most astonishing ways. He wrote some of the longest and the shortest sonnets in the language. While for the most part paying due regard to the formal requirements of the sonnet form, octet, sestet, and rhyme scheme, he paid these dues to the sonnet form in such an unusual rhythmic and structural manner as to subvert the form almost entirely. In his hands the thing became something more than infinite riches in a little room; something more like simple pieties framed by wild and expansive rhythmical and verbal irregularities. Certainly his sonnets are neither elegant nor formal; their effect is powerfully bewildering and sometimes grotesque and the reader is always left with the problem of reconciling the rich dialectic of the linguistic structure and the simple, didactic vision the poem frames.

Together with his fellow Victorian poets Hopkins escaped the pressures of the urban, industrial society around him and concentrated his attentions on the countryside. He was from his early youth an ardent Wordsworthian student of nature. Indeed, as his note-books make plain, his interest in nature was fastidious to the point of being botanical. His note-books also make clear that he was, as a priest, conscious of the squalor and distress created by urban living but when he tried to write poetry about his experience of the industrial landscape he wrote well below himself, as in the grotesque and strained performance of 'Tom's Garland'. There is no doubt in his mind that if God made the countryside and was visible in created nature, man made the towns in his own squalid image. None the less, in his study of the countryside he clearly valued the idea of 'truth to nature' and in his sketches and in his descriptions of the minutiae of the natural scene he seems to have interpreted truth to mean fidelity to observed detail; in other words he is guilty of that kind of pedantic realism that characterises the paintings of the Pre-Raphaelites. Also, as with the Pre-Raphaelite painters, although he aimed to transcend sensuous experience and achieve metaphysical significance, he often falls short of symbolism and into simple allegory although, in his case, allegory is supported to some extent by traditional Catholic inconography whereas the allegory of the Pre-Raphaelites is supported only by Victorian pieties. But clearly, as with the P.R.B., what Hopkins valued most was the intensity of observation and it was this idea of contemplative intensity of natural phenomena that he called upon the theories of Duns Scotus, and upon the eccentric vocabulary of instress and inscape and so on, to support and thus to confer religious and metaphysical respectability upon an aesthetic that the P.R.B. were content to leave in the realm of aesthetics.

In a sonnet such as 'The Windhover' the flight and move-ment of the bird seem to be precisely delineated but the language in which the bird is described is continually drawing in disparate areas of experience so that the intensity of the observation and the language of contemplation in which the observation is recorded at first seem to be at variance, and then to diverge, until the bird itself is, in the sestet, completely lost sight of and the contemplation entirely dominant. The bird, even regarded as controlling image, is lost from view. The impression is one of a poet trying to control intractable materials in order to come to grips with experience but looked at more closely it seems that the language is struggling with itself, that a kind of verbal in-fighting is taking place, as images of kestrel, chivalry, discipline, freedom and ploughing contend or combine to produce a feeling of vague, but undoubtedly sensuous, significance. As in most of these characteristic Hopkins sonnets the effect of richness is produced by disorder, by image rapidly following upon image, a riot of images both visual and abstract to which the sonnet form cannot hope to give shape or form. The connections between images are often there, an under-meaning running parallel to the over-meaning, but too often these links are pure associational, accidental or personal. To return to 'The Windhover', for example, the crucial word 'buckle' is, to put it mildly, ambiguous and the images of ploughing do not appear to be part of the bird imagery or of the chivalric imagery. Of course it could be argued that if the description 'a poet's poet' was ever a meaningful description then there is no reason why we should not have 'a critic's poet' or why we should not accept Hopkins on these terms. Certainly no other poet, perhaps with the exception of Donne, responds half so well to analytic techniques.

In the way that Hopkins uses it the sonnet form comes very near to parodying itself; the effect is not one of order, concision and finiteness but of anarchy, expansiveness and lyrical rhetoric. Even the later, so-called terrible sonnets are austere and precise only in comparison with his own more characteristic performances. It is important also in regarding these terrible sonnets and in generalising about Hopkins's 'development' on the basis of them, that they are not the product of a particular period of his life in so far as while writing these sonnets he was at the same time continuing to experiment in his more familiar and assured mode. In other words there is no evidence to support those who wish to argue that in 1885 his whole attitude to life and poetry changed fundamentally from joyful and expansive optimism to misery and introspective pessimism. Indeed some of his most extravagant and buoyant experiments in language were written after 1885 although he also tries to achieve a more severe plainness in some of the sonnets. Even in these more austere sonnets themselves, however, he is unable to subdue entirely that rhetorical lyricism that too often throughout his work introduces a note of mild hysteria at a point where controlled meaning seems to be called for. To illustrate again from 'The Windhover', in the sestet where we expect some kind of resolution of the experience and conflict of the octet, we get the magnificent gestures first in one direction;

> AND the fire that breaks from thee then, a billion
> Times told lovelier, more dangerous, O my chevalier!

(where 'chevalier' rhymes with 'ah my dear' and 'here') and, in another direction;

> . . . blue-bleak embers, ah my dear,
> Fall, gall themselves, and gash gold-vermilion.

These rhetorical gestures are successful in so far as they conclude the poem on a wave of ardent affirmation, an emotional up-beat. Gestures of this kind open themselves to varying interpretations and I. A. Richards feels that 'the close has a strange, weary, almost exhausted, rhythm and the word "gall" has an extraordinary force, bringing out painfully the shock with which the sight of the soaring bird has jarred the poet into an unappeased discontent'.[6] If we are in a position at the close of the poem to regard these lines as ardent affirmation or 'unappeased discontent' we can at least agree that there is an impressionistic vagueness of meaning here that admits these contrary interpretations. In the octet of this same poem the rhetoric, although excited, is controlled, in the first sentence at least (the first seven lines that is), by the concreteness of the imagery and by an almost Yeatsian sense of phrasing (though Yeats, we suspect, would never have committed all eight lines to the single repetitive -ing rhyme). It is in the sestet of the poem, where we might expect a hard currency of meaning, that we are put off by gestures that appear to amount to little more than a blank cheque—an expansive gesture in any circumstances but here an open invitation to draw upon the reserves built up in the octet. Hence the uncertainty whether 'Buckle' has the force of strengthening or weakening, coming together or falling apart, (or whether it means both) or whether the poem ends on a note of triumphant affirmation or of frustration. It is in this area of tone and mood that Hopkins so often fails and where he might have learnt so much from Tennyson. Hopkins moves his poems from breathless excitement to blank despair but both these extremes court the dangers of hysteria; nowhere for long does he successfully manage the disciplined control of tone and mood that enabled Tennyson and the Victorian masters of poems expressing moods and states of feeling to gather the meaning of their poems together in one final and satisfying gesture of the kind that Tennyson, particularly in the lyrics of 'In Memoriam', manages time and time again.

None the less, it is in the area of meaning, of intellectual content, that Hopkins was once thought to be superior to his fellow Victorian poets and yet it seems that so often it is by impoverishing content, by limiting his range and narrowing the implications of his poetry that he best succeeds. In poem after poem he raises those problems that proved so imponderable and intellectually harrowing to his contemporaries only to dissolve them in rhetorical gestures of emotional affirmation or in a brilliant display of linguistic dexterity. The colour and energy of his language turn the reader's attention away from the content towards the linguistic surface and verbal structure. His best poems represent the triumph of form over content, of language over meaning, and he generates a confidence that persuades the reader to accept the poem on the poet's terms without questioning the doctrinal assumptions on which the content depends. In the end Hopkins's experiment is an investigation into the nature of language, an investigation that has without doubt enriched the technical resources of poetry itself. His beliefs, even if he felt he had not lived up to them, were never in doubt. He never suffers the torments of doubt reflected even in the minor poets of his age, in the work of Christina Rossetti for instance. If Hopkins succeeded where his contemporaries had failed, he did so by severely restricting the area of experience about which he wrote. The vast area of ordinary human experience and human relationships receives little or no mention in his poetry in which he returns time and time again to the same theme, the theme that was to him as a priest of over-riding importance, and it is not surprising that most of the traditional common-places of human life find no place in his poems. In so far as his priesthood resolved the central intellectual, emotional and spiritual problems in a way totally acceptable and totally committing to the man, he could afford to concentrate on the problems of language; the argument as to how many angels can balance on the end of a pin is undoubtedly a fascinating and absorbing exercise for those who never doubted the existence and qualities of angels. To compare his poetry with that of Tennyson and Browning is entirely inappropriate in so far as he was restricted by his vocation and his faith to a narrow segment of human experience. He believed that the only just literary critic is Christ, which indicates his intense seriousness and the terrifyingly high standards he set himself. It is also the point at which commentary is silenced or, at least, the point at which commentary moves into areas properly belonging to faith and conscience.

NOTES

[1] *Poems of Gerard Manley Hopkins*, 3rd edn., rev. and enlarged, ed. W. H. Gardner (1948), p. 205.

[2] A 4th edition, ed. W. H. Gardner and N. H. Mackenzie, was published in 1967.

[3] 'Protestantism', H. W. Schneider, *The Nineteenth Century World*, ed. G. S. Métraux and F. Gouzet, Mentor Books (1963), p. 325.

[4] *The Gothic Revival: An Essay in the History of Taste*, Kenneth Clark (1928; Penguin reprint 1964), p. 174 n.

[5] *Gespräche mit Eckerman*, 23 March 1829.

[6] *Dial*, September 1926.

See also *The Shaping Vision of Gerard Manley Hopkins* by Alan Heuser (1958), and 'Instress of Inscape' by Austin Warren, *Kenyon Review*, VI (1944), pp. 369-82.

INDEX